FOOTPRINTS IN A DARKENED FOREST

Fulton J. Sheen

FOOTPRINTS
IN A DARKENED
FOREST

MEREDITH PRESS · NEW YORK

331

Library of Congress Catalog Card Number: 67-16514
Manufactured in the United States of America for Meredith Press

ACKNOWLEDGMENTS

The author wishes to express his gratitude to the authors and publishers who have granted him permission to quote from their works.

Quotation on page 103 reprinted from *The Plague* by Albert Camus, translated by Stuart Gilbert, by permission of Alfred A. Knopf, Inc. Copyright 1948 by Stuart Gilbert.

Quotations on pages 13 and 17 from *Four Quartets* by T. S. Eliot. Reprinted by permission of Harcourt, Brace & World, Inc., publishers.

Quotation on page 104 from *An Episode of Sparrows* by Rumer Godden, by permission of The Viking Press, Inc., publishers.

Quotations on pages 251, 252, and 254 from *Markings* by Dag Hammarskjöld, translated by Leif Sjöberg & W. H. Auden. Copyright © 1964 by Alfred A. Knopf, Inc. and Faber & Faber, Ltd. Reprinted by permission of Alfred A. Knopf, Inc.

Quotation on page 252 reprinted with permission of Charles Scribner's Sons from *Dag Hammarskjöld: A Spiritual Portrait*, p. 48, by Sven Stolpe.

Quotation on page 24 from *Skipper next to God* by Jan de Hartog, copyright 1945, 1947, 1949 by the author. Reprinted by permission of the author.

Quotations from the works of Ernest Hemingway which appear on page 24 are protected by copyright and have been reprinted by special permission of Charles Scribner's Sons.

Quotations on pages 24 and 25 from *If Winter Comes* by A. S. M. Hutchinson. Copyright 1921 by A. S. M. Hutchinson. Published by Little, Brown and Company. Reprinted by permission of the publishers.

Quotation on page 49 from *Fair Bride* by Bruce Marshall, Houghton Mifflin Company, copyright 1953 Bruce Marshall. Reprinted by permission of A. Watkins, Inc.

Quotation on page 246 from "Renascence" by Edna St. Vincent Millay from *Collected Poems*, Harper & Row. Copyright 1912, 1940 by Edna St. Vincent Millay. Reprinted by permission of Norma Millay Ellis.

Dedicated to
THE LADY
WHOSE SON
LEFT ON EARTH
THE FOOTPRINTS OF HEAVEN

Contents

I

MAN

CHAPTER ONE

The Ages of Man

Shakespeare has depicted seven ages, enumerating not always **what** is best, but what he found most natural to each age:

> All the world's a stage,
> And all the men and women merely players.
> They have their exits and their entrances;
> And one man in his time plays many parts,
> His acts being seven ages. At first the infant,
> Mewling and puking in the nurse's arms.
> And then the whining school-boy, with his satchel
> And shining morning face, creeping like snail
> Unwillingly to school. And then the lover,
> Sighing like furnace, with a woful ballad
> Made to his mistress' eyebrow. Then a soldier,
> Full of strange oaths, and bearded like the pard;
> Jealous in honour, sudden and quick in quarrel,
> Seeking the bubble reputation
> Even in the cannon's mouth. And then the justice,
> In fair round belly with good capon lined,
> With eyes severe and beard of formal cut,
> Full of wise saws and modern instances;
> And so he plays his part. The sixth age shifts

Into the lean and slipper'd pantaloon,
With spectacles on nose and pouch on side,
His youthful hose, well saved, a world too wide
For his shrunk shank; and his big manly voice,
Turning again toward childish treble, pipes
And whistles in his sound. Last scene of all,
That ends this strange eventful history,
Is second childishness, and mere oblivion,
Sans teeth, sans eyes, sans taste, sans everything.
　　　　　　　　—*As You Like It.* Act II, Scene VII

Instead of treating each of the seven, which would involve too much detail, we will revert to Chinese and Hebraic wisdom and reduce the ages to three. Solomon is traditionally credited with having written three great books of the Bible: The Song of Songs, which is one of the most poignant love stories ever written; the Book of Proverbs, which is full of axioms, advice, criticisms, witticisms, and sententious remarks. And finally, Ecclesiastes, the burden of which is the old man looking back on life and saying: "Vanity of vanities, all is vanity."

These three ages of Solomon—youth, middle age, and old age —correspond to the three ages of Confucius. The Chinese sage described each age in terms of its dominant passion: Youth is impelled by the instinct of lust, carnality, and sex; middle age has as its principal fault or drive the quest of power; while old age is apt to fall into the vice of greed and avarice.

It is interesting to bring Confucius up-to-date and to note how the three great psychiatrists who have most influenced the modern world have each specialized on one of these drives or thrusts: Freud, Adler, and Jung. According to Freud, the basic drive of man is sex. To Adler, it is the desire of superiority and the satisfaction of the ego in power; when repressed, this comes out as an inferiority complex. Jung, on the contrary, affirms that the basic urge of man is for security, the piling up of wealth to bolster an inner emptiness. Each of these psychiatrists is one-third right and two-thirds incomplete. A true psychological understanding of man would be one which combined these three insights in a more complete interpretation of man. Sex, egotism, and need for security are three inseparable fires set blazing inside the human condition. Though they do not necessarily succeed one another in a clear-cut fashion, one is generally more dominant than another in the three seasons of life.

Nor is there any guilt necessarily associated with these different and dominant urges; wrong enters in only when there is disorder. Sex is not wrong; otherwise marriage would not be a source of happiness. The search for superiority is not wrong; otherwise man would never seek to develop his natural talents. Desire of property is not wrong, for property is the extension of personality. It is the excesses of these drives which make such evils as immorality, breakdown of the family, and undue concentration of wealth. Dust is good on the road, but it becomes dirt on the dinner plate. Nor are these thrusts limited to any age group, though there is more emphasis on one at one period of life rather than another.

From a *biological* point of view, each of these ages represents a crisis. The crisis of youth is puberty. The crisis of middle age is experience, when a man who has lived long enough can look back to give a summary of his trials and conflicts. The last stage, biologically, is the reaching of limits, physical and mental, which enforces a kind of detachment from the turmoil of life.

Characteristics of These Stages

The two outstanding traits of these successive ages are: (1) continuity of personality, (2) a conviction that life is a pilgrimage.

Whether one divides man into the seven ages of Shakespeare or the three of Solomon and Confucius, there is a constant—a personality which abides. There may be a "stream of consciousness" as William James explained it, but the stream of every river has a bed. Despite the changing of moods, affections, ideals, and even philosophies of life, despite appearances, airs, and hypocrisy, behind them all is an enduring subject—a string on which all are attached as beads. A man of eighty, when he uses the personal pronoun "I," subsumes all the experiences of life. He may deny that he is guilty of any vices, but he will not deny that he is to take credit for his virtues and successes in every period of life.

Cohesion of experiences in a personal substratum is not to be explained wholly by biology, because while the cells of the body change, the person remains identically the same. If the ego were explicable in terms of biology, then a man who is arrested at fifty for a crime which he committed at thirty could plead that he was not the same person.

Furthermore, in the three stages of life man can reflect upon himself, which material things cannot do. I can bend a piece of paper upon itself, but the paper does not become a thinking subject; but I can know myself, be pleased with myself or be angry with myself, see myself as in a mirror, which no material thing can do. Something changes in me, but something does not change. And so man can be pleased with himself and displeased with himself. He can enter into introspection, analyze himself on a couch, because he has an underlying substratum which endures through vicissitudes of life.

Life as a Pilgrimage

Looking through the three ages of man progressively, one notes a second characteristic: Man is on a pilgrimage; he seems to have here below no lasting city. Pilgrimage is rather deeply rooted into human experience, in dreams, myths, parables, allegory, and inner development.

Many of our dreams depict an unconscious journey in which there are encounters with various persons and objects which are projections of our inner psychic states. This dream, which actually happened, revealed the pilgrim character of personality.

The facts behind the dream were as follows: A young girl fell in love with a young man who was about to be called into the Army during the First World War. The spirit of both of them as they went along with their sexual affair was "eat, drink and be merry, for tomorrow we die." The girl particularly had thrown aside all moral standards, saying, "Why not?" But after a time she had a longing to be married; her boyfriend refused. She allowed herself to become pregnant, hoping to force him into marriage on the ground that the social mores would be too strong for him to refuse.

Just about the time she was to tell him, he was called into service. Afraid to tell her mother, she arranged to have an abortion. The doctor said to her, "You had a fine boy. Why did you have to destroy him?" This brought home to her the consciousness of what she had done. (It reminds one of the words of the Swiss psychiatrist to a young woman who came for an abortion, saying, "I wish you would get rid of these extra cells I have." The doctor asked, "What did you intend to name the cells?")

Later on in life the girl had a dream in which she saw that the basement of the house had been burned out. "We could rebuild it. The walls were standing, but the inside was gutted. I felt that the house could be made very nice if the cellar could be refinished." Here was a tie-up between the devastated part of her life, which corresponded to the cellar, and the hope of a future life, which was related to the building of a new house or a new personality.

Does not one also find the instinct of pilgrimage in boys who like to live in tents and in huts away from the stability of a home? The Winnebago Indians had a medicine rite in which the neophyte was instructed that in the morning he must start on a journey which would lead him to a wide road. He would find four footprints of those who had passed into life before him; if he followed them, he would have a renewed life.

One of the very earliest accounts of pilgrimage was in Homer, and many centuries later there was an account in *The Canterbury Tales* of Chaucer, who said that "all folk love to go on pilgrimages."

Among the Muslims there is the hajj to Mecca, after which one is allowed to dye his beard.

Dante wrote of pilgrimages in company with Virgil through purgatory and hell. The quest for the Holy Grail is a search for happiness quite beyond the present.

In the Middle Ages one of the books that was best known was *The Pilgrimage of the Human Life* by William of Deguilleville, which was written in the fourteenth century. It was an allegory about Everyman, describing the many adventures he meets on his way through life. Perhaps the best known of all outside of Chaucer is John Bunyan's *Pilgrim's Progress,* written during the twelve years the author spent in prison. One wonders whether or not one should include here the mobility of the American, one out of every four changing his residency every four years.

Dr. Samuel Johnson was once taken by Boswell to see the Giant's Causeway in Ireland. He arrived there in a disagreeable mood, after having traveled long on horseback. He shrugged his shoulders contemptuously as he gazed at the basalt rock, considered one of the wonders of the world. Boswell asked him, "Isn't this worth seeing?"

"Yes," replied Johnson, "worth seeing, but not worth going to see."

But beyond all of these pilgrimages is the forty years which the Israelites passed in the desert, making progress, then slipping back, but ever having before them the Promised Land that was afar. Man looks to the future. He draws on the expectation of other days for the enjoyment of the present. The wilderness wanderings were a type of man's struggle with the power of evil. The Israelites dwelt in tents; they knew there were mansions in store for them, and even after they entered the Promised Land, they continued to have the Feast of the Tents or Tabernacles to remind themselves that they were strangers on earth. The paschal lamb had to be eaten standing, for they were sojourners. Their feet were to be shod, for they were on their way. They were to bear a staff in their hands to reveal they were sojourners.

In view of the fact that personality endures and memory records all our deeds, good and foul, and inasmuch as we are all on a pilgrimage, it is time to ask in any of the ages of man, "Who am I?" "What am I here for?" and "Where am I going?" The failure to answer these questions is the base of our cult of sadness, in which we are perpetually angry with ourselves for being caught up in self-love. We would not keep a gadget in the house ten minutes without knowing its purpose. Why then live through the seven ages of Shakespeare or the three of Solomon without seeking the goal and meaning of life? Even the game of football has to have goal posts, and baseball a home plate—why not a goal and a home to life?

The meaning to these ages is not here, for we know we ought to be happy, and we are restless. We do not mind seeing a worm in the mud—that is its destiny. But to see a bird with one wing broken and dragging in the mud tears out one's heart. But it is a great, wide, wonderful world when you know where you came from and where you are going. Whether long or short, there is always time to say "Aye" or "Nay" to the Eternal Love Who made us.

CHAPTER TWO

Getting Out of the Rat Race

Man lives through many ages, and all of them are spent in time. This brings up the problem of why time weighs so heavily on us. Adults call it the rat race. Alienated youth speaks of getting kicks. To them "kicks" means escape from the rat race, the monotonous daily round and grind of being on the treadmill, the lassitude which comes from the mechanized life. As Camus, who showed such an outlook, wrote: "We constantly live toward the future which we should dread because it is death in disguise." A little boy reflected it, too: "I do not want to grow up and have work to do like you, Dad." Aldous Huxley, feeling this nausea with life, wrote: "What we are looking for in some way is getting beyond our vomit—beyond this piddling twopenny and halfpenny personality." Shakespeare described it:

Creeps in this petty pace from day to day. . . .
And all our yesterdays have lighted fools
The way to dusty death. . . .

We shall try to explain the meaning of the despair which comes from meaningless existence both in adults and in alienated youth. For normal people, time has a past, a present, and a future. All three are essential. Any one note in the symphony is intelligible only in terms of what has gone before; the music heard up to the present moment anticipates what is to follow. All who are psychologically sound realize that they cannot think a present thought without going back into their memory; from that storehouse come thoughts, recollections, and emotions which serve as foundation stones for building the future. One could not construct a house unless he remembered that he had laid foundations and also had in mind the plan of what the house should be. There is hardly anything more regrettable than amnesia, which is the forgetfulness of the past that we trod.

The future is as important as the past, for the future with its ideals, hopes, aspirations, and dreams gives urgency and action to the present moment. Every youth has to ask himself the question "What next?" when he finishes any separate period in his life. Consider a trip between New York and Washington. Washington is the goal or the purpose of the journey. If one were lacking this future plan, one would not be setting out from New York. Furthermore, every present moment in that trip is made intelligible only because it has a starting point and conclusion. The present, therefore, is a link in a chain binding together origins and destinies. This brings us now to the questions: What is the essence of the rat race? Why is youth concerned only with the present moment?

The rat race and the meaningless existence of some youths who live for kicks is founded on the false philosophy that life has only a present, a now, a moment. The past and the future have been knocked out. The past has been destroyed through rupture of all relatedness to parents, home, tradition, experience. Youth was meant to live very much like wheat in a field, not to be pulled up until it was ripe. Today youth, pulled up from the roots, lives its own present life without memory or tradition. One becomes like a pendulum outside of a clock, a carbon paper without an original, who calls all parents square. Where the past is not consciously repudiated, there is considerable unfamiliarity with it. Modern youth has little knowledge of two world wars, knows nothing of the Depression, and rather despises history as bunk. Convention is looked upon as a kind of restraint, a restriction, a manacle, a straitjacket; the culture which formed them is rejected; hence the fondness for placards, protests, adding signature to signature against anything which presently exists, whether it be religion, government, schools.

Those who are suffering from the nausea of life not only reject the past; they have even knocked out all thoughts of the future. Modern technology has played a small part in this, because modern youth knows that twenty years from now there will be jobs in the future which he never imagined. Before, change was rather accidental in civilization, such as the discovery of the compass; now, it is the very fabric of civilization, and in some instances it is planned, and in other cases it is unguided; but the net result for youth and the rat racers is: "Why bother about tomorrow because one cannot know where it is going?" The future to them is also unthinkable, because the atomic bomb may blow us all into nothingness. Tomorrow disappears with all of its hopes and ideals. Why bother working toward any profession, since the day might never come? Why save, if inflation is inevitable? But most of all, just as soon as a man admits there is a tomorrow, then there is a responsibility. Hence, the best way to escape responsibility is to cut out the future.

What Is Left?

What is left from this point on? If there is no past and there is no future, there is only the immediate, the present, the now, and sensation. To understand life one must think of an avalanche descending on a village at the base of the Alps. One thinks away the mountain, one thinks away the snow, one thinks away the village, and one has left just the sheer emotion. Man is no longer pictured as one who sits on a hillside and looks back at the land over which he has traveled and the beauties that lie before him. He is rather like one on a jet plane who has feelings of unrelatedness and unconnectedness with the ground, and thinks only of the present moment. This is the essence of the rat race, or kicks or the meaninglessness of

life. Modern man is not active; he is passive, in the sense that he is
acted upon by forces which rush him to his own destruction. He is
concerned only with the process and not with the product. That is
why beatniks and alienated youth and bored writers of the rat race
have a hatred both for the conventional, which refers to the past,
and also for the future, which frightens them because of the absurdity of their lives. They think that by cutting off both the roots and
the fruit that they avoid any commitment or responsibility. They
avoid falling in love, for that means involvement for tomorrow;
love affairs are for the moment. This makes them bizarre, deviants,
the oddballs, and always rebels; but while strong in hates and nega-
tions, they are weak in lasting loves and affirmations. Life is a process, not a program, and one must be angry with it, because one is
angry with oneself.

Time Need Not Be a Burden

For the Greeks, time was cycles, not an upward pilgrimage to a
mountain height; it was constantly coming back to new beginnings,
an Eternal Return.

But the modern man is burdened by time. Because life is
meaningless and has lost coherence, one second does not differ from
any other second. Architecture just piles brick on brick, but it
builds nothing; the needle draws threads, but it creates no pattern.
All moments are so impoverished that life is nothing but the adding
of zero to zero. All is a muddle, a junk heap, a drifting wreckage.
As T. S. Eliot puts it:

And the way up is the way down, the way
    forward is the way back.
. . . *time is no healer.*
                    —"The Dry Salvages"

Some radio stations give nothing but news, feeding the mind
no interim of reflection between one murder and another, one ca-

lamity and another; events have no significance in the mass production, excessive details, bulletins, flashes, oppressive closeness in an
overpopulation of happenings. This colossal density and overcrowd-
ing of the mind is really an attempt to escape time by minimizing
the significance of each event; what becomes important is what will
happen next. Nothing holds time together; there is no spool on
which this kaleidoscopic turmoil may be wound.

In the crazy circle of the rat race, any one day of life has no
meaning, except to usher in night. Existence is a perpetual inconse-
quence. Sartre's play *No Exit* portrays the contradiction of endless
meaninglessness by one character saying to another in hell, "What
is the point in your using a toothbrush? That's right! Why sleep?"
There is no sense in being clean, no division between activity and
resting; no reason for doing anything, because life is meaningless.

Because time is a bore, the common man must "pass time,"
"kill time," or escape it in some way. Literature does this by appealing to myths. James Joyce appeals to the myth of Ulysses, but how
different was the journey! On the basis of the Homeric *Odyssey*,
Joyce dehydrates the life of Leopold Bloom into a single day, hoping
to give it importance by relating it to the myth. Thomas Mann,
Proust, Virginia Woolf, and Dos Passos try to conquer time by making characters recall their lives and thus live again, remembrance
being more real than actuality. This artistic manipulation of paral-
lels between contemporaneity and antiquity is a literary way of escaping the uncongenial present. But they are all verbal ruminations
without a pole star, ships standing still in a raging sea without point
or compass. On the contrary, the past, present, and future all have
significance, as the following legend portrays.

There is a legend of the sybil offering to sell the King of Rome
three volumes of oracles. The price for the three was so high that
the king refused to pay it. She, in his presence, burned one of the
volumes. He returned later on and asked for the price of the two,
only to discover that the price for the two was the same as the price
for the three. Having been again refused the price, she burned the

second. Later on, feeling that the price of the surviving volume would be less than the other two, he was surprised to learn that it was the price of the three. The three volumes had to deal with youth, manhood, and old age.

Men are apt to think that the price for happiness is too high. In youth, they feel that it might mean giving up the carnal life, and so they refuse, and one third of their life is consumed. For manhood, the same price is asked—namely, the renunciation, the denial of self, the vision of eternity and the goal. When that is refused, then there is only old age which is left. Here renunciation becomes more difficult and seems harder because of fixed habits. If the price were paid at the beginning, one would have had the three volumes and happiness.

The Present Solves Nothing

The present itself is meaningless, unless there be some reference to the past or to the future. If a young man wishes to become a doctor, it is this ideal which encourages him to study through college and medical school; and it also gives meaning to each and every moment of preparation. But once the "now" moment is isolated from other moments in life, it has no meaning; those who live only for the isolated present fall into despair and occasionally into suicide. There is no joy or happiness looking at life through a keyhole. One would never enjoy a motion picture, if he were sentenced to look at one single frame of a motion picture reel, always in isolation from what went before and what followed.

There is a law of life that the more conscious we are of any moment of time, the less we are enjoying ourselves. The clerk who always has his eye on the clock does not like his work. On the contrary, the less we concentrate on any moment, the more happy we are. For example, listening to a conversation or to a symphony, we say, "Time passed like anything." Because we are in time, we cannot make a club sandwich of pleasures; we cannot march with Napoleon and march with Caesar; we cannot take tea with Shakespeare and Francis Thompson, or ski and swim in the same moment. I had an experience of the happiness that comes with timelessness in a retreat which I recently preached to the Trappists in Gethsemane, Kentucky. They have no radios, no television, no clocks, no newspaper; there is only a large bell which summons them to the various offices of study and work and prayer during the day. They keep perpetual silence. One of them wrote, "Time does not exist for us here. It is hard to distinguish between one year and another. That is probably why we are so happy."

Since our happiness and joy depend on getting outside of time, it follows that there is really no perfect happiness until one reaches eternity. Eternity is not the last of the series of present moments; it is something outside of the series which gives meaning to everything in it. Eternity is not the ultimate moment in a series, like a train which one might watch until the last boxcar has passed. Eternity is something outside of the series, as the engine is outside of the series of boxcars and thus gives movement to the cars. The last moment is not the final moment; it is a kind of sum of all moments and yet more. Just as one might draw a line under the addition of twenty plus twenty, so at any moment God can draw the line, and the sum is what constitutes our character for eternity.

One finds a suggestion of the relationship between eternity and love in the fondness of lovers to make vows under the moonlight. They are very conscious that their experience of mutual attraction is not something that is going to last. They escape the "now" moment by an appeal to eternity, by invoking an oath that their love will be stronger than death. Somehow or other, they know the ephemeral, or the present moment, does not explain love. Perhaps this is why all of the love songs have a ring of eternity about them: "Until the sands of the desert grow cold . . ."

Eternal Love also gives salvation from the daily routine of the rat race. The vision of eternity makes it possible to deal with the long haul. What is happening for the moment becomes insignificant in the light of eternity. Disappointments and trials and so forth can be borne because one does not buckle under crosses. It is not what one suffers that is unbearable in life, it is not knowing why. "One can bear any 'how' when he knows 'the why,' " said Nietzsche. It is Eternal Love which makes life both a drama and an expectancy.

Simone Weil, who lived through the madness to escape monotony and meaninglessness, wrote: "We must get rid of the superstition of chronology to find eternity." The religious mind does not seek to escape time but to redeem time; time is a novitiate in which one may say "Aye" or "Nay" to eternal happiness. Life is not cycles or a running round in circles but a pilgrimage; it may even be a nostalgia or a yearning for the Love from Whose hands we dropped. Particularly since that day when Eternity became incarnate and intemporalized, life became a moment of response to the Eternity. Every now and then we transcend time in a moment of prayer or communion. But, in general, time is not to be escaped; it is to be redeemed.

T. S. Eliot, in the face of the common man's escape from time into happenings and the literary man's escape by telescoping it, has said that the redeeming of time is not the work of an astrophysicist or a psychoanalyst, but rather:

> . . . *an occupation for the saint—*
> *No occupation either, but something given*
> *And taken, in a lifetime's death in love,*
> *Ardour and selflessness and self-surrender.*
> —"The Dry Salvages"

Francis Thompson, in flight from his home and his profession, from time, and from his very soul, would stretch out half-dead on a bench, dying of hunger. In his *Sister Songs* he described better than anyone else the desire to escape from the burden of time:

Forlorn, and faint, and stark,
I had endured through watches of the dark
The abashless inquisition of each star,
Yea, was the outcast mark
Of all those heavenly passers' scrutiny;
Stood bound and helplessly
For Time to shoot his barbèd minutes at me;
Suffered the trampling hoof of every hour
In night's slow-wheelèd car;
Until the tardy dawn dragged me at length
From under those dread wheels, and, bled of strength,
I awaited the inevitable last.

"Redeem the time" is St. Paul's counsel of urgency, to leap at it, seize it, turn it into goodness. The stream is ever passing before us. No sighs or tears will bring back one moment. Failing to redeem seconds means that they remain captives forever.

Eternity is not to be understood in terms of mechanical time which is measured by sundials, clocks, and chronometers. Eternity is better represented as something experienced, as in the legend of a magician who asked a caliph to dip his face in a basin of water. The caliph did as he was bidden and lived a full life's experience, followed by a succession of other lives—as a man, woman, sage, etc. During that last existence something startled him, and he noticed that he was just lifting himself from the basin of water. In a brief time, he lived a long life.

Eternity is without succession, a simultaneous possession of all joys. To those who live toward Eternity, it really is not something at the end; it is that which influences every moment of the "now." The reason for the Sabbath or the rest on the Seventh Day was to make man stand off from the flux of a workaday world to contemplate his origin and destiny. Nor is the end of the series the point where God is found. He is not outside the world; He is within it. "In Him, we live and move and have our being." The Immanentism is a kind of temporalization of Eternity; God became flesh and dwelt in our temporal order. Actually, the biblical view does not stress the "morrow"—but rather leaves it in God's care. We live in the interim between two comings, the last of which will be the complete dominion of Him Who already reigns in some hearts.

The Old Testament affirms that beneath the surface of the time-rhythms there is a movement toward the consummation of history. The location story in Genesis is the first telling of the whole human history, namely that of light dispelling darkness and leading up to the ultimate fulfillment of the Seventh Day.

What meaning and purpose are to reason, the Eternal in time and the Word made Flesh are to the order of grace. Time is, therefore, good; it is the stage in which Divine Love works its way out and where man makes decisions. In every prayer there is at least a brief wedding of time and Eternity. Those, therefore, who would escape time through drugs, LSD, and laziness are destroying that which lets in the Breath of the Eternal into our suffocated subways and bedarkened hearts. History, then, becomes understood as dotted by meaningful moments or appointed times, *kairoi* or "moments of visitation" or opportunities for grace. New creative moments flash in a continuous salvation history.

The breakthrough of the Eternal into time was so total that it split time into B.C. and A.D. With Christ something new appears, a complete renewal of temporal creation and the possibility of a "new man"—the time of the world in its totality is rooted and measured by Christ Who came in the "plenitude of time."

Time, then, is not a rat race. It is a race—but a race in which not everyone receives a crown; a race which is not cyclic and in circles, but an ascension, in which a tremendous injectus or push of Love is given at the first second of existence, and in which the open Arms of Eternal Love are held out at the end, like a father encouraging and aiding his child to keep striving, not falling, for the "sufferings of the life are not worthy to be compared with the joys which are to come."

CHAPTER THREE

Loneliness

A politician running for office christened his campaign with a beer party, asking for volunteers. So many young women descended on the hotel that there was almost a riot. Was it politics which interested them? No! It was partners! One of the first questions was, "How many men showed up?" They were a segment of the thousands and thousands of lonely young women in our modern urban civilization.

An elderly woman would stay up until midnight every night to hear an announcer say, "We are now signing off. Good night. Have a good sleep." This was her one contact with the world which relieved her loneliness. Others send for doctors who are their sole tie to the world, while others go to psychiatrists to find one who is interested in them, even though it costs a dollar a minute. The paradox of modern loneliness is that those who love only themselves hate to be with themselves. An old person said, "I am not afraid of dying, but I am afraid of living until I die."

Men who are leaders are lonely; the top man on the totem pole is lonely because separated from the life of the people. The masses are lonely as the bottom men on the totem pole, out of fear of being absorbed in the collectivity through an increasing lack of spiritual values and a sense of community. The infant is lonely if he lacks contact with his mother. The child is lonely if he lacks parental participation in play. The teen-ager is lonely if rejected by his fellows or because she has pimples.

Most people forget what they were like when they were children, but recollection will reveal a terrible loneliness. Five million children have parents who are divorced. The tension between the adults has a psychic repercussion on children. One mother who had been away for a year came back and said to her child, "Why, I almost forgot I had you." One of the effects on the children is to withdraw from others in order not to be hurt too easily again. When children quit school early, it is not just the lure of wages; it is the hope of finding acceptability in another environment.

Girls are lonely when they find themselves unattractive to boys. Loneliness is in part overcome by daydreaming and indulging in fantasy. The flight into gangs is to love oneself in a totality. Thus a totalitarian politics is born. The gang provides the members with a pseudobravado, which individually none of them possesses. Almost all the boys will say, "To go with others and start doing daring things takes you out of yourself. You feel small on your own, and you get lonesome and bored. When you're a gang, you talk big and think big."

Dante begins one of his finest poems with:

At the mid point of my life
I came to the dark wood.

The dark wood is when one loses the zest for life. Tolstoy, at the age of fifty, said as he passed through it:

All took place at a time when so far as my outward circumstances went, I ought to have been completely happy. I had a good wife who loved me and whom I loved; good children and large property which was increasing with no pains taken on my part. I was more respected by my kinsfolk and acquaintances than I ever had been; I was loaded with praise by strangers; and without exaggeration I could believe my life already famous. Moreover, I was not insane nor ill.

Canyons of Loneliness

Loneliness begins when we want to be with someone and cannot find anyone, and when we want someone to be with us and he refuses. Loneliness is an inability to find atoneness. A basic loneliness exists even in all human love simply because we become used to it or take it for granted, as the jeweler becomes used to handling precious gems. The most terrible penalty of all love is that one is no longer thirsty at the border of a well. To escape this loneliness in the later ages of life, some resort to a succession of spouses, adding zeros to zeros, where there is a substitution for love rather than a deepening of it. The last thing anyone expects when he gets married is to be lonely. But later on there can be the "loneliness together" when all stories have been told and all conversations exhausted.

But even in the deepest moments of true love, where there is the ecstatic union of husband and wife, there descends a great loneliness afterward, when one is thrown back upon himself and herself. Regardless of how much one desired to be lost in the other, one finds oneself alone—sated, satisfied, and yet not wholly complete.

A fear also exists of being betrayed in human relationships, and this makes one more lonely, because there cannot be a complete commitment to another. A strange man and woman met at a well. One said to the other, "I will not hurt you, if you do not hurt me." To love is to make oneself vulnerable and softens one to a point of becoming a target to the "slings and arrows of outrageous fortune."

Another loneliness is to be found in young women whom men do not treat as persons but as functions or machines. Young men will plead love to them, but what they love is themselves and not the one whom they praise. The result is that young women find themselves labeled as replaceable parts in an IBM civilization. Drink the water, forget the glass.

The penalties of loneliness are crucifying. Children, when they find that they are unloved, will sometimes begin to steal, finding their consolation in things rather than in hearts. How often a dog, when he is left alone in a house or an apartment, will begin to tear up furniture, papers, and telephone wires, as a protest against the fact that he is unloved.

Dr. René Spitz has given an account of ninety-one infants in a foundling home with all of the care that our comfortable modern civilization could give them in the way of food, clothing, toys, etc. But there was one thing lacking—the love of a mother. Each ten children had a nurse, which means that each had a decimal point of a mother. After three months, Dr. Spitz noted great changes in the children. Without mother love, 30 percent died the first year, and twenty-one who survived their time in the home were so scarred by life that they could be classed almost as idiots. No report was given on the other thirty-two who found their fulfillment in being cared for by foster parents.

Every lonely person is a hurt person, and that hurt may be on the inside or the outside. It is on the inside when someone whom we loved has wounded us. This is one of the deepest sorrows that can come to the human heart and made Christ say to Judas, "Wouldst thou betray the Son of Man with a kiss?" Said Caesar to his friend, "Et tu, Brute?" The outside hurts are those which cut us off from others, either because of our accent, our race, our color, our defects, our failings. This separation or exile is actually a kind of death, for the essence of death is detachment.

The Excessive Demand to Be Loved

The lonesome have an abnormal complex to be loved. Nothing is wrong about wanting to be loved, for by nature we are incomplete, bows without violins, saucers without cups, and hearts without affections. The danger is in exclusively wanting to be the object of affection without ever showing love. Then we become like the Dead Sea, which receives but does not give. The fresh waters of the Jordan pour into it but, having no outlet, its waters suffer no living creatures to flourish therein. It condemns itself to sterility because it does not serve.

Lonesome people may sometimes be religious—but it is better to say demireligious, for they separate love of God from love of neighbor. Love of God without that love concretized in neighbor is not piety but pietism. In one of the plays of Jan de Hartog we find this admirably brought out:

1938: Captain Joris Kuiper, a Christian who has transported a shipload of Jewish refugees to the New World, is told by a South American consul that they cannot enter his country and that he had better take them back to Nazi Germany.

> KUIPER: "These men are men; that's enough for me. . . . I've got a heart that feels, and a conscience that must answer to God, and a soul that's immortal. And so have they, even if their faith is not the true one. . . . For five years now, by the grace of God, I have lived in peace with my conscience and the laws of the world, growing in the Faith like a tree. What good would these five years have been if I let myself be felled by the first gale He blows at me to try my roots? I'll bend, sir, if God wills it; I'll let myself be split and splintered if God wills it; . . . but I will not take these people back."
>
> —*Skipper next to God*. Act I

In *If Winter Comes* by A. S. M. Hutchinson we read the story of Mark Sabre, who argues that despite what others may be saying about his motives, he is going to care for a wayward girl:

> " '. . . I felt that the girl had a claim on us. . . . she'd turned to us in her abject misery for help and that alone established a claim,

even if it had come from an utter stranger. It established a claim because here was a human creature absolutely down and out come to *us*, picking *us* out from everybody, for succour. . . . you've got to respond. You're picked out. You! One human creature by another human creature. Breathing the same air. Sharing the same mortality. Responsible to the same God. You've got to! You can't help yourself. . . . You can't get out of it. The same earth as your earth is there at your feet imploring you; and if you've got a grain, a jot of humanity, you must, you must, out of the very flesh and bones of you, respond to that cry of this your brother or your sister made, as you yourself are made.

The basic cause of loneliness is the excessive desire to be loved, for this creates an atmosphere of lovelessness. The more we seek to be loved, the less we are loved. The less we are loved, the less lovable we become. And the less lovable we become, the less capable we become of loving anyone else. Like a bird caught in a net, we deepen our tragedy.

As an example of such excessive desire to be loved, there was the young woman engaged to a young man who counted every telephone call that she received and every note. Adding them up, she felt that she was not sufficiently loved, so she began to write herself threatening letters. To make the fiction even more realistic, she lodged a complaint against the character in the city as the writer of the note. The result was that she who refused every means to become lovable had made herself very unlovable.

A mother had a daughter in college. The mother would call the daughter almost every night and keep her on the phone unpardonably long. Finally, the daughter, in order to avoid these long calls, which exasperated other students who wished to use the phone, told her mother that calls were not allowed. Later on the daughter was told to call back at a certain hour but was unable to do so because she had a class assignment. A friend put in the call; the mother, exasperated, claimed she was not loved at all by her children. Her desire for love had created lovelessness.

The same condition prevails among hypochondriacs who are constantly complaining about their aches, their pains, their sicknesses, in order to get attention. It is not long until very few people are willing to listen to their complaints; thus they who set out to win attention by showing their wounds finally reach a point where there is no one around to heal them.

A wife constantly demanded attention from her husband, saying that she was not appreciated. He would often stay away from work in order to take her on trips. He began to begrudge the time that was to be given to her, because love should be freely given; to demand love is to kill it. Then she began to suspect that there was another affair on the part of her husband, which indeed there was not. Thus the marriage was ruined. To pity oneself is the most weakening of all emotions, and loneliness, by a curious paradox, is begotten of the madness of the arms open to be embraced but never extended to serve.

The Indifference of the Nonlonely

Because the lonely isolate themselves, others feel justified in ignoring them. Their contribution to sinking into lower levels of isolation is a refusal to listen. Listening is a therapy for the lonesome.

A psychologist formulated an intricate marriage problem involving financial, moral, sexual, and legal elements. He presented it to one hundred priests and ministers; with a stopwatch in his pocket, he found that the average length of time that they listened before giving an "off the cuff" solution, or saying they were too busy, was two and one half minutes. No wonder the distressed desert the rectories and pastoral houses. Psychiatrists are better listeners. They get paid for it, of course, but they do listen. However, seeking a cure for loneliness on the psychological level, rather than on the moral and spiritual, often increases loneliness.

In George Bernard Shaw's *St. Joan*, King Charles said to her,

"Why do not the voices come to me? I am king." And Joan answered, "They do come to you; but you do not hear them. You have not sat in the field in the evening, listening for them. . . . If you prayed from your heart and listened to the trilling of the bells after they had stopped ringing, you would hear the voices as well as I do."

This is also one of the reasons why prayer is so imperfect. We do all of the talking but never listen. We would not go into a doctor's office, rattle off our symptoms, and then dash out. We mumble prayers, not giving ourselves time for response and for hearing that whisper which cannot be heard in thunderbolts, storms, and the noise of the highway, but only amidst gentle zephyrs and peace.

When there is no one to listen or sympathize, loneliness becomes a moment of confrontation with the whole mystery of life. There is nothing else in loneliness to which a man can appeal except self. There is no landscape to distract him, no sunset to admire. One is confronted with that mysterious double which is himself, imprisoned in a hall of mirrors. It is this which drives the high-school boy to the drugstore corner, the college boy to the café, and the lonely woman to endless routines of shadows at the movies.

A Cure for Loneliness

The most immediate cure for loneliness is to show kindness to others. The search for happiness by turning one's back on humanity kills happiness. The slums, the city hospitals, the missions, the unloved, the ugly, the socially disinherited—all these are potential remedies for the darkest of souls.

There is no cure for loneliness in distraction, in amusement, or in momentary excitement. Being outside us, they leave the inner man sometimes even more destitute. In any case, it is not things that make us lonely; it is rather persons or the absence of persons. Our healing then must involve personal relationships. Even negatively this is evident, for we know that some persons can hurt us more than they can heal. Even when they come back to bind up our wounds, their very attempt to solace is in itself another wound. But granted this abuse, it only proves that the balm for hurt minds is hidden somewhere in personal relationships.

Even the love of God for lonesome people is to be shown through persons who love God. If my love is inspired by a desire for pleasure or reward or the emotional satisfaction, then there is not a deep personal relationship. If, however, the love that I have is inspired by God, then the other person feels less lonely because truly loved. It is my friendliness that must make others feel loved. It is my trust in them which must make them feel worthwhile, just as my own anxiety and nervousness can lead to their anxiety and nervousness.

One wonders if there has ever been a lonely missionary in the world—certainly not, if he was serving either the body or the spirit of another. I saw an American missionary living in a leper colony in a piano box—not a grand piano box but an upright piano box. The side was on hinges; each night he would put himself into the base of the box and pull up the side—this was his home. He found the lepers after the camp had been broken up by an invading army. Gathering them together, he resolved never to leave them and is with them to this day. The moment we begin to put love where we do not find it, two things happen: we find the other person lovable, and we become less lonely.

To love the seemingly unlovable requires effort, but it is no great effort once we realize that God loves us. What is there in any one of us that should make us pleasing to God and worthy of His Redemption? If, then, I who am unlovable am loved by God, then I can begin helping the unlovable. Otherwise, their unlovableness will bring out this bad reaction in me. Once I begin to accept other people as they are, then I begin to find that others will accept me as I am.

The Best Consoler

The best healer is the person who himself has been hurt. The best consoler of the lonely is one who knows what loneliness is. Counselors who have never felt aloneness can never impart a true sense of caring. Somewhere, somehow, there has to be hidden in the healing universe hands that have been hurt and scarred. There has been much condemnation of Thomas the Apostle because he doubted; but he has been very much misunderstood. Thomas said, "I will not accept any healer for the agonies and tortures, doubts and darkness and loneliness of my soul, except Someone Who Himself has been rejected, hated, despised, separated from men, and still had made light come out of that darkness."

Lonely persons should never seek advice from those who have not suffered. It need not necessarily be a hurt of loneliness, but it must be someone who can go beyond words which are empty and cheap. It is not so much the one who speaks who heals, but how much the healer has suffered, even in seeing the affliction of another.

In the story of the good Samaritan, the priest and Levite passed by. It is possible that they were on their way to temple services. Sometimes liturgical offices must be abandoned when a neighbor is in grave need. A man of another race picks up the wounded man, brings him to an inn, and cares for him. The priest and the Levite walked round the wounded man—that is, made a detour in order not to see him. This is what the rich man did when Lazarus was at his door. It was not because he was afraid of his lice or his leprosy, but simply because he did not want to *see* him. Looking at a neighbor's misery is one of the first steps in brotherly love. Love begins with the eyes, and then it goes out to the hands. When the poor sinful woman came into Simon's house, Our Lord asked him if he *saw* the woman. Brotherly love begins with *eye* control.

Some Loneliness Is to Be Expected

What makes lonesomeness more oppressive is the belief that we should never be lonesome. Many believe that we should never have tensions. If we had no tensions, we would be abnormal. How can we avoid not having tensions, since we are like batteries with a negative and a positive pole? Our body and our spirit do not want the same things at the same time. It is rare to find an athlete who is also a brilliant student, because the care of the body forces some neglect of the mind, and a dedication to the books often means a relaxation of the muscles. Our ego has two landing fields: one of pleasures which are generally associated with our feeling, and one of joys which are at the other extreme of the spirit.

So it is with lonesomeness. This earth is not our final home; we get what we want, and then we do not want it. Possession dulls. Romance thrills and marriage may become monotonous. We were absolutely sure, as we looked forward to something in life, that if we obtained it, we would be at peace—we got it, and with it boredom. We are on an endless quest, and because we are not quite sure of what it is—or being sure, we are afraid of losing it—we are anxious, uneasy, and in pieces rather than at peace.

Loneliness is indigenous to our state of life here below, partly because we are pilgrims on a journey to a Promised Land, partly because complete happiness is impossible here below, partly because, like young people who do not come into an inheritance until they reach majority, we do not attain fortune until death has intervened. As Augustine said: "Our hearts were made for Thee, O lord, and they are restless until they rest in Thee."

By nature, we are panting creatures; we taste and we hunger again; we drink and we thirst again. When the bird refuses to sing, we regild the cage; when we are unhappy, we keep adding externals and opiates to quiet our feverish souls. Many a man thinks he is becoming better because he condemns himself for this restlessness;

but self-severity is a vain comfort. As yet we are as plants which grow not perfectly in alien soil.

It is not the pursuit of happiness which makes us unhappy but the pursuit of what might be called the misplaced infinite. We put marble busts on the stem of the rose, and it cannot bear the weight. So, too, lonesomeness increases as we misunderstand the nature of our pleasures. Pleasure is not a bride but a bridesmaid. It is a by-product, something that follows what we do or ought to do, but it cannot be sought directly or it escapes.

But pleasures are like poppies spread,
You seize the flower, its bloom is shed; . . .
—ROBERT BURNS

Even the beauty of great paintings is lost by looking at them from the wrong angle or even in the improper light. The true flower of pleasure is thrown into our lap when we are thinking of something else. We cannot acquire absolute rights to God's great estate; we are only tenants.

To set up as a standard "to have a good time" is not to enjoy oneself; happiness is outside time. The less conscious we are of the passing of time, the more we enjoy ourselves. The more time weighs upon us, the more miserable we are. "Kill time" is really right; in order to have perfect happiness we have to get outside time where there is no succession, no before and after, but where all things are enjoyed at once.

We are now speaking here of metaphysical loneliness—the absence of God, while limiting loneliness to everyday experience. So long as we are on the earth, we will be lonesome, not always in a social sense but in a spiritual sense. We fall short of perfect Love. But as soon as one identifies this with God, one is met with the challenge, "What interest does Love have in our loneliness?"

Does God know the loneliness of a poverty so wretched as to be born amongst animals with no other cushion than hay? Was He ever as lonely as a refugee, an exile with no civil rights, obliged to flee a dictator hundreds of miles? Was He ever so lonely at home that He fled to a big city as a boy? Does God know what it is not to have a white-collar job and to have hands so callused as to alienate one from a soft-hand society? Does God know how lonely it is to be driven out of a home town after an attempt on His Life? Does God know the loneliness of spending your life with the dull-witted, the ignorant, the slow, and with those from the wrong side of the tracks? Does God know what loneliness there is in deafness and dumbness, and become so identified with them that He sighs, as if they were His own? Does God know bereavement, sorrow, and the loneliness of losing a devoted friend, or a weeping widow in tears at a grave?

Did God ever shed a tear, such as a patriot sheds at seeing his country decay or as a father sheds at the sight of the moral rottenness of a son or as all humans have done at a grave? Did He ever fear facing death? Did He know what it was to have the cards stacked against Him? Did He ever feel abandoned? Were His lips ever betrayed? Did He know anything about the hunger of the slum dwellers who go even four days without eating? Did He ever face the absurd in which it seemingly does no good to be good and where even the lover of truth is nailed to a scaffold?

Was He ever shadowed by bureaucracies, by police, by intellectual snipers? Was He ever falsely accused of being an alcoholic? Was He ever lost, wandering about asking and answering questions of men? Did He ever have to do dirty work like washing the feet of dirty men? Did He ever go into darkness? Did He ever so much immerse Himself in human anxiety and loneliness that He could cry out, "My God, why hast Thou abandoned Me?"

There are two answers to these questions. One is to gather up these doubts, fears, abandonment, and incorporate them into a system saying: "Life is absurd." "God is dead." "Hell is my neighbor."

The other answer is to say if God did enter into this human

condition—this muck, doubt, darkness, and loneliness—and make them a part of Himself and still overcame them, then I can go on. Once this Figure plunged into this cauldron of loneliness—then, we are face to face not with some superior Celestial Command hidden in an atomproof shelter, who is indifferent to anyone who presses a button to atomize this loneliness and anxiety. Rather, we have Someone Who plunges into them, crosses a line into their clawing fingers, and never goes back until He has conquered.

Identification was so complete that He claimed no immunity from the ills and sufferings of mankind. If you were the only one in the world who had eyes, would you not be a staff to the blind? Love never isolates itself from the misery of others, taking a glance and then crossing back to a point where they cannot be seen. Love incarnates itself with suffering humanity.

So one was He with lonely men that on the gallows He speaks for the forsakenness of man but never loses sight of God. He calls upon Him to witness the load that He is carrying—namely, that there is not a wound in all the world that He would not carry, no sin He would not have thrust into His conscience, and no robbery that He would not feel as if its guilt were in His hands; no rotten thought that He would not feel in His own crowned head; no excesses of carnality that would not be His as His flesh hung from His Body like dirty rags; no alcoholism that He would not feel as His own as He suffered thirst; no prodigality and delinquency of youth that He would not experience in His feet riven with steel to make up for their wanderings; no pornographic visions that would not lay their viciousness upon Him as blood congealed in His eyes; no blasphemies that ever curled from human lips that would not resound in His ears from volcanoes of hate and craters of blasphemy at the foot of the Cross; no adultery, false love, forgetfulness of vocations that He would not feel in His side perforated with steel; no human grief of sorrowing mothers that would not be His grief, as He looked upon His Mother with a kind of mystical sword running through her pure heart; no loneliness that He would leave unexperienced as when our fellowmen desert us in trial and only one of His Apostles was at the Cross.

No breath,
Without Him, sorrow draws; no feet
Wax weary, and no hands hard labour bear,
But He doth wear
The travail and the heat:
Also, for all things perishing, He saith,
"My grief, My pain, My death."
—LAURENCE HOUSMAN

Here is loneliness and meaninglessness that fled to God. As soon as one sees all this in the light of the Resurrection, then one may never overcome loneliness, but one is never *overcome*. Perfect Love casts out fear. Faith is only when the chips are down. As the old woman said, "I am not afraid, because I know to whom I can run, if anybody chases me." The universe is fatherly. I do not have to go about looking into abysses, voids, writing dirty plays, hot with blasphemies.

In the loneliness of life one does not ask "Why?" but "To what end?" One thing is certain, God would not have shared all this loneliness if loneliness did not fit into the Divine Plan. I may have to walk through dark forests, but I see footprints leading to the City. I may live on a cross, but I see the glory of the empty tomb. I may have to battle, for life is a struggle, but in any case I fight not under a Captain Who has never sensed a wound, but One Who stumbled to His Throne.

CHAPTER FOUR

The Treasures of the Subconscious

Service of others is one of the cures for loneliness, but there is an-other within man himself—his subconscious mind. The mind, from one point of view, is made up of what is called the conscious and unconscious. The conscious mind is like the first floor of a home where visitors are entertained, where we wear our best face and make ourselves presentable. The subconscious, on the other hand, may be likened to a cellar into which we throw a number of our unpleasant experiences, failures, embarrassments, and rubbish we do not like to think about, such as a relative who was hanged for sheep stealing. We keep all these out of decent company whom we hope to win as friends or to influence. Not only do we throw junk and rubbish into that cellar, but it has its own measure of the noi-some, vexing, and uncongenial, such as environmental rats which come up from the outside, water which seems to seep up through the floor, or termites and mold.

Besides the unsavory thoughts and experiences we hurl down into the cellar, there are also certain basic instinctive drives, the deepest one of which, according to Freud, is the urge to pleasure or sex, though others say it is the urge to superiority (Adler) or secu-rity (Jung). Were we born with them, or did they come from out-side? They came from outside us in the sense that all our experi-ences, unpleasant or pleasant, have resulted from our contact with environment. Other psychologists would say that these drives come from the outside also, because they are a part of our evolutionary hangover or descent from the animal; and because we inherit from humanity myths and symbols which often appear in dreams.

It is not easy for these impulses and stimulations to get up into consciousness, because at the top of the cellar stairs is a "censor" who is a kind of a protector of the taboos, conventions, and morality. Freud calls this the superego. Just as soon as one little impulse goes up the step, the censor cracks him over the head. The instinctual drive, as a result, begins to chafe and be unhappy because denied expression, repressed, and stepped on. If it be the sex urge, it has to disguise itself, put on some mock livery to slip by the censor at the gate. It generally does this when the censor is asleep. But being so often repressed, the strangled instinct comes up as a dream—but a disguised dream. The dreamer may not always know what it means, but it is the business of the psychoanalyst to tell him its meaning. This is the view of Freud.

Some "sexiatrists" interpret every dream in terms of sex, thus making it the key to man instead of man the key to sex. They recommend wholesale abandonment on the ground that all repression is bad. This theory forgets, however, that every expression involves repression of some kind. If I repress stealing, I express honesty; if I repress anger, I express compatibility.

The Other Side of the Subconscious

But has psychology revealed totally the mystery of the subconsciousness? Besides these libidinous instincts, repressed desires, drives to pleasure and sex, and the collective myths of our human ancestry, is there not another drive? Our consciousness and anthropology reveal a great treasure in the depths of our being. The subconsciousness need not be just a cesspool, something we are so ashamed of that it takes constant prodding to bring it to the surface; it is not always a sewerage and drainage system full of the muck and rot of our lives.

Besides the *id* there is another neglected area for which we have to find a name. Since Freud used the Latin word *id* to signify that cellar of repressed desires, we will use a Greek word *pneuma* to describe the other aspect, though we could use the Hebrew word *ruah*.

Both the *id* and the *pneuma* are in the subconscious levels of our mind; through them pass suggestions, desires, urges, drives, and impulsions which seek entrance into the conscious level of life and conduct. They are also the same in that there is a little censor at the top of the stairs who can keep down the dynamisms, drives, and thrusts of the *pneuma* if it does not like them. In fact, there are seven censors battling against the *pneuma*: Egotism, Lust, Greed, Anger, Laziness, Intemperance, and Jealousy. But there is one big difference: the *id* is principally concerned with the drive to pleasure. The *pneuma* is concerned with a drive toward peace, harmony, integration, and happiness. There is in us a double drive: one toward giving release to our carnal nature, the other giving freedom to our deeper spiritual nature. One is an urge to flaunt conscience and the moral law and to be bad; the other is to grow in goodness and love of neighbor; one is to exalt our own ego, the other to serve neighbor and to crush our selfishness.

We are, therefore, solicited in two ways: one toward release of what is egotistic, the other toward a harmony and perfection of our nature. In other words, we are tempted also to be good.

Turning Temptation—A New Look at Temptation

How far we have gotten away from the total understanding of our subconscious mind will be clear from one word. When I say the word "temptation," what images and ideas are conjured up in your mind? "Sex"? "Get drunk"? "Rob"? "Steal"? and so on. Why do we always associate the word with what is rotten, immoral, and antisocial? Why does the subconsciousness always have to be considered a Gehenna or a drainage ditch? Why do we assume that every solicitation we have is something we would be ashamed to admit in polite society? Analyze yourself, and you will find this astounding fact—that you have more temptations to be good than you have to be bad.

How many times have you been tempted to help a poor family, and how often you felt sad if you did not and happy when you did? How often you were tempted to give up excessive drinking, bad temper, stealing, to "see what is in the Bible," to be kinder to your wife, more gentle to your children, less cranky with your employees, less sarcastic to your neighbor, to try praying, to share your wealth with the hungry, to be more interested in community welfare? It is not only devils who walk up those stairs to the conscious mind; the stairs are really like Jacob's ladder with angels on every rung. And as regards repression, we knock more good thoughts over the head than we do bad thoughts. If, as some say, repression of our primitive instincts is wrong, why is not the repression of our meaningful instincts also wrong?

Why must we think of our subconscious always as a garbage pail instead of a dinner table? Why conceive that the energy of electric power is to give us a shock and not to light and heat? Are there only snakes underground, or do we also find gold? Does not the depths of the soul shoot up oil and fountains of water, as well as being the centers of earthquakes? The time has come when psychiatrists must see the subconscious not just as a mudhole where pigs love to wallow but also a runway where planes take off for a flight into the sky. The subconscious may be a basement, but it is one not only where we throw out refuse, but also keep our groceries, our hobbies, and our playroom and our wine.

What Is This Voice?

What about the origin of this *pneuma* which transmits urges and drives from the subterranean part of our lives? Where does it come from? As psychiatrists say, the *id* has its origin outside us; so does the *pneuma*. The *id,* they say, is due either to contacts with our environment or more remotely with our animal ancestry, or it is cultural lag in the evolutionary process, a result of the collective unconsciousness of the race.

As the origin of the *id* is external—that is, not wholly of our making—and yet that through which all our drives function, so the origin of the *pneuma* is external, even much more so, though it, too, functions through our subconsciousness. In fact, it is very mysterious, something like the wind which is invisible and yet strong. We pass over naming the source of the *pneuma* to concentrate on its silent, enigmatical intrusion into our subconsciousness.

How often we have been moved by an inspiration to change our lives; we know that it does not come from ourselves, for when we have it, we say, "I don't know what made me do this." A truck driver in Los Angeles, speeding down a highway, saw a large paper carton ahead of him. Generally, he said, he would drive over it and crush it, for it gave him a sense of power. But this time, he suddenly swerved to avoid it, stopped, got out of his truck cab, and went back to take it off the highway. Lo and behold, it was moving! A little boy had crawled into it and was propelling himself across the road. When asked what made him do it, the driver answered, "God! Because I never acted that way before."

How often a soldier in battle will be suddenly inspired to crawl out of a trench in the face of murderous shellfire to rescue a wounded buddy in a veritable no-man's-land. Braver than ever before in his life, he is praised for his rescue but will disdain it, saying, "Anyone else would have done it. I deserve no credit." In other words, "I did not do it—*something else moved me.*"

A characteristic of the upsurgence of the subconscious mind is what might be called sensing a crisis. H. G. Wells expressed it well: "At times in the silence of the night, and in rare lonely moments, I come upon a sort of communion of myself and something great that is not myself . . . it takes on the effect of a sympathetic person and my communion has a quality of fearless worship." What is present is a kind of dissolving of the elements of consciousness, as if some new chemical had been poured into the soul, and there begins to be a surrender to what the individual believes to be a higher power.

Thus there pass through the subconscious mind inspirations, insights, new values, and motivations which never before were entertained. They did not come from ourselves, and if we correspond with them, they completely remake us. They change fear into love, indifference into enthusiasm, hate into service. This *pneuma does not belong to our nature as such*, though the *id* does. But it is so constantly introduced into our impoverished nature that it seems to be a part of our life. When it touches us, it seems to affect principally our intellect and our will: the intellect, by enlightening us to see a truth we never saw before, and our will by giving us a power to do something we never had the strength to do before.

But the healing and elevating power of the *pneuma* always sets up a counterresistance on the part of our disordered human condition. We are not easily persuaded to give up our sinking ship. The *id* revolts against the *pneuma* and the *pneuma* against the *id*, making our heart the battleground. The egotistic self is threatened with its conceits, lusts, imtemperance, anger, and the like. To die to them is not easy, even though the prospect of peace is so appealing and desirable. But once the *pneuma* is at the helm of the ship, the psychic regions are filled with an indescribable joy and delight.

A New Heart

Just as not everyone gives way to the sexual license which the *id* may suggest, so not everyone accepts the temptation of the *pneuma* to reorganize one's life. But when one does, among many effects which might be mentioned we concentrate on but one—a complete change of life's direction.

If I take a ball and roll it across the floor, it will move in one direction unless diverted by a superior power. So, too, our lives very quickly become grooved through habit. They will roll by mere inertia in that same direction of crime, insensibility, mediocrity, emptiness, banality, unless some outside power or force alters their direction.

A law runs through nature that the lower is taken up into the higher. Chemicals are taken up into plants, plants into animals, and animals into man. Everywhere there is an upsurge to life. Lower life is meant to be born to a higher life. But there is one condition—the carbons, phosphates, oxygen, nitrogen, and other chemicals are never privileged to live in a plant kingdom, unless two things happen: The plant must intercept them, incorporate them into itself, and the chemicals, in their turn, must die to their lower nature. It is as if the grass and the trees and the roses said to the chemicals, "Unless you die to yourself, you cannot live in my kingdom. You must be reborn from above."

Plants, in their turn, can become one with the sentient, mobile life of the animal, if the animal comes down to them, descends to their lower life, and takes them up into itself. The plant, in its turn, must be pulled up from the roots. The same is true of the lower orders living in our body—to become one with the living, thinking, loving being, man must humble himself and go down to their lower state; they in turn must submit to the sacrifice of the knife and the fire, and thus the law is fulfilled: "Unless you die to yourself you cannot live in my kingdom. You must be born again from above."

Now the *pneuma* which works inside us is a summoning presence, a kind of alien intruder, but one which always respects our freedom. Animals do not consult plants nor carry on a dialogue with them before using them as food. But the *pneuma* does not violently possess us; it solicits quietly, it tempts, it leads us into a desert, it begs us to die to what is lower. Once we freely consent to absorb the élan and drive of the *pneuma*, there is a peace which the world cannot give and a joy which surpasses all understanding. Most of us miss the exhilaration, because we prefer to move in the horizontal areas of monotony instead of the vertical heights where there is new knowledge and deeper love.

There is not a single person in the world who has not experienced both the *id* and the *pneuma*, though greater priority is given to the *id* than the *pneuma*, because it titillates the flesh and makes no demands on the ego. The *id* belongs to what William James has called the once-born; the *pneuma* to those who are twice-born. We have three ways of knowing: One is by our senses, such as the clasp of a hand. The second is by abstract ideas and scientific training, such as the science of physics. Over and above both feeling and intellect, there is another kind of knowledge which a husband and wife have after many years of married life—they have come to know one another by loving one another. This kind of knowledge the *pneuma* gives, only its love is more intense.

A new heart is created within us by a response to the *pneuma*. From the fleshy heart, there goes forth blood to the body and then a return flow to it. The heart understood psychologically also is understood as the center from which flows our mental and moral activity. From it comes all our character-worth, and to it returns all our good merits; but the heart can also be the center of depravity which corrupts the whole circuit of life. "Out of the heart comes forth evil thoughts, murders, adulteries, fornications, thefts, false witnesses."

A boy in a family could not be induced to keep himself clean: dirty fingernails, hair hanging like a mop, clothes unpressed, dirty shoes. The parents begged, pleaded, coaxed, and even tried to bribe him into cleanliness. It did no good. But one day he appeared clean, brushed, and neat. He did not slam the door as he went out. What made the difference? He was in love with Suzie! This is the key to *pneuma* which reorients life; it is essentially love but not an earthly love.

As there are compulsive drinkers and compulsive addicts in the *id* world, so there are compulsive lovers of humanity and compulsive lovers of Love in the *pneuma* world. We are no longer in the presence of demons and pink elephants, but of a Light which unfailingly allows us to follow footprints in the darkest forest of life.

I knew a man in London who told me that he had been an alcoholic for years; so enslaved was he that he would take off his shoes at the saloon door and sell them for a drink. This particular year he was seated on a bench at Hyde Park, musing about his miserable condition. Suddenly he felt a strong urge to reform his life. He professed ignorance as to where the resolution came from, but he said that it was not from himself. Following this inspiration was easy, but putting it into practice was difficult. He went into a church, and there came over him immediately an intense craving for drink. He ran to the rear of the church to escape, but he knelt down at the door. From that time on, the goal of his life was changed. He now spends his time caring for his fellow alcoholics in the same London dive where he lived for years. The day the inspiration seized him, he knew only one thing—it came not from himself. He had been hell-bent, and suddenly he was, after a struggle, on the heaven-bent road to inner happiness. The *pneuma* confronted him on the inside of his being, but it came from the outside. It was as if another Presence was in his life, acting like a radar bringing him to the port of Peace.

Another example is given by the Russian novelist, Tolstoy. His despairing nature drove him to the thought of suicide. Then, as he put it, something contrary to his mood seized him:

I felt [says Tolstoy] that something had broken within me on which my life had always rested, that I had nothing left to hold on to, and that morally my life had stopped. An invincible force impelled me to get rid of my existence, in one way or another.

Yet, whilst my intellect was working, something else in me was working too, and kept me from the deed—a consciousness of life, as I may call it, which was like a force that obliged my mind to fix itself on another direction, and draw me out of my situation of despair.

During the whole course of this year, when I almost unceasingly kept asking myself how to end the business, whether by the rope or by the bullet, during all that time, alongside of all those movements of my ideas and observations, my heart kept languishing with another pining emotion. I can call this by no other name than that of a thirst for God.

The Inner Thermostat

We have in our subconscious a mass of dead ideas, lifeless hopes, faded childhood memories, and lost faiths. We would like to get back to their innocence and joy, but they are cold and sepulchered. Then what was crucified by us suddenly rises from the dead; what was cold is now hot; what was crystal now becomes a living cell. What was on the periphery of life now becomes a center; what we ignored now is valued. And we know very well that this old building in which we lived, with its leaky plumbing and cracked walls, did not suddenly become a mansion without some builder from the outside. If my life is traveling in the direction of "confusion worse confounded," and all of a sudden changes its course, with new goals, then the Latin maxim applies: *Nihil movetur nisi per aliud movetur.* "Nothing is moved unless it is moved by another." The new mental arrangement of ideas, the sudden thrust of some alien motor efficacy, demands a source outside of me and yet working inside me and principally through my subconsciousness.

The classic playboy of all antiquity was Augustine, who combined the greatness of the intellect with a sexual abandon which he justified by rationalization. One day the dissension between his sex life and his higher aspirations became so intense that he picked up St. Paul's Letter to the Romans; in it he read that not in wantonness, immorality, strife, and envy do we work out salvation. It acted as a thunderbolt in his soul with his wasted young life. Changing the direction of his life after the impact of the *pneuma,* he cried out: "Too late, O Ancient Beauty, have I loved Thee!"

A spiritual knowledge under the *pneuma* is arrived at so quickly that the intellectual is left behind; one is not able to find a cause for the change in any previous thought. No one goes from the life of sin to holiness without some intervening cause which is sufficient to account for the change. There has been what is nothing less than a Divine-Human encounter. A power enters into the subconsciousness which regenerates, changes direction, alters the moral character, making precious what was previously vile and vile what was previously precious.

No new faculties are created. They are just regenerated. What happens may be likened to putting a lamp inside the Japanese lantern. It was nothing but a crisscross of crazy patterns. Once the light was put in it, there was a unification of color and line so that a pattern was revealed. The change may also be likened to a new kind of vision. We have the same eyes at night as we have in the day, but we cannot see at night because we lack the light of the sun. So a new light is given which enables us to see things that before we could not see.

There is never any violation of personality. No invasion is there like to what has been described as possession. But there is a *surrender* of self to Another. Looking back on the evil that one has done, one never sees it as a violation of the law, but rather as hurting someone we love. A new master center takes possession of personality and gives it what Frankl calls "a will to meaning." The whole life begins to be organized, not merely as a sum of parts but rather as a whole, very much the same as the melody which is heard very differently from the distinct notes on the paper.

Id requires analysis, because the mind is all mixed-up. The *pneuma* synthesizes. To analyze the waters which pour into a sinking ship is not to save the ship; to plow by constantly looking back to see if the furrow is crooked may even make life more zigzag. Under probing, the true essence of life vanishes. Our physiological life demands harmony, the tiny cell choosing from its environment what it is able to assimilate; the psychological demands similar peace. A regulator, a kind of thermostat is at the center of our organism, seeking to establish constants, such as temperature, blood pressure, and digestion. The automatic control is ever working to synthesize harmony and meaning.

So, too, there functions in the depths of our being another kind of regulator, or constant, summoning us back to order and to peace. Little warning lights begin to flicker as they do in the cockpit of a plane when anything is wrong, such as an unlocked door or an overheated motor. That is, organized sensitivity to the body becomes spiritual sensitivity in the conduct of our lives. A carpenter uses a gauge containing a colored liquid. He lays it on a board to see if it is level. Once he finds it off center, he begins to make the adjustment and correction. So, too, in us is an adjuster which makes us rediscover inner peace and the true center, even in the midst of errors and excesses.

It has been proved medically that the power of healing wounds at a certain age increases when the temperature of the body is raised by four degrees. It is conceivable that the power of the *pneuma*, which increases the joy and the love in a person, may also accelerate the healing of the anxiety and chaos in the depths of being.

Now, what is this *pneuma*? *Pneuma* is the Spirit, the Spirit of God, the Spirit of Christ. As my body lives, thanks to my soul, so my soul begins really to live, thanks to the Spirit. Because this Spirit comes from outside us, and is not either of our making or of our deserving, it is free or gratis or what is commonly called *grace*. The *id* draws to pleasure of the flesh; the *pneuma* to the joys of the spirit. It might be well to cut down on the temptations of the *id* and begin giving way to the temptations of the *pneuma*.

CHAPTER FIVE

The New Taboo

What adds to loneliness and diminishes the joy of the *pneuma* is the new taboo. In the Victorian days it was sex. A discreet silence was kept on anything that had to do with birth, generation, and the carnal expression of love. That taboo has been done away with, though its elimination has not diminished problems associated with it, as was claimed. What is the taboo of the twentieth century which corresponds to the nineteenth-century taboo on sex? The taboo of death.

In the more Christian days, death was something that was always kept in mind and for which we were to be prepared: *Memento mori*. Now the physicians shrink from telling the patient that he is dying, that he might prepare for it either legally or spiritually. Patients are sometimes kept alive with a network of tubes from oxygen tanks long after consciousness has departed. Besides depriving a person of his death through silence, there is an awkwardness in the face of death itself. Mourners do not know what to say to the bereaved. Preachers are instructed not to refer to it but rather to gardens, fresh flowers, and gentle winds blowing through meadows.

The same evasions that were told in the Victorian days about sex—namely, the stork bringing babies—are told today about death. Funeral cosmetics are used to destroy that borderline between life and death; mourning, widows' weeds, black bands, plumed horses, elaborate hearses, all conspire to cover up the inevitable. Even when it is spoken of, it is covered up with words such as: "It has to come to all of us," or "Everyone must die."

Bruce Marshall in his novel, *Fair Bride*, writes:

> Down in the street, the municipal hearse flashed by on one of its daily journeys to the cemetery. From the high window the naked corpse lying in the unlidded coffin looked like a doll in a cardboard box. There were no mourners and no priests. There was no hope, no despair, no mystery. Everything was simple and clear: life meant something only because it meant nothing.

Tennessee Williams in *Camino Real* makes the last receptacle of our outworn humanity not the graveyard, but the garbage pail.

This taboo on death has brought on what might be called the Second Fall, when understanding of immortality is lost. Perhaps now we have reached an age when we may speak of the two falls or two types of humanity. The once-fallen had hope in the Redeemer; the twice-fallen live in a universe that is silent, where radar sends back no sound, where the center of the universe has fallen apart, and belief in future life has vanished. One is asked to be brave when life is meaningless. This is what is called "heroism with its eyes out," as Carlyle described the ethics of John Stuart Mill. The humanity of the Second Fall is disillusioned with nature, with humanity, and with society; nothing makes sense. The only point of death is its absurdity. Karl Marx once described belief in life after death as "pie in the sky." In the Second Fall, there is neither a pie nor a sky. Camus expressed it well for the Second Fall: "There is but one truly serious philosophical problem and that is suicide." Why stay alive in a meaningless universe? In that meaningless universe, he died as he crashed his car into a tree.

Some grow old physiologically while they attempt to remain young psychologically. They try to stop the clock of life, or else to turn the hands back, hugging to childhood. Sexagenarians put on rouge, imagining themselves to be in their teens; they are as pillars of salt, fixed in their flight from death, with no close bond either to the youth which they seek to imitate or to the living reality of their present hour.

The Reason for the Taboo

In previous ages, men lived in existence at which there were two ends, neither of which belonged to existence itself. One was birth, the other death. Birth and death were the two questions which made one ask: "Where did I come from?" "Where am I going?"

Birth itself was not explicable by existence, for it was before my existence. Otherwise we would have to say that the egg was the cause of the chicken which laid it. Death, too, is not explicable by our existence, for it is its negation. Suppose now one cuts off these two terminal points of birth and death from existence—then life becomes meaningless. As long as men pondered about their origin and their destiny, neither of which were explicable by their finiteness, they could find answers to the riddle of life. But once these great questions were no longer pondered, the universe ceased to be transparent like a window; it became opaque like a curtain. The sacred was written off as the unreal, and one did his best to settle down to a kind of cosmic coziness which was never very cozy. The old became afraid to die, the young afraid to live.

What we cannot explain we disavow and ignore. The time span of life becomes meaningless, since it was without an origin and a destiny, as a journey is meaningless without a point of departure and a point of arrival. The subject of death thus became a taboo in which there was a disavowal of death through face-lifting, the refusal to recognize one's age, the denial of responsibility, the glorification of the absurd, and fondness for death songs among the youth. Playwrights came to the rescue by staging, as Ionesco did, a corpse which gradually rose until it floated away as a balloon to nowhere. The periodical injection of paraffin into the corpse of

Lenin is the Communist way of avoiding the taboo of death and giving immortality, which it denies, to mortality.

Despite the disavowals, there are some psychologists who deplore "the slick, smooth operation of easing the corpse out by saying no to weeping, wailing, and expressing grief and loneliness. What effect does this have psychologically? It may mean that we have to mourn covertly, by subterfuge—perhaps in varying degrees of depression, perhaps in mad flights of activity, perhaps in booze." Another psychologist recalls that it might result in "a callousness, a rational preoccupation with the fear of death and vandalism."

Decades of Communism have not hidden the desire for something beyond the temporal. In *Dr. Zhivago,* the work suppressed by the Communists, Boris Pasternak writes: "It was not until after the coming of Christ that time and man could breathe freely. It was not until after Him that men began to live toward the future. Man does not die in the ditch like a dog—but at home in history, while the work called the conquest of death is in full swing; he dies sharing in this work."

Psychiatry

The psychiatrist best equipped to deal with this subject is a Jew who himself saw tens of thousands of his people, as well as Christians, go to the awful furnaces of Auschwitz and other concentration camps. Only he who lived with death knows anything about it. Dr. Viktor Frankl writes in *From Death Camp to Existentialism* that psychological observations of thousands of prisoners revealed that men who let go of the inner hold of their moral and spiritual selves generally fell victim to the degenerating influence of the camp. But what was this "inner hold"? It was "a goal to reach." The man who lacked this inner hold generally fell into retrospective thoughts, contrasting his early experience with those of the present, and thus fell into a blue mood. Dr. Frankl then further defines this inner hold:

It is a peculiarity of man that he can only live by looking to the future—*sub specie aeternitatis.*

. . . The prisoner who had lost his faith in the future was doomed. . . . Some prisoners had dreams that on a certain day they would be released. They immediately picked up in the light of that illusion. But when they were not released on that day, they died almost immediately. As Nietzsche has said: "He who has a *why* to live for can bear with almost any *how.*"

One woman told the doctor that she was grateful that life had hit her so hard, for in her preprison days she had wasted her opportunities and ignored her spiritual development. Now, she said, "I am happy, for I have a tree out there in my loneliness. And that tree speaks to me every day, and it says to me: 'I am eternal life.' "

Another prisoner made a pact with Heaven that his suffering and death should save the human being that he had loved the most. He did not want to die for nothing. What threatens man is an existential vacuum or nothing to live for. What gives him hope is something in the future to which he can dedicate his life. Then "the sufferings of this life are not worthy to be compared to the joys which are to come."

When anyone gave up the future, he said: "I had nothing more to expect from life." In prison, as long as men were living for a future, such as a wife and children or a home or medical books to write, they were sustained in the present.

If a temporal future so much sustains, how much more strength was given when the future was a goal? As a result of living so close to death, Dr. Frankl, out of his prison experience, developed what he called logotherapy—man is not dominated by the will to pleasure nor by the will to power but by the *will to meaning.* Without this, man suffers an existential void. He then began to put into practice a lesson from the Talmud: "Whoever destroys even a single soul should be considered the same as a man who destroyed the whole world. And whoever saves even one single soul is to be considered the same as the man who has saved a whole world." The saving of the soul is giving them not just a hope for the future, but a goal and a destiny.

In contrast, Ernest Hemingway wrote of the crash of 1929 when men who adored money lost their "god":

> Some made the long drop from the apartment or the office window; some took it quietly in the two car garage with the motor running; some used the native tradition of the Colt or Smith and Wesson; those well constructed weapons which end insomnia, terminate remorse, cure cancer, avoid bankruptcy, blast an exit from intolerable positions by the pressure of a finger; those admirable American instruments so easily carried, so sure of effect, so well designed to end the American dream when it becomes a nightmare, their only drawback is the mess they leave for relatives to clean up.
>
> —ERNEST HEMINGWAY, *To Have and Have Not*

In another work he wrote:

> "Last week the old man tried to commit suicide," the old waiter said.
>
> "Why?" asked the second waiter.
>
> "He was in despair."
>
> "What about?"
>
> "Nothing."
>
> "How do you know it was nothing?"
>
> "He has plenty of money."
>
> —ERNEST HEMINGWAY,
> "A Clean, Well-Lighted Place"

The thought of the future makes it possible to bear some of the trials of life. Imagine a child who is given a ball to play with. He is told that it is the only ball that he will ever have in his life. The natural effect will be that he will be afraid to play with it too much, afraid to lose it, afraid of its wearing out—the thought of ultimate dissolution will be a constant harrassment to him, even when he bounces and throws it.

But suppose that he is told that maybe next year or maybe in five years, but sometime in the not-too-distant future, he will be given another ball which will never wear out and which will give him happiness the like of which he has never before known. The natural reaction of the child will be not to be too much concerned with the first ball, because he is going to have another. The belief in the future world sustains the trials of this, for thus one fits meaning into the universe.

Freud holds that every one psychologically has a belief in the future, inasmuch as he is a spectator to his death.

We have tried to keep a deadly silence about death. After all, we even have a proverb to the effect that "one thinks about something beyond, as one thinks about death." After all, one's own death is beyond imagining, and whenever we try to imagine it, we can see that we really survive as spectators. Thus the dictum should be dared in the psychoanalytic school: at bottom, nobody believes in his own death. Or, and this is the same: in his unconscious everyone is convinced of his own immortality.

The Law of Death in Nature's Life

Every mortal has both an outer life and an inner life. The outer life is his reaction to environment, his wealth, his amusement, and his pleasures. His inner life is his character, his spirit, his motivation, his heart. Man is very much like a barrel of apples. The apples that are seen on the top are his reputation, but the apples down below represent his character.

It is a law of life that while the "outer man begins to grow older, the inner man is often renewed from day to day." The spirit can grow, while the body is decaying. How often the beauty of the inner life appears even amidst the decrepitude of a perishing body. Milton lost his sight, but his poetic vision increased.

A man is very much like a plant. Divinely endowed with one impulse that tends to push him out into the world, he has also a companion impulse that inclines him to the earth. If a plant were conscious, there might be a danger that it would throw all of its vigor into the roots or that it might concentrate wholly on the bloom and fruit. This would be to forget that in the realm of matter, as well as in spirit, all laws are twins. Each one is balanced by an opposite. The visible must be balanced with the invisible, the material with the spiritual, the love of God with the love of neighbor on earth. Man is two worlds at one and the same time.

Because man is rooted in both the physical and the spiritual, it is possible for him to share in the evolutionary process and to undergo the transformation that he finds in nature. One basic law running through all nature is that no realm ever enters into a higher one, without death to that which is lower. This process has been called the catabolic. Plant life says to the carbons, the phosphates, the sunshine, the rain, and all the chemicals about it, "Unless you die to yourself, you cannot live in my kingdom." Only if you surrender your lower form of existence in the chemical order, will you begin to be a part of the kingdom of vibrating vegetable life.

If the animals could speak, they would say to the plants and to the chemicals: "Unless you die to your lower existence, you cannot live in my kingdom." But if you surrender yourself, mortify your lower existence, you will become a part of sentient life, a feeling, seeing, moving creature. Man, in his turn, speaks to the chemicals, the plants and animals and says, "If you will die to your lower existence, if you consent to be plucked up by the roots, commit yourself to knife and fire, and even to the shedding of blood, you will live in my kingdom—you will be a part of a thinking being that can know the stars, write poetry, and even take a trip to the moon."

This law of immolation in the lower order is not voluntary, simply because the lower orders are not either conscious or endowed with reason. But in virtue of their immolation, they do not cease to be what they are—chemicals, plants, and animal life—but they are transformed and elevated, reborn and ennobled in a higher life.

This evolution of the universe should not stop with man. He has no right to say there is no higher life above him, any more than a rose has a right to say there is no life above it. Certainly there should be some nature, some kingdom above man into which he can be assumed, in order that his nature might be reborn. The law that would operate would be the same—he would have to die to his lower nature before he could live in the Divine. Nothing is born to a higher life, unless it be born from above. Chemicals would not be born into plants unless there was a higher life to take them up. Animals would not be born into man unless there was human life to assume them. Man cannot be reborn unless there is the kingdom above him. "Unless the grain of wheat fall into the ground and die, it remains alone." God would first have to come down to man, and man in his turn would freely have to consent to be taken up in the Divine order. The lower kingdoms are seized; man is free, he must consent. The tragedy of life is not what men suffer but how much they miss by refusing to follow the evolution of the universe. What is struggle for existence in nature becomes sacrifice and self-denial for man.

Could we but crush that ever-craving lust
For bliss, which kills all bliss; and lose our life,
Our barren unit life, to find again
A thousand lives in those for whom we die:
So were we men and women, and should hold
Our rightful place in God's great universe,
Wherein in heaven and earth, by will and nature,
Nought lives for self. All, all, from crown to footstool
The lamb, before the world's foundation slain
The angels, ministers to God's elect;
The sun, who only shines to light a world;
The clouds, whose glory is to die in showers;
The fleeting streams who in their ocean graves

Flee the decay of stagnant self-content;
The oak, ennobled by the shipwright's axe;
The soil, which yields its marrow to the flower;
The flower which breeds a thousand velvet worms,
Born only to be prey to every bird—
All spend themselves on others; and shall man,
Whose twofold being is the mystic knot
Which couples earth and heaven—doubly bound,
As being both worm and angel, to that service
By which both worms and angels hold their lives—
Shall he, whose very breath is debt on debt,
Refuse, forsooth, to see what God has made him?
No, let him show himself the creature's lord
By free-will gift of that self-sacrifice
Which they, perforce, by nature's law must suffer;
Take up his cross and follow Christ the Lord.

The power to find life through death makes the seed nobler than the diamond. In falling to the ground it loses its outer envelope which is a restraining power of the life within it. But once this outer skin dies, then life pushes forth into the blade. So, too, unless we die to the world with its vices and its concupiscences, we shall not spring forth into life everlasting. If we are to live in a higher life, we must die to the lower life. If we live in the higher life of Christ, we must die to the lower life of egotism.

To put the whole law in the beautiful paradox of Our Divine Lord: "If you wish to save your life you must lose it"; that is, if we wish to save it for eternity, we must lose it for time. If we wish to save it for the Father's mansions, we must lose it for this dull world. If we wish to save it for perfect happiness, we must lose it for fleeting pleasure of mortality. The transformation of nature through death, which is the law of evolution, cannot exist everywhere in nature, except in man. This upward surge, this progress toward greater perfection must be allowed to man as well as to fish, only it must respect his freedom. Once granted a thorough evolution, death is the doorway to life. Then all the trivial mortifications of life become rehearsal for the ultimate self-denial of death, which opens the seed to Resurrection and Life.

The fall doth pass the rise in worth;
For birth hath in itself the germ of death,
But death hath in itself the germ of birth.
It is the falling acorn buds the tree,
The falling rain that bears the greenery,
The fern plants moulder when the ferns arise.
For there is nothing lives but something dies,
And there is nothing dies but something lives,
Till the skies be fugitives,
Till Time, the hidden root of change, updries
Are Birth and Death inseparable on earth;
For they are twain yet one, and Death is Birth.
　　　　　　—FRANCIS THOMPSON

When the struggle for existence in the physical order becomes self-denial of pride, lust, avarice in the psychic order, one sees that death is the prelude to a higher life. In man this might be called excentration—he moves out of himself as center, to another Center Who has obeyed the same Law by undergoing a Good Friday for the sake of an Easter Sunday.

Death Is My-ness

Every man must do certain things for himself; blow his own nose, make his own love, do his own sleeping, and die his own death. Heidegger added, "Dying is something that nobody can do for another." In Vienna there is a sardonic saying: "So many people now die who never died before." This means they are undergoing a form of "self-denial" which they never practiced before. La Rochefoucauld said, "One can no more steadily look at death than at the sun." But he forgot that by looking at the sun, we begin to understand its mysteries. It is thanks to the inability to look at the sun that we see everything else under the sun. As Chesterton said, "We can see the moon and things under the moon, but the moon is the mother of lunatics."

Man differs from all other creatures, inasmuch as he knows that *he will die*. Out of the present he orients himself to the future. Even nature has something of this, for out of any chemical facts a scientist is able to predict future combinations.

Could it not be that our attitude toward death is very much what our attitude would have been to birth, had we been conscious? Would we not have shrunk back just as much from the portals of birth as we do now to the portals of death? Is not a beginning either in time or eternity the cause of an equal reluctance? There is only One Who has ever made such an affirmation of preexistence. When Our Lord was reproached, saying He was not yet fifty years old, His answer, as casual as a man looking over his shoulder, was, "Before Abraham was, I am." He did not say, "Before Abraham was, I was." He speaks of a beginning from all eternity and not the uncounted billions of years, but the very principle of life itself.

Because death is something every man must go through, it is not a problem but a mystery. A problem is something we see from the outside; a mystery must be seen from the inside. A problem is mere objectivity, such as how to send a rocket to the moon. A mystery is a participation and a sharing in the problem itself. Imagine three men holding a copy of Shakespeare's soliloquy of Hamlet, "To Be or Not to Be." One cannot read, though he sees all the letters just as well as any reader. The second can read, but he knows nothing about Shakespeare or the plot of the play. The third is so familiar with the background of the soliloquy that, when he reads it, he transcends it and sees in it the mystery of existence and nonexistence. We are so used to science and technology that the only information we consider as valid is that which comes unrelated to ourselves, something which we approach from the outside, rather than something into which we are submerged. What cannot be investigated as a scientific problem, we are apt to ignore as unreal, forgetful that much technological knowledge is based on substitution, such as the airplane for the train; while a profounder knowledge is based on the deepening of a mystery, such as comes to husband and wife in marriage.

Death is not a problem but a mystery, inasmuch as it personally concerns me, however much I may seek to avoid it. What heightens its mystery is not only that it will happen to me, but that neither I nor any one else has direct experience of it. It cannot be experienced from without. Each and every one has to undergo it himself.

The only answer to the mystery of death would be for someone to break the death barrier, as we have broken the sound barrier, so that, as sound and fury are left behind in speed, so death would be left behind in the newness of life. Someone must pierce the mystery from within. Man could lift his hands in protest against heaven, unless in some way God tasted death. How often a mother, before she gives medicine to a child, takes it herself and says, "See! Mother does not mind." Should not God also take His own medicine, namely, Death?

God Takes His Own Medicine

On Good Friday men announced, "God is dead." They set watches, they sealed a tomb, and they signed the death certificate. There had to be a moment like this—when it was absolutely certain God was dead—before an ultimate reason could be given to the mystery. The skepticism should be greatest, not among the unbelievers but among believers—the kind of people who accepted death as final, so final that they would bring spices to anoint the body, impugn witnesses who would say He was alive, and shrug them off,

saying, "A woman's tale." Never was the world so close to bright-
ness and the solving of the riddle of death as when learned professors, lawyers, and scribes of temples of philosophy trumpeted, "God
is dead!" This fact had to be first before there could be hope.

The veil of the mystery could be lifted only by the most persistent and convinced of all the God-Is-Dead-ers—the type of man
who would absolutely refuse to believe those who saw the empty
tomb and the Conqueror of Death in the transformed glorious state
of the Victor. That skeptic, whose name was Thomas, would have
to give to future generations the one test: "I am not going to believe
anything beyond death, until I can apply the same test I apply to
men who say they have been to war. What care I if they wear
medals on their breasts—these can be bought! I want to see the
marks inflicted by the God-Is-Dead crew; I want proof that He has
been to war against death. What proof is in an unscarred hero who
says he has been in a shell hole or a ditch? Let me see the place
where the God-Is-Dead-ers drove in nails; bayonet wounds when
they pierced His side, the Feet so dug with steel that He had to be
carried off the battlefield on a stretcher. Once I see these scars of
One Who battled death and conquered, then—and then only—
shall I believe."

When this President of the Society of God-Is-Dead-ers throws
himself prostrate before Him, saying, "My Lord and My God"—I
will believe. Then, my faith rests not on just the testimony of those
who saw Him, but in the response of the scientist who probed
Hands, Feet, and Side to bring to final conviction that He Who was
dead lives.

There is no other answer to the riddle of death. Philosophies
and world religions can never enlighten the mystery until someone
crashes the impregnable wall. And when that Death was preceded
by poverty, hunger, thirst, hatred, miscarriage of justice, intellectual
barbarism, and scourgings, and the seeming abandonment of
heaven and flies that could not be brushed away from a bleeding,

crown-pierced Head, then I know that nothing that happens to me or anyone else can be worse and that it is eventually to be swallowed up in joy and peace.

From that day to this, we say to Him Who stumbled to His Throne, "How can You allow polio to strike down a child, cancer still the hand of the musician, and death lay its cold hand on a young mother?"

And Christ answers, "Can you not see that everything that touched you first touched Me; that every tightening of a violin string is not for the sake of pain but to give a richer melody, that every stroke of a hammer on the marble is not to punish stone but to bring out the beautiful form hidden therein? I am in the midst of your sorrows; your tears run down My cheeks; your thirst is but an echo of My parched cry of the Cross. Every demon I drove out leered at Me; I died the very death that I conquered. Who among you fears death, and I did not fear? Who among you dies, and I did not die with you? In fact, I am the First Born from the Dead. Suffering and death are hostile powers. You struggle against them. So did I. But everything that strikes you first struck Me. It had to pass through My Hands before it touched your hands. No greater truth was ever announced on this earth than 'God is dead.' Once you know this, you are on the road to the next chapter of the Book: 'He Who is dead is now alive. See the place where they laid Him.' "

The Resurrection

Just suppose a man is put on trial for murder, the evidence against him being complete except for the fact that the body of the murdered man was not discovered. All the evidence that was brought out in court revealed the exact time of the murder, the testimony of hundreds who saw it, the instruments of torture used in the crime, and the official documentation of police, military, and religious authorities.

Suppose that immediately after the judge had sentenced the

guilty man to death, the one who was murdered walked into the courtroom alive! The judge would have to say that the *corpus delicti* was a living man. How dare accuse one of murder when the murdered is living? There would be nothing to do but to release the condemned man.

Something of this kind is present in the man of faith who believes in the Resurrection. His guilt is beyond dispute; he has even confessed it. His rebellion was heartless; his sin indelible. But at that point, where he shamefully admits to crucifixion, lo and behold! the Crucified appears not only alive but as Life. The trial is over. All his sins are swallowed up by faith in the Resurrected Man Who brings forgiveness.

Hence there are two ways of facing death. One is the way of the pessimistic existentialist whose novels, poetry, and plays revolve around the one theme: Find a lonely man, tell him that he is under the threat of death, and he will be more lonely than he was before. He will make a philosophy out of his loneliness, ridicule his friends and his neighbors who are afraid to face up to the fact that they will die; he himself will always have it before his face. He invites it; he scorns it. He boasts that it clears his head. He stands on the edge of precipices, on the railings of bridges and of ships, spitting in the face of death. He calls everyone else a coward who is afraid to face death in this absurd life.

The Christian has always faced death but not with such morbidity. He makes a rehearsal for death by many acts of self-denial: "I die daily," and, "I am crucified with Christ." His mortification is a daily death, a kind of preparation for the ultimate.

The existentialist dies for his own sake, and the Christian dies for Christ's sake. One is centered in self-consciousness, and the other is centered in Other-consciousness.

Hammer and the anvil, the potter and the clay, the sculptor and the stone, the surgeon and the ulcer, the gold and the fire—out of the hammering and the beating and the purging and the flame something takes shape. But in order that it might do it, there must be some kind of cooperation. As Augustine put it: "Without God, we cannot; without us, He will not."

Behind the transformation is love—love for God Who was Dead. This fact became the basis of a story by Tolstoy, *The Death of Ivan Ilyich*. Ivan, as well as all the other members of his family and his group, uses the expression that "one dies" without ever personally relating it to himself. There is, however, one in the group, a poor servant, who knows that he has to die, and he turns to changing the attitude of Ivan, bringing great love to bear upon him. Ivan begins to see that what is important is not so much that he is dying of a diseased kidney, but that his life has been pointless, wasted, frustrated, and to no purpose. Under the impact of love, he then begins to care for others, to feel sorry, and for the three days preceding his death he keeps repeating, "Life! What joy!"

Love, therefore, has a double effect on the attitude toward death. First, it changes our sense of values and turns blessings into curses and curses into blessings. It does this through a sense of forgiveness. Secondly, it changes the selfishness of life into service, as it did with Ivan Ilyich. One of the supreme examples of turning the blessing into a curse was the thief on the right, to whom pain was the worst of all evils except impending death. Then suddenly, the light flashes, and he asks to be taken into Paradise, to which there comes the answer: "This day." And the thief died a thief because he stole Paradise.

Finally, in *The Brothers Karamazov* by Dostoyevsky, we have the whole story of how we come to the solution of the mystery, where we hear the anguished cry of a woman:

Life beyond the grave . . . what a tremendous puzzle. The mere thought of it shakes me to the point of anguish, torment, and even terror. . . . Do I live only to disappear without a trace, except for the weeds growing on my grave, as some writer said? It is a terrifying outlook. What shall I do? What am I supposed to do, in order to recapture my faith! . . . As a child I accepted faith spontaneously without question. . . . But how shall I go about finding the truth now? Where am I to look for the proofs? Not a soul, in fact, hardly anyone in this world today, seems to be concerned with these things. Yet, I myself cannot bear the burden of my own ignorance. It is a terrible feeling.

[Father Zozima answers her question] No doubt, this is a terrible nightmare. No one can really prove these things. And yet, it is possible for us to convince ourselves of their truth. . . . But how? Through the experience of active love. Try to love your neighbor with relentless, active, affective fervor. As your love grows, you will become more and more convinced of both the existence of God and the immortality of the soul. And if your love for yourself reaches the heights of complete mystery, there will be no doubt left. This is a sure, proven way.

II

MAN in SOCIETY

CHAPTER SIX

The Origin of Man in Society

Sometimes the young give indications of the great future which awaits them. Napoleon loved to play with tin soldiers. Pascal, as a boy, without ever having studied geometry, worked out all the propositions of Euclid in the ashes of the fireplace, using a poker as a pencil. Young Teilhard de Chardin, living in a majestic eighteenth-century manor house in France, kept in his room a small telescope and on his table a number of rocks dug from the surrounding countryside. Rocks were the absorbing passion of his life. As a child of six he seemed to have more than a childish intuition of the unity and goodness of the concrete things of the world.

One day he was holding in his hand a piece of iron which he loved, but his mother told him it was only a rusted piece of a ploughshare. While crying at its worthlessness, she began speaking to him about the Sacred Heart of Christ and His great love for the world. Suddenly he saw that the iron he loved was real, good, and full of being, because the Heart of Christ had made it. Swords were to be beaten into ploughshares, said the prophet, but now broken ploughshares were to be beaten into a synthesis of sciences. At a period when science was beginning to construct a synthesis of the laws of matter and life—that is, of chemistry and biology—Teilhard was thinking of adding to them psychology, so as to produce a union of physical energy and psychic energy. As he wrote shortly before his death: "Since the time of Darwin, evolution has passed beyond the narrow limits of zoology and has become a general process, covering the atom as well as the cell." Evolution to him was not just a biological theory; it was an essential part of all sciences.

His life was spent digging into the earth, finding in its rocks, its strata, and its bones the secret of the universe. Among all his achievements as a paleontologist, the most famous was his codiscovery of the famous Peking man—who actually turned out to be a woman, whom he named Nellie.

Born on the first of May, 1881, the fourth of eleven children—(his mother was the sixth direct descendant of Voltaire's sister)—until the day of his death, the tenth of April, 1955, he gave to the world the most complete theory of evolution it had ever known, setting it down in nine books, which have sold over a million copies since his death.

Darwin had said that his study of science had dulled his capacity for poetry, music, and the spiritual things of life. With Teilhard de Chardin, it was just the opposite. To take but two incidents out of his life to indicate how he wove together science, theology, poetry, saintliness: He was on an expedition into the Ordos Desert of Inner Mongolia. One day, unable to read Mass, he offered his prayer:

Since once again, O Lord, in the steppes of Asia
I have no bread, no wine, no altar
I will raise myself above those symbols
To the pure majesty of Reality,
And I will offer to Thee, I, Your priest,
Upon the altar of the entire earth,
The labor and the suffering of the world. . . .

Receive, O Lord, in its totality the Host
Which Creation, drawn by Thy magnetism

Presents to Thee at the dawn of a new day.
This Bread, our effort, is in itself, I know,
Nothing but an immense disintegration.
This wine, our anguish, as yet, alas!
Is only an evaporating beverage.
But in the depths of this inchoate mass
Thou hast placed—I am certain, for I feel it—
An irresistible and holy desire that moves us all,
The impious, as well as the faithful, to cry out:
O Lord, make us one!

The Sufferings of Teilhard

During World War I, he was assigned as a stretcher bearer in the Moroccan Regiment. He became "Arab," exchanging the Field Service blue for the khaki of the African troops and also wore their red fez. He was in the Battle of Verdun, Second Battle of the Marne, and in the final counteroffensive which brought him into Germany.

Baudelaire said of Paris: "You gave me your mud, and of it I made gold." So Teilhard took the trenches of war and turned them into gold, one being his very famous vision of the Heart of Christ expanding into the universe. He refused the rank of a captain, saying that he could do more good among the men as a soldier. He spent most of his time in scientific work among the diggings in Asia, so he spent his wartime, for the most part, serving the Muslims. He shared the lot of the troops and shouldered his own pack in marches. One day a major, walking alongside of him, noted that he was tired and asked if he could carry his pack. Teilhard refused, saying, "A corporal does not give bad example." The Muslims trusted him and went to him when they wanted advice and wanted him near when they died.

Teilhard also suffered a great deal from his own brethren, from misunderstanding of his books. When a young Communist and an angry agnostic were with him in China and asked him about the reactions of some of his brethren, he said, "I am quite beyond revolt."

Personality: Earth and Heaven

There has always been throughout human history a belief that the world, and all that is in it, is wicked. Oriental philosophies insisted on the extinction of desires. In Christian history one of the greatest of all heresies was Manicheanism—namely, that there was an absolute principle of evil working in the world, hence, not all creation is good.

Teilhard de Chardin sought to bridge this gap between the world and God, or between physics and theology, as St. Francis before had bridged the gap between the Divine and the human. Francis found all humanity lovable; Teilhard found the cosmos lovable. As all mortals, even the weakest, told Francis of God, so the physical universe told Teilhard of the Divine. His background, he said, prepared him for seeking the union of the two:

> By education and intellectual training, I belong to the children of heaven. But by temperament and through my professional studies, I am a child of the earth. Placed thus by life at the heart of two worlds whose theory, language, and feelings I know, and because of intimate experience, I have not erected any inner partition in my mind. . . . Now at the end of this process, after thirty years dedicated to the pursuit of inner unity, I have the impression that a synthesis has taken place naturally between these two currents which had been making contrary demands upon me. The one has not killed the other. Today I probably believe in God more than ever before—and certainly I believe more than ever in the world.

On October 7, 1946, he wrote that all his thought was in one direction: "A rethinking of Christianity on the scale and dimensions of the universe as it is revealed ever more clearly to us."

What Chardin strove to do was to avoid the dichotomy and the divorce between revelation and science, the commitment to the eternal and the commitment to the temporal, between loving God and loving the world.

Having lived many years of his life in a non-Christian civilization, he saw a vast civilized humanity growing up outside of the consciousness of Christ. This to him was not exclusively a tragedy; it was merely a summons for a new type of Christianity, which would be, at one and the same time, more involved in the world and more detached from the world. As he wrote: "The saint is the man who Christianizes in himself all that is human in his own time." He felt great pity "for those who live only for their own times and whose love extends no farther than their own country."

As one looks at the various trends in our day, one sees that Teilhard's conception of spirituality is in the forefront. He knew that he had to pass through many hazards, but his was directed principally to the cosmic world. Others have been directed to the human world. This does not mean to say that Teilhard limited himself to anthropology and physics. His fundamental orientation was "to attain heaven through the fulfillment of earth. Christify matter."

It is very likely that within fifty years when all the trivial, verbal disputes about the meaning of Teilhard's "unfortunate" vocabulary will have died away or have taken a secondary place, Teilhard will appear like John of the Cross and St. Teresa of Avila, as the spiritual genius of the twentieth century.

Teilhard in Relation to Previous Thought

Our education is made up of many different courses like dishes in a cafeteria. The student picks and chooses among them, and somehow selections do not always jibe with one another, like ice cream and lobster. Think of what a jumble the human mind is which has economics at nine o'clock, Spanish at ten, modern poetry at eleven, psychology at twelve, etc. Great minds in history have sought a synthesis of all sciences, trying to relate them one to another, like the various cells and organs of the body. In order to see what Teilhard did for knowledge, contrast his view with the great minds of the past.

The model for the arrangement of various disciplines of the mind in the past was astronomy. The ancient system was the Ptolemaic, in which the earth was the center of the universe, with the sun and other planets revolving around it. When Aristotle began constructing his system of philosophy, he had to find a center around which other branches of knowledge revolved like planets. This he made philosophy or what he called metaphysics. Around it revolved all the other disciplines like mathematics and physics, zoology and botany, psychology, music, and the like.

The Middle Ages accepted the same system of astronomy in which the earth was the center of the visible universe. But there was a change: Philosophy had been the center of all knowledge for Aristotle, but for the thinkers of those days, theology was put at the center of the intellectual world, and all other branches, like planets, revolved around it: metaphysics, physics, mathematics, logic, ethics, economics, politics, etc.

Then came the Copernican revolution; the earth was no longer the center of our universe. The sun became the center of the universe and around the sun revolved the earth and the other planets such as Mercury, Venus, Earth, Mars, Jupiter, Saturn, Uranus, Neptune, and Pluto, these being the satellites of our solar system. But there are many other systems in the universe much vaster than our solar system.

Now that we had a new astronomy, would anyone attempt to synthesize all the other sciences around it as Aristotle and the Middle Ages had done? No! The field was too vast; the spectrum too complicated. All our ideas about the cosmos and the history of man had to be changed. The revolution was as complete in each science as it had been in astronomy. Instead of a synthesis built on the plan of a central point with satellites revolving around it, the sciences now were almost unrelated to one another, like shelves.

In physics, the old idea was that the universe was constructed of atoms or unbreakable billiard balls. But the new physics revealed that the atom was not a billiard ball at all; it was made up of electrical charges of protons and neutrons. In the field of biology and zoology there was another revolution. Aristotle had held that all species were fixed and separate; a dog always remained a dog, a bear always remained a bear. Darwin suggested that there could be such a thing as the evolution of species, through fortuitous changes in environment.

Psychology was the science of the spirit, reason, and consciousness. Freud, Jung, and Adler appeared on the scene to suggest that the subconscious is also important for a complete understanding of man. Paleontology and anthropology made us revise all our thinking about the age of the universe and man's time-space in it. Philosophy had been abstract, dealing in universal concepts or with "objects out there"; now it became concrete, personal, empirical, and related to the person, or what today is called existential.

The New Synthesis

No one attempted a synthesis of the new departments of advanced knowledge until the time of Chardin. What Aristotle had done in pre-Christian times, what Thomas Aquinas did in the Middle Ages—and both on the basis of the old astronomy—what Descartes attempted in philosophy, Teilhard did but without appeal to astronomy. He introduced two changes: In place of astronomy as the basis of the universe, he used evolution; instead of making it like a solar system, he saw all sciences and all knowledge, from biology and paleontology up to theology, as a cone or a series of cones, one inside the other.

Why a cone? Because the universe was growing in complexity, from the primitive spark to man. But there was also another reason

—the older themes of evolution could not explain consciousness. According to the ancient idea, there began to be a chance combination of atoms—of carbon, nitrogen, hydrogen—forming clusters, until so favorably structured, they produced life. Life, in its turn, through the vast stretches of time and through the operation of natural selection, finally began to produce a man who was capable of choosing love over hate, justice over injustice, of writing the *Summa* of Aquinas, of composing music like Mozart, and of throwing a vault like Michelangelo's against the dome of heaven's blue. There were several fallacies in this theory. Let (a) represent chemicals, (b) plants, (c) animals, and (d) man. The evolution of the universe would then be explained as follows:

How did an animal come into existence? $a + b = c$

How did a man come into existence? $a + b + c = d$

But there is something new at each stage which is different in quality from the preceding stage and which is not in the antecedents: $a + b + c = abc$, not d. One cannot get the greater from the less. This was the basic idea behind Lloyd Morgan's Emergent Evolution. It might explain lower realms of life, but it could not explain consciousness. One could build a huge electronic computer that might unravel all of the processes of evolution, but one could never make that machine conscious of itself. Man is something new in evolution, inasmuch as he is self-conscious. Furthermore, when he studies the universe, he is not a part of it, otherwise he could not explain it.

Teilhard contended that the mere physical and chemical forces of and by themselves do not manufacture any new energy. On the contrary, they have a tendency to disintegrate unless sustained from without. For example, the sun will use up all of its hydrogen atoms in about fifteen million years and then die. There must exist some other kind of energy working within the universe itself, capable of producing higher forms of consciousness and preventing universal decay, as it unfolds through the three stages of prelife, life, and self-conscious thought.

How then explain the appearance of consciousness and also the new energies? There are not only environmental forces (tangential) which are outside things to modify them, there are also forces inside them (radial) which bring them to new complexity. There had to be an Alpha Point at the beginning of the universe which explains everything that will unfold in an orderly fashion, as an author has the plan of his book in mind before he writes it. Every word, paragraph, and chapter are the unfolding of this original idea. The Alpha Point explains the origin of self-consciousness. Teilhard posits consciousness on the "inside of things," or better, a protoconsciousness, even in the lowest forms of matter. Reversing the laws of the gradual decay of energy, the law of complexity consciousness tells how the universe unfolds into greater and greater complexity. In the evolution of animals this complexity consciousness becomes instinct; in man it becomes moral judgment, freedom of choice, and spirituality. This Teilhard calls the noosphere.

As the unfolding of evolution has not only an Alpha Point; it also has an Omega Point. There is a target for the arrow and a bow which shoots it. A little architect exists on the inside of everything to make it what it is. He thus makes consciousness rather coextensive with life. As Huxley put it, "Man is nothing else but evolution becoming conscious of itself." The Omega is not the end product of natural evolution; it is "the prime mover ahead . . . the principle which at one and the same time makes this cosmic coiling irreversible and moves and collects it."

Alpha-Omega

What is this Alpha-Omega, this Center of Centers of all things? It is Love.

Empedocles postulated love as the underlying activity of the universe. Plato said that love was in everything there is. Aristotle held there was a natural appetite in all things that drives everything back again to God. Aquinas said that all things—mineral, vegetable, animal, and human—possess the capacity of natural love: "Natural love is found not only in the powers of the vegetative soul, but in all the potencies of the soul, and indeed in all parts of the body and universally in all things." Love is a kind of iceberg inasmuch as only a small part of it is visible, and even its visible part is but little known.

Love appears as chemical affinity, unification of electrons and protons in an atom, sympathy, solidarity, and friendship in the social order. Love, says Teilhard, has "its presence in an inchoate form in everything that is." What is the Source and Object of this love to which Teilhard refers, which draws to itself all of the personal energies of the world?

It can be seen that Teilhard was not concerned only with the outside of things, but with the "withinness." All reality has an inner face and an outer face. This withinness is difficult to detect the farther one goes back to primitive forms of life and to matter. But the more it becomes complex, the more it is observable. Just as families go to pieces without love, so the universe could also disintegrate and dissolve without the drawing of the Omega.

This Alpha-Omega from which all comes, toward which all tends, and which gives energy to all things is "outside the last term of the series, and also *outside all series;* not only does it crown evolution, but it closes it. If it did not escape from time and space which it gathers together it would not be Omega."

This Alpha-Omega has three notes: It is immanent and central, in order to unite all things. It is personal, in order to personalize all things. It is transcendent, in order to consolidate all things.

It is a first mover and also the point of achievement. What Teilhard has done is to break with the sharp dualism between matter and consciousness, which was introduced into philosophy by Descartes. For Teilhard, there is a continuity between an animal seeking food and a magnet pointing to the north; between a male and female uniting in the act of generation and two atoms uniting to form a chemical compound. The meaning is not the same in each instance, but there is more than a mere figure of speech in this unification. Atoms are not alive, it is true, but they have what might be called prelife.

What then is evolution? It is not a sudden appearance of life and consciousness and sensitivity, but an elaboration, an organization, a centering of something *which was there inchoately from the beginning.* This Alpha-Omega is Christ "in whom we live and move and have our being."

Man is the final result of the clustering and synthesizing of all the labors of the universe; in him consciousness becomes self-consciousness, related to the lower forms but transcendent to them. In all things there is an outside and an inside, a within and a without, or what scholastics call matter and form, wherein the world is charged with the grandeur of God.

The day Teilhard held the iron and heard about the Sacred Heart, he united what he called the cosmic sense and the Christic sense, and in his conception of the Omega Point he said, "I should never have ventured to envisage it, if my consciousness as a believer had not already known it."

Evolution, therefore, is not a push from below; it is a gift from above. It is not a getting of a greater from the less but the unfolding of supreme Intelligence in matter to more and more complex forms of life. "Everything holds together from above." It is no mechanical thrust from below, but an attraction from above. His theory is the opposite to the idea of gravitation. Things are not pulled down; they are pulled up.

But his vision of the universe goes beyond this. At the top of the large cone which represents the unfolding of matter, life, and consciousness, thanks to Alpha and Omega, there is also another spiral or cone at the top. Could it be a Superman? Not in the sense of a higher developed brain or a new species? No! While Homo sapiens is not developing as preman did, evolution has not stopped.

"No evolutionary future awaits man, except in association with all other men." Invention, communication, international politics all demand greater unity out of this multiplicity. Humanity is facing, therefore, either brotherly unity or atomic disintegration.

Christ—Center of Convergence

Knowing, however, that Love which is the Alpha and Omega will not cease loving, it is fitting that as man reached a point of convergence of the whole universe beneath him, all men should have a Center of Convergence which would pull them together, and that is the Incarnation of the Son of God. This is a truly supernatural intervention but one long prepared by the Spirit of Love:

> The long ages which preceded the Nativity were not empty of Christ, but penetrated by His powerful influx. It is the shock of His conception which put the cosmic masses in motion. It is the preparation for His Birth which accelerates the development of instinct and the flowering of thought on earth. All these preparations were cosmically and biologically necessary before Christ could set foot on the human scene. . . . When the Virgin's time came, the final and gracious purpose of the universe was suddenly revealed.

Christ, then, is the emergence in concrete Personal form of the Word Who was immanent in the evolution of the universe from the beginning.

This recalls the medieval question: "Would Christ have become incarnate if there had been no sin?" St. Thomas Aquinas answers in the negative, contending that Scripture revealed no other reason than to atone for our sins. The Franciscan school answers in the positive—the Birth of Christ was necessary for the perfection of the universe. Teilhard holds to the latter view. "Without biological evolution which produced the brain, would there ever be sanctified souls? Similarly, without the evolution of collective thought, which alone can realize on earth the fullness of human consciousness, would there ever be a consummated Christ?" Christ of Nazareth is the Personal center for the material universe and for man. "The supernatural plenitude of Christ receives support from the natural plenitude of the world." He was, as St. Paul says, born in the "fullness of time," and Teilhard would add in the fullness of evolution, for Christ is "the organic center for the whole universe."

Faithful to his priesthood and his faith, Teilhard said that the Catholic Faith gives us an intense dynamic drive toward unification because it has the three following characteristics of the Incarnate Christian God:

"(a) Tangibility, experimental in order, the result of the historical entry (by His Birth) of Christ into the very process of evolution.

"(b) Expansibility, universal in order, conferred on the Christic center, in virtue of the 'Resurrection.'

"(c) Finally, assimilitative power, organic in order, potentially integrating in the unity of a single 'body' the totality of human kind. . . .

"What constitutes the invincible superiority of Christianity over every other type of faith is that it is becoming more and more conscious of being identified with a Christogenesis; that is, with the rise, collectively recognized, of a certain universal Presence, at once immortalizing and unifying."

"It is in Him that you find your completion; He is the fountainhead from which all power and dominion proceed."—Col. 2:10

"In this new Man of God's design, there is no distinction between Greek and Hebrew, Jew or gentile, foreigner or savage, slave or free man. Christ is all that matters, for Christ lives in them all."—Col. 3:11

But Christogenesis, because it brought Personally in the world the love of God and because it redeemed man, prepared the way for the mystical union of all souls in Christ, in the Church. He calls the Church a phylum. A phylum is a zoological group or branch with similar characteristics, a kind of bundle of unities. The Church is the phylum of love growing within the human phylum, or a spiral in a spiral, a cone above a cone. "In Rome we find the Christic pole of earth," the axis for all the love of the universe.

Teilhard's thoughts were cosmic, human, and Christic. As Cuenot has summarized it: "Teilhard's synthesis between 'the God above' (the immanent God Whose Face has been revealed in evolution) is not a synthesis on paper. The whole world is ascending toward Christ the King, even the irresistible surge of the ocean tides under the Pull of the moon and sun." The human is the bond between the cosmic and the Christic, and thus the three stages for Teilhard are cosmogenesis, anthropogenesis, and Christogenesis, or the evolution of the universe, the evolution of man, and the crowning of man's evolution with the Incarnation.

Because he was misunderstood, because he was maligned by his brethren, because he was suspect in his orthodoxy, he asked God that if He was pleased with his life and work that he would die on Easter Sunday. Without any previous warning, he dropped dead on the Day of the Resurrection (April 10) 1955.

CHAPTER SEVEN

The Amorization of Humanity

"L'amour, toujours l'amour" is a French song that almost everyone knows. *L'amour,* the French word for "love," is taken from the Latin word, *amor;* from it may be built up the word "amorization," which means "Making love prevail in humanity." But this is not without difficulty, for the word "love" can be used in different senses. For example: "I love crepes suzettes," or, "I love Paris in the springtime," or, "I love the Mets," "I love Suzy." If one were to build up a hierarchy or scale of love, it might break up into three kinds, each succeeding one higher than the preceding:

It-Love;
Service-Love;
Gift-Love.

Each has to do with our relation to a person: It-Love is interested not in another person, but the pleasure that person can give. Service-Love is interested in the person simply because he is a bearer of value and without any regard for what is given in return. Gift-Love is a discovery of the origin of all the love there is in the universe; it is a Gift from God Who loved us first.

It-Love

It-Love may be described as outlined by George Orwell in his work *1984,* which predicts what society will be like in that year. Sex will be apart from marriage and will have no relation to persons. The hero of this book, before tousing the heroine, demands reassurance. "You like doing this?" he asks. "I don't mean simply me; I mean the thing in itself." He is not satisfied until he gets the answer: "I adore it." True love wants the beloved. The It-Love wants only the pleasure. The symbol of the It-Love is the circle—the circle circumscribed by its own egotism—or the serpent with the tail in its mouth slowly devouring itself. It-Love is paper-cup love—you drink the water and throw away the cup. Love, which normally means wanting the beloved and contemplating the beloved, now wants an it instead of a person. He does not want the cigarette; he wants the carton. There are some writers who would go so far as to say that even love spoils the erotic. One is the flax, and the other is the fire. The erotic slays what it loves and, while loving, turns into hate when it is not satisfied.

This kind of egotism has been called Eros-love, which is not altogether just. Plato wrote profoundly about *eros,* but it was not for him altogether sexual, carnal, passionate love. It was the state of being in love, a glow that was enkindled by the sight of another and eventually led to a love of virtue. *Eros* was always related to the ecstatic, the intellectual, and the eternal. For Plato the *eros* was born out of the *penia* (poverty) and therefore had its root in need and emptiness.

But today the *eros* has become the erotic, which means one drinks the water, destroys the vessel—the pleasure enjoyed, the person ignored. The ego projects itself into another, pretends that it is worshiping the other when actually it is only idolizing its ego in the other person. The partner, then, is something only functional. Young men and women become like replaceable parts in a machine.

While the loved one is irreplaceable, the sex partner is always replaceable. As one young man who seduced a young girl said, "All is over. I do not wish to see her anymore. A young girl is a feeble creature, and when she has given all, she has lost all."

This kind of love is found in the writings of Proust, Freud, and Sartre, in which the existence of the other is at least mentally annihilated. Love becomes equated with war—violent moments in which the other is dispossessed. Making love is a receptacle for self-love, a mirror in which one sees reflected his own image, the partner being only a means for making a conquest.

The prevalence of It-Love is sometimes called the revolution in morals, which is a way of justifying it: Since everybody is stealing, honesty cannot be right. The sense of justice is so deep in man that, even when he does wrong, he wants it to give the appearance of right. He cannot look at a picture hanging crooked on a wall without straightening it. He cannot turn his instinct for love into egotism without justifying it, arguing that only by giving primacy to the libidinous and the erotic can he be truly free.

But why is so much rationalization bound up with It-Love? The reason is this: As we rebel against conscience, or resolve upon a way of life contrary to it, we invent a false value in its place. Once God is driven out of His Heaven; Baal is put up in His place. The inner remorse and unhappiness which one feels is now set up as the "authentic"—a very good modern word—while all else is called the "inauthentic life." Actually this is just a travesty on inner weakness. Young men who practice barnyard ethics consider others as "sissies," because they have not ravished a girl. The new ideal is "manhood" or "conquest." On the other hand, young women in college dormitories who have lost their virginity ridicule others who are still virgins, because they have not yet "known life" or "come to fulfillment."

Darkness thus becomes light and light darkness, and those who do not subscribe to this egotism are immediately put on the defensive as being "out of the swim," "antiquated," "behind the times."

One finds this rationalization true in the field of law, as well as in sex. They who flaunt law by disobedience will always be those who exalt liberty to the sky, comparing those who are not rebellious to "slaves." Those who refuse to have children will exalt "life." They who are selfish, greedy, and grasping will exalt "justice." All others are robbers and cheaters. Ultimately there comes along someone like Jean Jacques Rousseau who wrote about his vices in his *Confessions* but called them virtues. In the same spirit, Nietzsche pleaded for the transvaluation of values, so that evil would become good and good become evil.

What happens to paper-cup lovers who love only the experience of love and not the person? The answer was given in the year 1875 by Dostoyevsky in his novel, *A Raw Youth*. The story concerns a character named Versilov, whose heart is torn between two women who represent virtue and beauty: one a married woman, the other an engaged woman. The first is Sonia, the other is Katerina. Versilov had stolen Sonia away from her husband Makar, showing neither respect for her married life nor for her virtue. Beautiful Katerina, on the other hand, becomes the object of his intense villainy, even at the time of her engagement. Beauty presented to him a kind of challenge, a city that had to be taken, a rose that had to be plucked. She will be his and no one else's.

The question now arises: Why did he seduce the virtuous Sonia and the beautiful Katerina? It was because he was irritated by their virtuousness. As a man in an office who leads a licentious life is irritated by the presence of a decent girl, or as an adulterous husband is made angry by the virtue of his wife, so he had to do something to besmirch the purity of others, in order to protect himself from his own conscience. He feels that he can keep his integrity by ridicule and by insult, for *eros* is always unhappy in its excesses.

Versilov returns briefly to Sonia and sees an icon on the table. These are his words as he describes the tension, the fission, and the split in his own soul:

"Do you know, I feel as though I were split in two?" He looked round at us all with a terribly serious face and with perfectly genuine candor. "Yes, I am really split in two mentally and I am horribly afraid of it. It's just as though one's second self were standing beside one; one is sensible and rational enough, but the very self is impelled to do something perfectly senseless, and sometimes very funny; and suddenly you notice that you are longing to do that amusing thing, goodness knows why; that is what you want to do, as it were, against your will; though you fight against it with all your might, you want to. I once knew a doctor who suddenly began whistling in church at his father's funeral. I really was afraid to come to the funeral today, because for some reason, I was possessed of a firm conviction that I should begin to whistle or laugh in church like that unfortunate doctor who came to a bad end. . . . And I really don't know why, but I've been haunted by the thought of that doctor all day; I'm so haunted by it that I can't shake him off. Do you know, Sonia, here I've taken up the icon again (he had picked it up and was turning it about in his hand), and do you know, I've a dreadful longing now, this very second, to smash it against the stove, against this corner. I'm sure it would break into two halves—neither more nor less."

A few moments later, the man with the split personality throws down the icon and breaks it in two, into exactly two pieces. The erotic man is always split—at war with himself. As John Donne put it: "Nothing but man of all unvenomed things, dost work upon itself, with inborn sting."

Then he comes to Katerina to avenge the insult that she has given him; namely, the insult of beauty accompanied by innocence. He assumes that it is a false innocence because nobody is naturally innocent. A bystander describes the scene:

She saw Versilov, suddenly turned white as a sheet and gazed at him for some moments immovable with indescribable horror and fell into a swoon. He rushed at her. I remember with terror his flushed, almost purple face and bloodshot eyes. He caught her up as she fell unconscious, and with amazing ease lifted her up in his arms, as though she were a feather and began aimlessly carrying her about the room as though she were a baby. . . . I ran after him. What I was most afraid of was the revolver, which he seemed to have forgotten in his right hand and was holding close to her head. . . . He suddenly waved the revolver over her, but as though realizing, turned the revolver and aimed it at her face. . . . He would have shot her and then himself, but since we would not let him get at her, he pressed the revolver against his heart; I succeeded in pushing his arms upwards and the bullet struck him in the shoulder.

The It-Lover seeks to kill that which taunts his conscience; he seeks a kind of reconciliation with himself by taking the life of another. Rapists often follow their It-love with murder. Here is a sickness that is not psychological nor physiological. It is a spiritual sickness. It is the sickness of the man who has become wholly erotic and cannot endure the sight of virtue or beauty. One hates oneself with the same intensity that one burns toward another.

At this moment, a man might react by humility, in which he discovers within himself the disfigured image of Christ; or he might revolt, which he sees as the only way of reacting against his depravity—to put on a bravado, to humiliate others as he has been humiliated. In the violence against Katerina, beauty is both desirable and hateful. He who is insulted now would despoil beauty as an insult. He cannot touch anything without spoiling it.

Service-Love

Service-Love begins to see persons each with a dignity because precious to God. This dignity is what might be called alien, in the sense that the value of the person is not derived from one's own esteem of that person but for the love which God bears to him. Service-Love takes one out of the sphere of liking into the sphere of loving. Liking is in the realm of feeling, glands, tastes, moods; therefore, it is not readily under control. Because it is a sensible, organic, physiological reaction, it is as immediate and unpredictable as the rumbling of a stomach. Arguments are rather useless to convince a boy that he ought to like spinach. But loving is in the will, not in the glands. It is subject to moral command and is under our control. The biblical command is not "Like thy neighbor," but "Love thy neighbor." Not every neighbor is likable, but every neighbor is lovable. It is hard to like certain neighbors who step on toes and make funny noises when they eat soup, but one can love them.

Another difference is that liking generally implies being liked. There is reciprocity in liking, which is the basis of friendship. "You love those who love you. What reward is there in this? Do not the heathens this?" Loving is something shown even when it is unreciprocated, as the wife continuing to love an unfaithful husband or a martyr loving the persecutors. A further difference is that liking often extends to the general, as a way of escaping the particular— for example, liking humanity. But loving gets down to the concrete and immerses itself even in the human who is not humanly very likable.

We can understand this distinction between liking and loving by asking, How do I love myself? Do I love myself always and at certain moments, such as when I am doing something embarrassing or when I hurt my neighbor's reputation? On the other hand, do I not love myself when I visit the sick, send money to lepers, or find a job for the father of a family? We discover that we love ourselves when we do what is good, and we hate ourselves when we do what is wrong.

So there will be certain things in the neighbor which will be loved, and other things which will not be loved. And they are the same things that were loved and hated in me. Hence, one can love the sinner, hate the sin; love the thief, but hate robbery; love the

Communist, but hate Communism. The Church will always accept the heretic back into the treasury of her soul, but never the heresy back into the treasury of her wisdom.

It is fortunate that in English we have two words to distinguish between liking and loving. The French have not this advantage. They have only the one word which is *aimer*.

Love Is a Verb

If humanity is to be amorized, it must mount to a love of persons, not only in friendship and marriage, but in helping fellowman. Man and woman are pulled up to new heights of love when person and sex become inseparable in the marital union; then the glass is as precious as the elixir. Sex is no longer just a function, a city to be taken by throwing a torch into it, to revel in as it is devoured by flames. The other person becomes a bearer of dignity, with whom communion is constantly established. The communion is of two kinds: One is the communion of words, in which there is a dialogue involving the common interests of life—work, children, problems, joys, pleasures. The other is a wordless communion, for those ecstatic moments when love reaches the ineffable moment too deep for words.

In this type of relationship, the other person is always looked upon as the more worthy. The lover is on his knees; the beloved is on the pedestal. As the centurion said: "Lord, I am not worthy that Thou shouldst take me under thy roof." This kind of love is one that does not seek to have but to be had; not to own but to be owned; not to possess but to be possessed. It is the giving of oneself for another. That is why one speaks of the arrows and darts of love, for love is a sacrificial seeking to serve.

But love of this kind must not be restricted to marriage, where there is a reciprocation of love. Service-love reaches a higher stage even when love is unreciprocated; this kind of love is found in missionaries, some social workers, Peace Corps workers, doctors and some civil servants, many of whom are like glasses which pour themselves out that a neighbor may be helped, poverty relieved, and a fevered brow calmed. This is the love of brotherhood.

Perhaps the best way to indicate Service-love is to find it in those whom we would expect to be served. The night of the Last Supper, the Divine Master gathered His apostles about Him. As they came into the upper room, they began to fight for first place at table. Despite three years of familiarity with Him, there was still the drive to superiority. (One wonders why it is called an inferiority complex when actually it is a superiority complex.) As they struggled for the best seats, they addressed Him as "Lord." At this point He gave the lesson that the nobler one is the more one must serve. Many great men cannot bow; despite integrity, rectitude, nobility, and self-respect, true love is not then achieved until they can stoop and serve.

Once before the Master had told them: "If any man desire to be first, let him be last of all." This was speedily forgotten. As they quarreled about priorities, Our Blessed Lord picked up a towel, circled it about His waist, knelt down, poured water into a basin, and began to wash their feet. Girding Himself with a towel was a symbol of how Divinity had girded Himself with our suffering humanity, becoming the servant to do dirty work, such as washing away our sins. Though they fought for the first seats, none of them fought for the towel. So he said to them, "You call Me Master and Lord and you say well, for so I am. If I then, the Lord and Master, have washed your feet, you also ought to wash one another's feet, for I have given you an example, that you also should do as I have done to you."

Here was something new in the amorization of the world. *Imperium est servitium*—Authority is for service. The higher one goes, the lower one must descend in helping neighbors. This action taught the supreme lesson that love is not a noun—it is a verb, and the verb is to serve. Love is not just to consume itself in beatific quietism but to prove itself Divine with a Body in useful and visible labor.

Here is a *service,* a lowliness which is not to be explained by the consciousness of loftiness, but rather by a desire to turn superiority into oblation and dedication. The example that He gave was that, if others called Him Lord and Master, which indeed He said He was, and He served others, then the highest type of human love is the caring for fellowmen. It does no good to tell men to face self-sacrificing humilities for the sake of others. This must be translated into concrete form by doing with His own hands what He expected others to do. That is why He did not call it a precept but an example.

Men are more anxious for primacy than they are for service. That is why it took Divinity to give this new concept of love. A man must sweep out of himself into a larger world, make himself one with the purposes of God, which is to help weak and stricken humanity. There is no bisection of the world into the secular and the sacred. Our everyday work, done with a religious motive, is a religious work. There are some who cannot carry the cross. At least, they can carry the towel. The world is full of weary travelers with aching and dust-stained feet, walking through all the humdrum, monotonous tasks that are so necessary for the welfare of the world.

Secularization or Amorization

A great and tremendous change has come over the world in our time, despite its wars and its failings—humanity is becoming amorized. It used to be that hospitals for the sick, charity for the poor, and education for the ignorant was wholly in the hands of religion; these were known as "works of charity." Today many of these activities are being taken over by the state. Some would call it secularization, but, rather, is it not amorization? Is not the yeast beginning to leaven the whole mass of our society? Foreign aid may have many defects, but still it represents a desire to help the poor of the world. Love is gradually shifting from the center of ourselves to others; what was once a circle is now more like an egg broken open for the manifestation of life.

Social workers, psychotherapists, psychiatrists, doctors—regardless of their background, their belief, or their want of belief—are nevertheless showing love to other humans. Every advance toward racial justice, every move toward the improvement of the actual human conditions, every striving of nations to unite in the peaceful settlement of disputes, every picking up of the pieces of the broken world and putting them together is a heightened form of service which is love. Every move toward dialogue, even with the widest varieties of ideologies, every move to save humanity from nuclear destruction, because one loves his fellowman, is another step in the amorization of humanity.

Gift-Love

The amorization of the universe can continue without being very conscious of its source. How few there are who know any of the secrets of the sun. How far is it from the earth? How many tons a day does the sun burn in atomic fission, to light and heat the world? But though there are few who have ever made inquiries into the nature of the sun, nevertheless all live and are lighted by it. The love in the human heart, which goes out to neighbor, to brotherliness, to social justice, to philanthropy, must have a Source. One may not know it. One may not even take the trouble to discover it, but it exists. Eventually it will become known.

When the feet of Peter were washed, he knew nothing of the action's meaning. It was no symbol; it bore no mystery. It had no meaning. It was only something done. Our Blessed Lord told Peter that at the present time he did not know, but later on he would know. So, too, those who are expressing themselves in service may not know to whom they render the service. It is the fact of service itself, which later on prepares the way for its consciousness and meaning.

Some men work best from the consciousness of that love, others secondarily. Some are inspired by Divine Love, as Our Lord the night of the Last Supper in washing the feet of the disciples. The other class, sometimes called the secular-minded, are really the amor-minded, who never investigate the mystery of the love but who work under its impact.

They start with a fact. They must see something, touch something, handle something; they proceed from the visible to the invisible, as the others proceed from the invisible to the visible. Men do not always have to work from the point of knowledge or understanding. There are moments in life when our highest powers of reasoning are set aside. We then become little children, just receivers. Let the thing be done; a meaning will come out later on! This was the answer of one of the characters of Dostoyevsky. Begin loving neighbor, and you will begin to find the meaning of the Love of God. Finally, the heart learns that all the love it gives it once received as Gift-Love from the Giver.

It is interesting that in the answer to the question: "Who is my neighbor?" (Luke 10:29), Our Lord told the parable of the good Samaritan and then asked the lawyer: "Which of the three do you think became the neighbor to him who fell among thieves?" It is to be noted that the neighbor-relationship was established by the event. It was not something that existed apart from it. It was not theoretical; it was practical. Everyone becomes my neighbor by my action or my speech; I enter into relationship with him. Or, because of his request or plea, he has entered into relationship with me.

The human heart eventually discovers the Source of all the waters that it has been drinking, even though it has been taken from paper cups, glasses, man-made wells, bottles, faucets, or earthly pools. Any love which one shows to neighbor is seen as Gift-Love, in the sense that one is first loved by God. Conscious of the fact that one has received this undeserved gift, one becomes prodigal of service and affection for all men. Changing the figure, he sees that if he enjoys a spark, there must somewhere be a flame; that if he has the segment of the circle, there must somewhere be the perfect round. The story of looking for the Source of Love can be found in the search for a new word to express the Fountain. The one word that had been used through antiquity to explain love was *eros,* which degenerated from the high noble view that Plato gave it into sensuality and lust.

When the fountain of love appeared on this earth, it was necessary to find another word to explain it, and that word was *agape.* Rarely was it found, even in classical literature. Only ten times does it appear in Homer. Three times it appears in Euripides. But it appears 320 times in the New Testament, the model being the Father Who so loved the world that His Son sacrificed Himself for us.

The difference between the *eros* and the *agape* is this: *Eros* is egotistic; *agape* is sacrificial. *Eros* is attracted to that which is beautiful; the *agape* pours out love and makes others beautiful. *Eros* is the circle enfolding upon itself; *agape* is the Cross extending its arms to embrace all humanity. *Agape* loves even when that love is not reciprocated. It extends to both the deserving and the undeserving: "He makes the sun shine on both the just and the unjust."

In *eros,* the desire is the cause of the love, the chance to make quick money, to buy a yacht, or whistling at a beautiful girl. *Agape* is, on the contrary, the cause of the desire. For example, I desire to help the poor family because I love them as my brothers. We cannot like everyone, but we can love everyone.

Conclusion

On the Sunday after the Resurrection, early in the morning, seven men were out fishing in a boat. One of those men, Peter, three times had denied the Divine Master. Three times he was asked if he loved, twice in a very sacrificial way, and the other in a human way. When all three questions were answered in the affirmative, there came the command to feed lambs, sheep, and firstlings of the flock. In other words, love is the condition of service. Professionalism is service without love.

We are knit to the Fountain by true affection, which is based upon the consciousness of our falls, our weaknesses, and also our reception of His forgiving mercy. Then we shall have the qualities that fit us in the impulse to serve and help our fellowmen. I do not say that there is no philanthropy apart from the Fountain, but I do say it picks and chooses, the rich generally giving to the rich. In the long run, they who are pressing Divine Love to their hearts are most equipped for efficient service in total surrender of heart. The peace of the world is conditioned upon the amorization of our hearts.

CHAPTER EIGHT

Caring for Humanity

When amorization of humanity becomes personal, it is caring. But caring can be difficult if there is inferiority or superiority.

Not having had time for lunch, one afternoon I stepped into a small grocery store to buy a box of crackers for a snack. As I entered, I saw a mother in the back of her store with a four-year-old child who had just pulled a bottle of vinegar off the shelf, breaking it into pieces. Standing over him, she said repeatedly, "Pick up those pieces!" With each command, he became more rebellious. It was evident that she would have loved to have slapped him, but she dared not because she wanted to appear compassionate before the customers. The father, waiting on them, enjoyed his neutrality, ignoring both the case of the mother and the son. However, it was very evident that as she was thinking, "The boy is just like his father, stubborn and self-willed," he was thinking, "Just like his mother's family, always making a show of authority."

The mother, leaving the spilled vinegar and broken pieces of glass on the floor, finally dragged her son off to a back room, like a child might drag a rag doll. Who won the battle? Was it the child who maintained his will through tears, for tears are the last refuge of the weak? Or was it the mother who seemingly renounced her strength, though it was evident she was forced to capitulate?

Here we are faced with a problem which has very well been

summarized by Dr. Jean de Rougemont: "If my neighbor is stronger than I am, I fear him; if he is weaker than I am, I despise him. If he is equal to me, I use subterfuge and find excuses for either asserting my superiority or for not obeying him."

The strong and the weak! Superiority and inferiority! The same tension exists in the rich helping the poor. Do the rich help the poor because of a kind of pity, which makes the poor feel their inferiority? Do the poor in their turn resent being helped by the rich, because it offends their dignity and degrades their personality by being made dependent? Do the rich maintain a kind of equality by helping only the rich, and the poor maintain theirs by helping the poor? An institution that is already worth $100 million can easily get another $150 million. Thus the rich keep on their level by enriching the rich—they also get an honorary doctorate at commencement exercises and tickets on the fifty-yard line at one of the football games.

Those with little, on the contrary, generally help the poor, for here there is a deeper sympathy and understanding of what another suffers. It is very likely that the rich man in the parable of Lazarus wrote out very large checks to philanthropic causes, but he probably drew his curtains whenever a funeral procession passed by and avoided the exit where Lazarus sat with his sores.

How Solve the Problem?

How solve this problem of the strong and the weak, the rich and the poor, with weak fearing the strong and the strong despising the weak? The real solution is not to be found in any kind of law, for law ignores personal dialogue with others and also secures its right by imposing penalties. Then too, there can be a respect for neighbor, because it happens to be a mood or a fashion, rather than an upsurge of love. There should be some other way to care for others which is not like a plastic flower pinned to a barren tree, but rather a blossom that grows out of the tree itself.

As the distinguished psychiatrist, Paul Tournier, has pointed out: The strong must see their own weakness; the weak must see their own poverty; the poor must see their own wealth; the learned must see their ignorance; the ignorant must see their peculiar kind of wisdom.

Let the strong ask themselves: *How strong am I?* Am I master and captain of my soul, or am I driven about by every wind of passion? How long have I been able to stay on a diet? Or on the wagon? What New Year's resolution have I kept? Have I not resolved as a mother to be kinder to my children—and yet blast them even when I take aspirin for my nerves? Am I strong enough to cut down to one pack of cigarettes a day, as I wish I could? Can I resist flying off the handle when someone in the office crosses me? Can I resist a second or third cocktail when I know that it causes me to make everyone in the office uncomfortable? How strong am I in resisting lust or dishonesty?

How *rich* am I when I look at the poverty of my inner life? I may *have* something, but *am* I anything? Am I not poverty-stricken as regards self-mastery, and, oh, how rich in egotism and selfishness! How wise am I? I may know all the Books of the Month, being proud of my college education, but have I ever discovered the meaning of life? Is there anything lovable in me at all? Am I not nasty and cranky? Do I not short-circuit every conversation with a fellow worker at the water cooler?

But I still love myself. I am good to myself. I give myself a good chair when I come into the room. I always order the best food, avoiding anything which does not flatter my palate. I avoid conversations which might embarrass me.

If then I can love myself, despite all of my weaknesses, failures, and faults, why can I not love my neighbor, despite all of his faults? If I am really not rich at all, except on the outside, but inwardly poor, then why can I not really love the poor, who are richer on the inside than I? Why cannot I love others, despite the way they are?

The Strong Seeing Their Weakness

Here is the answer to how the strong can avoid despising the weak and the rich humiliating the poor: The strong must see their own ignorance.

Our Divine Lord said, "Love your neighbor as yourself." Why did He not say, Love your neighbor *more* than yourself? Because when we see how much we love ourselves, despite the fact that we are unlovable, then the greatest love we can show our neighbor is to love him despite his unlovableness. How many there are who say they hate themselves. But do they really? Let anyone else tell them how hateful they are, and they flare up in love for themselves.

But over and above all this, I am loved by God despite all my faults, failures, and infidelities. There is nothing in me that should make me lovable to God. Then why does He love me? Because He puts some of His love into me. He loves me as a mother loves a child with a dirty face; her image is in the child, and it is this the mother sees and loves. If then I, who am not worth loving, am loved by Love, the least I can do for others is to do what God has done for me. Once I no longer regard myself as a superman, who refused to share the struggle of others, then when others are weak, I am weak; when they are poor, I am poor; when they are tearful, my cheeks are damp. Then I see not that I am loved because God loves everybody; but rather that, if God loves me, as miserable as I am, then He *must love everybody.*

Only when I am as weak and helpless as my neighbor can I help him. Then there is no spirit of judgment, no sense of superiority, no superciliousness, no looking down one's nose at others. I am his companion in repentance. I too am waiting for grace, just as he did.

We notice how much intimacy this creates with another when a patient is faced with a serious operation. If a doctor tells a patient that an operation is necessary, the patient becomes frightened at the prospect. If, however, the doctor says, "I have had this operation," then the patient has an assurance that is based upon true sympathy. Incidentally, this is one of the reasons why, in seeking counsel, we should never go to a person who has not suffered. It need not be just physical suffering; it can be moral or spiritual. Only those who have been wounded really know how to bind up wounds.

From another point of view, are not the hearts of the strong and the chivalrous captured by weakness which solicits defense? Every language uses the diminutive to express tenderness, even to such a thing as a baby elephant. Beauty is bound up with the petite, not generally with the fat. There is a greater love of chicks than of chickens, of lambs than of sheep, of puppies than dogs, of kittens more than cats.

Love Is the Reason

One moves out of the realm of rights, law, civic equality, as soon as one is governed by love. It changes not only ourselves; it changes others.

Once there was a girl born of parents who constantly quarreled and made her feel that she was unwanted as she was certainly unloved. They finally separated. She had to shift for herself in a world that was a kind of jungle. She had no faith in those whom she met. She did not even have faith in herself. The rough, coarse ways of her home seemed to have left their mark and made her unhappy on the outside and afraid of others.

Then one day a miracle happened. She met a young man who came from loving parents. Despite all of the seeming commonness of the young woman, he saw her basically sweet manner and a potential for devotion and dedication. Her life completely changed in a moment. She was loved, appreciated, and cared for! She suddenly realized that she was beautiful, not because she had ever thought she was, but because he loved her. A song asks whether a young woman is loved because she is beautiful or is she beautiful because she is loved. The true beauty is that which is created by love. This kind of love that cares, that never seems superior, is creative, making the other person a true self, even nobler than self.

A wealthy American visiting one of our leper colonies in the Pacific came across a nun who was caring for about three hundred lepers and said to her, "Sister, I wouldn't do that for a million dollars." She said, "Neither would I."

A woman visiting a neighbor said, "I would give my life to have two children like that." The mother answered, "That is exactly what it costs." That much love, that much life, that much care!

Concern

It has been said that happiness is a twin, which means that we are really never happy unless we share. We were made for openness to the world. Our five senses put us in contact with the universe; our intellect enables us to understand it. Some, indeed, cut themselves off deliberately from its science, its culture, its music, impoverishing their joys and hardening themselves to the thrill of knowing. Man cannot exist without Encounter or without Care, which is a responsible being reacting to others, thus helping others to grow and develop. Fellowship or humanity is the matrix womb of our existence; we were born out of it—the family, the nation, the world. To it, we return, to become whole and even normal. A character in the novel of Johan Bojer, mindful of his ties to impoverished humanity says, "Here I am, for instance, sitting among clean people and eating with a silver fork at my table with a white cloth, and yet—well, I can't quite manage to feel only joy and gladness over it all, for half my inner consciousness is with the thousands that at this moment haven't even salt for the soup."

We Are All Part of Humanity

Albert Camus, in his work, *The Plague,* described a city whose hotel was ridden by rats, thus frightening the entire population:

"Are our city fathers aware that the decaying bodies of these rodents constitute a grave danger to the population?"

The manager of the hotel can talk of nothing else, but he has a personal grievance too—that a dead rat should be found in the elevator of a three-star hotel seems to him the end of all things. To console him, I said: "But you know everybody is in the same boat." "That's just it," he replied. "Now, we're like everybody else."

It was hell to him to be like everybody else. He refused to see himself a part of the muck and mud, the poverty and the starvation of all his brothers. He wanted to be different, alone, isolated—which in the end would make him frustrated. Every self-centered person is a self-disrupted person. Nothing has happened to him—he did something to himself: He no longer cared.

The Refusal to Share Our Humanity With Others

William Whyte in his *The Organization Man* pictures a world where people are encased in their organizations, institutions, and firms, and thus become totally oblivious of everything outside their jelly mold. David Riesman in his *The Lonely Crowd* describes similar people who want to be part of the "in" group, where one must be aware of trends within the group, such as swallowing martinis followed by an olive, followed by a lemon, followed by another martini. There is no place for the "outs"; they live in another world.

There must be one to see and care. Rumer Godden in *An Episode of Sparrows* brings out this lesson:

"It is not old-fashioned to say that God is good," said David Wix. "Remember, that not one sparrow can fall to the ground—"

"But they fall all the time," said Olivia. "We knock them down. We knock them, crush them, carelessly or carefully, it doesn't matter which, and they fall. That's what humans do to humans, so don't talk to me about God. . . ."

"Wait," she said, "humans to humans? Is that how it works? Somehow one person at least is meant to see the fall and care? See and become the instrument. I have seen. I wish I hadn't. . . . But I have, and I shall keep my eyes open."

Because Someone cares, we care; because I am loved in my miserable self, I must love others who certainly are better than I. If Someone took on my burden of guilt, then I must be foregiving to others. After all, I can never know their bad points as well as I know my own. But, if I love myself, knowing myself undeserving as I am, then shall I not prolong that love to others. This is happiness —service, encounter, responsibility, availability to all in need for Love's sake.

Caring As a Therapy

Most people are frustrated, miserable, and unhappy because they do not care. A self-centered life is a self-disrupted life. Egotists do not need psychiatrists, though patients with true psychoses and neuroses do. The egotistic are always out of sorts with themselves and with others. Instead of turning to others in care, they turn to themselves in self-pity. A house divided against itself cannot stand.

The punishment of self-pity is inherent; every egotist brings on his own punishment. Budd Schulberg in *What Makes Sammy Run,* after tracing Sammy's egocentric life, sums it up in these words:

Unconsciously I have been . . . hoping to be around when Sammy got what was coming to him. And now I realize that *what was coming to him* was not a sudden payoff, but a process, a disease, . . . a cancer that was slowly eating him away, the symptoms intensifying: success, loneliness, fear. . . . I thought . . . you can't have your brothers and eat them too. You're alone, pal, all alone! That's the way you wanted it! That's the way you learned it. . . . All alone in sickness and in health, for better or for worse, till death parts you from your only friend, your worst enemy, yourself.

In the play, *Peer Gynt,* the hero visits a lunatic asylum where he believes that people are out of their minds or out of themselves. The director corrects him: "It's here that men are most themselves —themselves and nothing but themselves—sailing without spread sails of self. Each shuts himself in a cask of self, the cask stopped with the bung of self and seasoned in a well of self. None has tears for others' woes, or cares what any other thinks."

The cure for this general malady of selfishness is to break out of our walled garden or glass cage. Existence is not opaque and unrelated to the universe and people about us. Existence has a relatedness to everything. That is why there is in us a nostalgia, a sense of nonfulfillment, until we complete it by having an encounter with others. Care makes one a responsible being, reacting to others, helping others grow and develop. Our fellowman, in a certain sense, is necessary for two reasons: First, humanity is the matrix womb of our existence. We are born out of the community, the family, the nation, and the church. Second, without our fellowmen, we could never exercise this role as being the servant and shepherd of others.

There is not a frustrated egotist who could not be cured by getting his back off a couch, getting on his feet to serve. His weakness would pass out through his fingers in what might be called the therapy of touch. Instead of having his guilt explained away, he could work it away with a love that covers a multitude of sins.

A British psychiatrist, Maxwell Jones, introduced into a hospital what he called community care. The project was that each person should have contact with those either in the same room or, if he was ambulatory, on the same floor; he was to consider himself a part of the healing community. No one was to talk about his illness but to bring solace to others. The orderlies, the nurses, the doctors also pledged themselves to be interested in others. Three results followed: Patients recovered more quickly, because they were loved. Doctors discovered that fewer formal interviews with patients were necessary, because of the new form of care on the part of the patients. Third, the doctor divested himself of unnecessary symbols of authority, such as the white coat and the stethoscope, and depended upon earning his status as a real person in the life of the patients and the personnel.

It is all very well and good to release men from certain anxieties, but the real cure does not come until one is released *to* a concern for the welfare of others. The cruelest words of tongue or pen are, "I could not have cared less." The ungiven self is an unfulfilled self.

Is Love Dead?

A popular mood in magazine theology is to say that God is dead. This has a shock appeal, very much like writing dirty words on back fences. But why do they say God is dead? Is it not rather that love is dead? We do not mean that love is dead in the sense of sexing, necking, fornication, lusting, adultery, perversity, homosexuality. Rather, we mean that love is dead in the sense of caring.

How can we know God if we do not know our neighbor? How can we see God if we do not see our neighbor? If we cannot see the visible, how can we see the Invisible? If God is not seen in the hungry, the distressed, and the despised brethren, then He will never be seen as the Lord of this universe. How many of those who have received rich royalty on the books announcing the death of God have ever given a substantial percentage of that money to the poor? Has national publicity worth millions to well-paid professors ever been balanced off by sharing it with the socially disinherited?

The death of God is not a question of semantics—that is to say, of finding a word which will express the divine reality. It is rather a question of optics. Let them visit any of the leper colonies that house ten million lepers in the world. Let them take a boy out of the *favellas* of Santiago or Rio and give him an education. Let them begin loving some polio victim who has been abandoned and forgotten. Then they will find that God was dead only because He had been crucified in their hearts when they fastened Love to a Cross. Why in the world, if our neighbor is not real to us, should God ever be real to us? If I do not love the ray of sunshine, my eyes will never look up to the sun. God made the birds with gorgeous plumage and sweet voices. But He gave them no wings. He laid the wings on either side of each bird and said to them, "I want you to care for others. Take these wings as burdens; carry them but in love, not in anger." They so loved their burden that they pressed them more and more to their breast, and finally they grew and became wings.

Sympathy

One wonders if there is not more sympathy in smaller communities than in great cities. One can live in apartments and not know the next-door neighbor, but there is hardly a village in which one does not know the next-door neighbor. There is probably less borrowing of sugar in all of the apartments of New York than there is in a village of five hundred. Not long ago, a picture magazine took photographs for one hour of people who passed by a wounded man on a subway stair. The magazine recounted in pictures the number who looked at the man and then went on their way without making a sympathetic inquiry. But the magazine itself forgot to state that the photographer was more interested in the click of his machine than he was in the tick of the heart of the wounded man.

This does not mean to say that sympathy is nonexistent, for the generous heart of Americans pours itself out in alms and in sympathy to the needy and the poor.

Sympathy is a temper or character which draws others together. It is what might be called conductivity. The Greek origin of the word "sympathy" implies "suffering with." It is a kind of silent understanding when heart meets heart. It is a kind of substitution, in which one takes the heart out of his own body and places it in the body of another man, and in exchange takes back the other's heart. It is not mere pity, for pity can be like the traveler in the Gospel who looked on the wounded man but did not help. Sentimentality can exist in low souls, but pure sympathy resides only in the noble.

Sometimes sympathy can be silent, particularly where there is grief. St. Paul told the Romans: "Weep with those that weep." The shedding of a common tear is far more eloquent than are honeyed words. This is well-proved in the case of Job, whose comforters sat silently seven days beside him; their consolation was far greater than when they broke their silence and gave so many false reasons as to why Job suffered.

The foundation of all true sympathy, and that which makes it universal, is love. The best of men can offer only human tenderness without understanding the mystery of pain and tears. But when one comes to the love of Christ, one finds both the tenderness of the human and the comprehensiveness of the Divine. In Him alone is united sympathy and the understanding of the mystery of pain. It was that that made Him weep over the death of His beloved friend Lazarus. Many men have a heart, but they lack the mind to embrace the mystery. On the one hand, there can be narrow good men and, on the other hand, ironhearted philanthropists; but in Christ, the tender heart and the Divine knowledge combine.

Hence, He bade us to have sympathy with all men, not in the way of condescension, not as the pure lifting their skirts from the impure; but as men touching to heal, as men hating the sin and loving the sinner. This sympathy alone can rid us of that modern pity which Chesterton so well condemns:

> The practical weakness of the vast mass of modern pity for the poor and the oppressed is precisely that it is merely pity; but pity is pitiful, but not respectful. Men feel that the cruelty to the poor is a kind of cruelty to animals. They never feel it is injustice to equals, nay, it is treachery to comrades. This dark, scientific pity, this brutal pity, has an elemental sincerity of its own, but it is entirely useless for all ends of social reform.

In many Oriental countries when traveling, one may stop at the house of anyone and ask for hospitality. It will be extended not only for the night, but even for a longer period. The natural sense of sympathy is deeper there than in our complex civilization where even giving a hitchhiker a lift is forbidden. Too many abused the privilege and made sympathy unsafe.

Christian sympathy extends to those who are unsympathetic. A legend tells us that Abraham received a visitor in his tent. Abraham killed his best lamb, gave him his best cot, and served him as a servant. But the visitor was displeased with everything. After three days, Abraham put him out. The Lord appeared to Abraham, saying, "Abraham, if I put up with him for forty years, can you not put up with him for three days?"

"Write a check!" This is one of the most common expressions of men who are called generous and philanthropic, when asked to subscribe for a cause, or to build a field house or a laboratory. They discharge the appeal by a stroke of the pen. While this immediacy of giving is very much to be commended, and while it never fails to rejoice the recipient, there is often wanting a spiritual quality which affects both the check writer and the check endorser. This is particularly true of very large donations. Andrew Carnegie, who gave away millions, once said that he never missed anything that he gave away; first because he did not know how much he had; second, all that he gave away was paper, and he could never notice any decrease in his paper, by which he meant checks, stocks, bonds, etc.

The nature of giving is best illustrated in the life of Our Blessed Lord, Who one day was approached by a leper who asked for healing. The Gospel tells us that Our Lord stretched forth His Hand and touched the leper. The Savior could have healed without the touch, as He healed the servant of the centurion at a distance. Why then, in the face of one of life's greatest miseries and a disease from which the healthy often recoil, did the Lord cure with a touch?

Because of a spiritual quality in the Giver—namely, compassion or the ability to suffer with others. Touch is the language of love. There are actually three intimacies in love: hearing, seeing, and touching. We could never love anyone unless we first know him or hear his voice. Next, after hearing a voice, one wishes to see the person. Vision is the second intimacy. Then finally, there comes the greatest of all intimacies, which only a few may enjoy, and that is the intimacy of touch. The Son of God made Man touched the leper in order to annihilate distance between the Giver and the receiver, between the Lover and the beloved, to prove sympathy by contact, to identify Himself with the woes of others. How different was the attitude of Shylock, who said, "I will buy with you, sell with you, talk with you, walk with you, . . . but I will not eat with you, drink with you, nor pray with you."

According to the Old Testament Law, Our Blessed Lord would have become ceremonially unclean until that evening because He touched the leper. How could He justify His exemption from the Law? Because the priests of the Old Testament in their contact with the leper were judged exempt from the law of defilement. How much more was He, the great High Priest and the Law Giver, exempt in cleansing the leper. Our Lord, however, did conform Himself to the Law, inasmuch as He ordered the leper to show himself to the priest in order that his cleanness might be authoritatively certified, thus restoring him again to society.

The Hand that touched was also the Hand that later on would be pierced with a nail, because He would take upon Himself the human leprosy of sin. The point is, however, that the hand was the extension of His personality and, therefore, a sign of His intimate compassion with the leper. Man is the only creature that has a hand that is creative, and with it he puts the stamp of his mind upon stone and gold, founds his sovereignty of civilization, and comforts his fellowman.

There was another moral effect equally important about touching—namely, the affection bestowed on the leper. Every diseased person has a heart, and the physician who heals the body as if it were a guinea pig, but awakens no human love in the heart, has failed in his mission as a healer. That leper was ostracized from society. He had need of a sip of the milk of human kindness. Up to that point the leper was despised and rejected. Now he was loved by Love.

Sometimes writing a check can be just as cold as flinging a dime at a beggar. The gift of the lover without the love of the giver is bare. It is part of my work to gather alms to support over four hundred leper colonies throughout the world. In twelve years in this work, we have never received a large check. Every gift was a sacrifice, something hard to give, something that demanded self-denial. In every single gift there was, therefore, a compassion with the suffering of the lepers and also a communication of love. Sometimes those who have little to give give with greater love, for after the example of the Master, they too "touch" the leper.

CHAPTER NINE

The War Against Affluence

In the economic order, the amorization of humanity becomes a war. Two wars are now being waged on the field of economics: one, the War Against Poverty; the other, the War Against Affluence. The rich today are on the defensive. It is important to make a distinction between those who use money as an end in itself and those who use money as a means. Here, we are not speaking of the former procuring the necessities of life, decent comforts, service of fellowman, and general well-being. Rather, we speak of those who treat money as a kind of a god or the supreme goal of life.

The affluent who are avaricious and make money the supreme quest of life generally reveal these psychological traits:

1. A passionate desire to accumulate;
2. A reluctance to give;
3. "The world owes me a living."

1. The desire to accumulate: Milton in his *Paradise Lost* describes Heaven before the fall of the angels. One of the angels, whose name was Mammon, went about Heaven with his head down, concentrating on the streets of gold. Since love is gravity, and he sought the things that were base, he fell. One of his lineal descendants was a young man who one day found a five-dollar bill on the street. From that time on, he always went about, like Mammon,

with his head bowed, looking for what he could find. After twenty-five years, he had collected 1,407 hairpins, 413 pins, 76 Goldwater buttons, thirty cents, and a stiff neck.

The affluent who desire merely to pile up money confuse *being* and *having*. A person is incomplete and needs things outside of himself to perfect his personality. Because one is worth so much in terms of dollars, he begins to think that he is worth something in character. These are the hollow men who stuff their barns and their vaults to atone for their own inner poverty. They who are most naked on the inside, as regards virtue and goodness, are most likely to go in for the excessive luxury on the outside. Adam and Eve did not need clothing until they recognized that they had lost their friendship with God.

2. Reluctance to give: It will generally be found that the affluent who make money an end are the poorest tippers. They will rationalize their greed by saying to anyone who would leave a good tip, "Don't spoil him," or, "What do you want to do, pension him for life?" The miser always pictures himself as being encompassed by people who want to take advantage of him. He, therefore, is obliged to mobilize all his resources against these fancied aggressors. Faster and faster, he builds up his own inner defenses, until at last he stands triumphant along with his hoard. He then becomes the real miser, enjoying not his own money, for one can never enjoy what one is afraid of losing, but enjoys only his conquest over those who would seize his wealth.

If the rich do give, it is generally to the rich. This keeps them on the same level socially and also enables them to receive more gratitude or praise for their gifts. It is generally the poor who help the poor; and it is the haves who help the haves. An institution with millions of dollars very readily receives many other millions, while those who have little generally have to depend on those who have nothing.

A parable on the curse of avarice is found in *The Brothers Karamazov:*

Once upon a time, there was a peasant woman and a very wicked woman she was. And she died and did not leave a single good deed behind her. The devils caught her and plunged her into the lake of fire. So her Guardian Angel stood and wondered what good deed of hers he could remember to tell God: "She once pulled up an onion in her garden," said he, "and gave it to a beggar woman." And God answered: "You take that onion then, hold it out to her in the lake, and let her take hold and be pulled out. And if you can pull her out of the lake, let her come to Paradise, but if the onion breaks, then the woman must stay where she is."

The Angel ran to the woman and held out the onion to her: "Come," said he, "catch hold and I'll pull you out." And he began cautiously pulling her out. He had just pulled her right out, when the other sinners in the lake, seeing how she was being drawn out, began catching hold of her so as to be pulled out with her. But she was a very wicked woman and she began kicking them. "I'm to be pulled out, not you. It's my onion, not yours." As soon as she said that, the onion broke. And the woman fell into the lake and . . . The Angel wept and went away.

This is the essence of avarice: "my security," "my goods," "my onion." It is a centering upon our own anxiety and resolving to save ourselves at all costs, regardless of the deepest needs of others; above all, it is a forgetfulness that we are stewards of the Mercy of God.

3. "The world owes me a living:" "I'll taste the luxury of woe," wrote Thomas More. Some love it. There is a difference between one who is *dependent* and a *dependee*. The *dependent* is one who has a claim on society for a just reason. The *dependee* is one who, though able to work and support himself, nevertheless claims, "I have a right to live, and the world owes me a living." There is a Yiddish word for one of this type—*Schnorrer,* a beggar who does not appeal to the heart alone but uses a veiled threat: "You had better comply with my wishes or else." A story is told of a *Schnorrer* who asked a friend for money in order to celebrate religious holidays, because he was unable to support himself. A few days later,

the one who gave him the money found the *Schnorrer* in an expensive restaurant eating caviar. His friend said to him, "How very inconsiderate, when you need money badly, to spend it on something so luxurious." The *Schnorrer* answered, "When I have no money, I can't eat caviar. When I have money, you tell me I shouldn't eat it. When do you suggest that I eat caviar?"

The *dependees* actually create situations of dependence, sometimes refusing to work or working briefly in order to put themselves on relief. They may even create a situation of dependence by maintaining that they are contributing to culture by their poetry or by their paintings, and therefore society owes them a living. Once they are refused help, they become aggressive and finally end by pitying themselves because of the injustices which have been done them.

A wealthy father may give spending money to an extravagant son, but when he refuses an exorbitant request, the son will say, "I hate you." Daughters, when denied a wish by the mother, will often retort, "I hate you." Ingratitude is always the note of the loafer, whether rich or poor. As Mark Twain put it, "If you pick up a starving dog and make him prosperous, he will not bite you. This is the principal difference between a dog and a man." The benefactor is hated because he does not repeat his gift. As Lord Byron put it:

Now hatred is by far the longer pleasure;
Men love in haste, but they detest in leisure.

What is given is always forgotten. That is one of the reasons why when one gives a gift, one should never remember that he gave it.

The survival of the infant attitude, in which one is perpetually supplied and in which there is little distinction between what is outside of me and what is within me, begets the avaricious man who says, "The world owes me a living." Chesterton said of the rich man, "I know of only one way for a man to become exceedingly rich, and that is to practice avarice."

The Origin of the Money Neurosis

The neurosis is to be traced to a great extent to childhood and the failure to rise above that infantile state. Although an infant has no sense whatever of being cloistered within the mother, there is nevertheless an inbred physiological dependence. Once the doors of the flesh are thrown open, this sense of being protected and cared for is continued. The child cries and is given milk. He cries, and his diapers are changed. Whether he cries or not, a warm blanket is provided. At night, if he cries, the parent walks the floor. He puts out his finger, the mother immediately grabs it. He is in the center of the stage, the hero before the footlights, a little king. If he is not a king, at least he is a president. He gets admiration as others do what he wants.

There is nothing wrong in this. Freud has made a very keen observation about infancy, saying that a child only gradually learns to distinguish between himself and the outer world. What is known to be outside comes later. He thinks everything is a gift which he gives himself. An immediacy also exists between the demand and the supply. If he could articulate his experiences, he would say not so much the world is mine, but, "The world, it is I." Could it not be also that the childish habit of sucking the thumb is merely a reflex of the child's omnipotence of himself supplying what is needed?

When the child grows out of infancy, there are refusals of requests and even delays. The child now begins to make a distinction between himself and what is outside of himself. He is trained for maturity by being taught self-discipline, restraint, self-denial, consideration for others, and obedience. When this type of home training is given to the child, it grows up to be normal, with little egotism but with a deep concern for others.

With the decline of morality, discipline, and religion, there is a permissiveness granted to children, in the sense that they are never asked to do anything they do not want to do. Incidentally, about the only place in our national life where discipline today exists in an organized way is in the Armed Forces. That is why in the decay of any civilization, the last remnant of order and decency is generally found among the soldiers, as is evident in the centurion at Calvary.

Along with the indifference to morality, parents also grant every whim and desire of the son and daughter. First the toy is supplied, then the red racer, with the result that the child never really matures. The birth certificate may register adult age, but the psychological age is between one and three. The avaricious man who piles up money is like the infant who cannot distinguish between the inside and the outside world. No matter how many hairs he has on his head, it hurts to have one pulled out.

The dependee is also a neurotic who has gotten out of his cradle but never out of its mentality. Everlastingly dependent upon another person or a group, he expects bottles to be brought when he cries, diapers to be provided, and toys when he has the mood. He may be an artist who expects society to provide him a living, or a person who takes just enough short jobs to remain within the pale of social security or unemployment insurance.

Socialism and the welfare state have a good origin and a bad origin. What is good about them is the recognition that we are brothers, live in a community, and are related as the parts of the body, each one needing his neighbor. The bad origin of it is the growing sense of irresponsibility, the refusal to work, along with the denial that one should make a social contribution to society.

The War on Three Fronts

The war against affluence may be waged on three fronts:

1. Among the rich themselves;
2. In religion;
3. In the youth and the new humanists.

1. The rich are negatively at war against affluence, inasmuch as they feel uncomfortable with their hoarded piles of disks called money and their paper rectangles called stocks and bonds. American society used to praise the rich man. Almost every commencement address, forty or fifty years ago, held up to emulation the man who started with a dime and then died worth millions. The most popular books for boys in those days were by Horatio Alger about poor youngsters who defended helpless persons, for which they were befriended by wealthy men, later becoming presidents of railroads or Wall Street tycoons.

How is the rich man carrying on a war against affluence? What does he do to escape the shock of knowing that one third of the people of the world go to bed hungry every night? He enters politics. The power which used to be linked with money is now transferred to the distribution of money—someone else's. By entering politics, the rich man is subconsciously defending his wealth by rendering a public service. He is less thought of as an accumulator of wealth; he now is pictured as one benefiting humanity. But how does he benefit humanity? By the spending of public funds. A study of wealthy men in politics will reveal that national and state debts always increase in greater proportion under wealthy men who have gone into politics than under poor men who have gone into politics. The wealthy man is under a psychological compulsion to justify himself. He is the "friend" of the downtrodden, the forgotten man, the poor, the slum dweller, the unfortunates of the world. But, the money that is touched is not in his own vaults nor in his own pocket but comes out of the pockets of the people. In any case, the affluent know that affluence is on the defensive.

2. Religion is also warring against affluence, both negatively and positively. Where it is affluent, it feels uncomfortable. In some instances, it has been an offender. However, many of the criticisms directed against religion are to be discounted by inquiring from the critics how much they have given to the poor. The Second Vatican Council was actually a pastoral affirmation of the value of poverty,

just as the Council of Trent was an affirmation of chastity against the immorality of the times and Vatican Council I was an affirmation of obedience against the license of the time.

Religion is beginning to see that the more prosperous it is, the less spiritual it becomes; that the vow of poverty must begin to take on new forms; that the invididual who takes the vow of poverty may not hide behind corporate wealth, knowing very well that there are several hundred million people in the world who would gladly take the vow of poverty today if they could live as well, sleep as well, eat as well, and be clothed as well as those who take the vow.

Granted this, there is a very strong affirmation on the part of all churches of the necessity of poverty, or rather the spirit of poverty. Some of the new religious groups stress poverty among their members; parishes adopt poor areas of the world, while a number of bishops have drawn up what they call Schema 14. Actually, in the Council there were only thirteen schemata. Schema 14 commits the signers not to live above the level of the people whom they serve, not to waste any time on administration but to deliver it over to the laity, in order that they might serve the socially disinherited and the poor of the world.

3. The third front is among the youth and what might be called the new humanists.

Could it not be that beatnikism, the crude dress of teen-agers, is a kind of protest against the lavishness, the affluence, and the emphasis on profit which has so characterized our civilization? Heartening indeed it is that many youths are protesting against expensive weddings and entering into careers where the stress is less on profit and gain, and more on service, such as research and the Peace Corps. Notable among them all, however, is what might be called the new humanism on the part of youth.

The New Humanism

The world today is undergoing a polarization: The bad are becoming worse; the good are becoming better. Here, the emphasis is on what is better. At the close of World War I the cry was: "Make the world safe for democracy," which was a plea for one type of government in the world. This led to a reaction of totalitarianism in its three forms of class, race, and nation. At the close of World War II we began to stress "One World." This slogan was physical or cosmic—we were one because we shared the same earth. It was also political, begetting the UN with its laudable bringing together of nations, not to one banquet table for a love feast but to one discussion table for tolerance's sake. But even this has run into danger of the nations dividing themselves into blocs.

The war against affluence is giving us something really new—not one world, but One Humanity. We are one, not because no airport in the world is over twenty hours away, but because we see that all of us have been made of one blood to dwell on the face of the earth. Humanity is not like a fence of separate poles, strung together thanks to political and economic barbed wire or red tape; rather it is like a giant tree which has been growing for centuries. Its leaves fall off now and then, but they are replaced by others, while the roots become deeper, and one mysterious energy or sap continues to flow, uniting the trunk and branches. Or it is like a human body, made up of many cells and many organs, and yet one because governed by one mind and vivified by one spirit. The arm cannot say to the leg. "I can do without your service." Nor can the eye say to the ear which is about to be struck, "I do not care; it is not going to strike me."

This new humanism is different from the veneration for humanity which was so general in the nineteenth century. It is easy to love humanity, because humanity is an abstraction. It enables one to escape his obligations: "I love humanity, but not that man." But the new humanism sees that there is no such thing as the problem of poverty; there are only poor men and poor women, famished bodies, leaky roofs, and untutored children.

The new humanism stands at the opposite pole of the modern egotism so well expressed in the drama of Sartre, where souls in hell gather to talk about their ills, their hates, their neuroses; no one listens; the others are impatient to tell their complaints when no one will listen. As the curtain goes down the last words of the play are: "My neighbor is hell."

Why are the new humanists warring against affluence in a constructive way? They feel an inner *void* and emptiness in our affluent society. They seek to fill up the void by serving humanity. Society, wealth, prestige, money, popularity—all these they have either tasted or have known, only to discover them as Dead Sea apples, beautiful on the outside, ashes within. Their emptiness is a summons; life should not be so hollow.

Poor in Spirit

What is this emptiness which draws them out of their egotism? It is the First Beatitude: "Happy, the poor in spirit." Since the Gospels were originally written in Greek, one must discover which word was used for "poor." The Greeks had two words for it; one was *penes*, which meant the man who was struggling for existence, living from hand to mouth, who barely had enough to feed and clothe his family and who could never lay anything aside as savings.

The other word was *ptochos*, which meant the destitute, the miserable, the slum dweller without a job, the man who through no fault of his own was reduced to beggary, the orphan child lost on the street, the man for whom there is nothing else but destitution.

Which of these two words was used in the beatitude? It was *ptochos*—the subhuman man. But how could such a one be happy? What blessedness is there in living in a *favella* or the dumps? The Lord did not bless destitution but multiplied loaves for the hungry, rather than send them away hungry; He pictured the rich man in hell because he refused to help the *ptochos* at the door.

Notice that the word "in spirit" follows the word *ptochos*. Hence, the beatitude means: "Happy is the man who in his soul is utterly destitute, who recognizes that he has nothing of and by himself, and that in his moral and spiritual life he is worthless." As the starving man is dependent upon the kindness of others, so the humble man recognizes his dependence on a loving Father; he sees himself as a spiritual pauper, bankrupt in himself.

This brings us back to what was observed earlier about the tension and the pull between the strong and the weak, the rich and the poor. How break down the superior condescension of the rich when they give and the humiliation of the poor when they receive? There is only one way, and that is for the rich to see their poverty. Once they see themselves poor—poorer than the most economically destitute—then they will begin not just to give alms but to feel the plague of their own heart.

Once one takes his eyes off what is on the outside—furnishings, jewels, games, glasses, china, and gadgets, and all the things which enter into us through the nose and the fingers and the ears and the mouth—then he is ready for introspection. This will take him to his inside poverty, his misery, his fears, his anxieties, his want of peace, his thirst for truth, his need to love, his fruitlessness, and his beggary.

He begins to understand what happened to St. Francis of Assisi. He had taken some of his father's bales of cotton, sold them, and given the proceeds to the poor. His father summoned him before the bishop to ask for restitution of his wealth. Francis said, "Up to this time I have called you, Pietro Bernadone, my father. From now on I shall call no one Father but God. I shall give back to you everything you have given me." He took off a sack from around his waist with a few pieces of gold in it, threw them onto the floor. Then he tore off his clothing—every piece except a hair shirt—and piled it on the money. He walked out on the frozen ground between the frosty trees. He could see himself as silly as a fly on a window-pane, but he did not mind being a fool; he would go on being the court fool of the King of Paradise.

Later on, when some of his followers had built a church for him because of what he did for the poor, he climbed up on the roof and began throwing the tiles onto the ground—the first step in the demolishing of the church. Why pay a tribute to him when he was so poor on the inside?

The largest check I ever received for the poor of the world was for $165,000. Upon inquiry, I found that it came from a young girl who was twenty-one years of age. She told me that it was the full inheritance she received from her parents; now that she was totally destitute, she would begin studying as a nurse to earn her living. On further inquiry, as to why she made such a total sacrifice, her answer was: "I received the gift of faith at a moment when my life was so empty. I want to help the poor in gratitude for my new wealth." The moment one begins to make oneself empty, then it is possible to be filled. A box that is filled with sand cannot be filled with gold; a heart that is drunk with the ego cannot find place for love of humanity. The new humanists are unhappy in our rich culture, our cutting of corners to pile up money, the new psychological aids of trying to be happy by lifting oneself by one's own bootstraps. As hunger drove the prodigal home, so they are driven to serve, to feed, to love the poor.

Filling the Void by Service

The new humanists seek a breakthrough into the world of the poor. The poor, first of all, have discovered themselves. Up until our times they accepted their poverty as fate, as destiny or "the Will of God." Now they rebel against it, because they *know* they are poor. They never before realized it. On the other hand, the new humanists have discovered the poor, not just in their own backyard but in the world.

With this discovery comes the desire to be identified with them; wherever there is pain, one wishes to share it; wherever there are slums, one goes into them. The new humanism is a breakthrough into humanity where it discerns need, sickness, misery. It is also an invasion, with baskets and bandages rather than with muskets and bullets, and the invasion has far more appeal than any form of space travel; the new humanism establishes a beachhead in enemy territory—the enemy being want, slavery, and injustice.

The new humanism is a disposability, in which some heroic souls are willing to consider themselves as used Kleenexes if they can only clean the bodies of their fellowmen; it is a vulnerability or a capability of feeling the wounds of others, like the Indian who sympathetically looked on a buffalo cruelly beaten by his master, only to find the scourges on his own back. The new humanism is not a togetherness but an otherness, as all its members bear the stigmata of the wounded, for they cannot stand apart from woe and misery.

Suffering is beginning to live in us—we see all the world's misery summed up, as it is said a drowning man sees his whole life pass before him in a second. Mozart once was asked if he "heard" the music as he wrote down each note. He said he did, even more than that: "Not only do I hear the notes successively in my imagination, but I hear them as it were all at once." The score was already completed. The blueprint is to an architect as visible as the building. When one composes a lecture—every teacher testifies to this—he sees the whole plan at a glance. Lacordaire, the great French preacher, was asked if he had finished his series of conferences. "Yes, I have finished them; all I have to do now is to write them."

The new humanist is like that; he sees injustices in his own land—hungry children, slums, lepers. They keep him awake at night; they worry him; he is groaning for the adoption of sons and the redemption of human bodies; he does not sleep well, knowing that there are people without beds; he is uneasy before his white tablecloth when he knows there are tables without even salt; he would like to ship the food left on his plate in a restaurant to prevent just one out of the ten thousand who daily die of starvation.

Pity

William Saroyan expressed it:

> Unless a man has pity he is inhuman, and not yet truly a man, for out of pity comes the balm which heals. Only good men weep. If a man has not wept at the world's pain, he is less than the dirt he walks upon because dirt will nourish seed, root, stalk, and leaf and flower, but the spirit of man without pity is barren, and will bring forth nothing—for only pride which comes finally, which must finally do murder of one sort or another—murder of good things, or murder even of human lives.
>
> —*The Human Comedy*

Love and sacrifice go together as with Elizabeth Pilenkoa, a young Russian who escaped Communism by fleeing to France; there she took on the wounds of the Russian refugees. She became a nun. During the persecution of the Jews in World War II, she founded a convent as a haven for the Jews. When the Gestapo found her, she was led to the concentration camp at Ravensbruck. During two and a half years she saw a block of buildings erected which were actually gas chambers, though the prisoners were told they were to be hot baths for the prisoners. She knew their real purpose.

One day a number of women prisoners were lined up before the buildings. One girl became hysterical. Mother Maria, for that was her name as a nun, was not among those selected. To the girl who became hysterical she said, "Don't be frightened. I shall take your turn," knowing very well she was going to her death. It was Good Friday when she died.

Those with pity become available in times of need. What they are used for matters but little. As Dostoyevsky said, "Could you not make me an old rag with which to stop up a hole in the corner?"

One would never have new humanists seeking a breakthrough into the poverty of the world, if there had not already been a breakthrough when He who was rich became poor. He domesticated poverty, slums, hunger, thirst, social injustice, the law's delay, the insolence of office, so completely that He could say, "This is My Body which is broken for you." All the social workers, all the fighters for social and racial justice, all the missionaries, Peace Corps men, nurses, doctors who are not working for gain but for service, all of these may not know it, but slowly after two thousand years a seed that has been planted has come to life. They may not know where the inspiration has come from, but there is nothing ever done in life that a great idea has not preceded. Everyone falls in love first with a dream; later on, the person who concretized that dream appears, and it seems to be love at first sight, but it is actually love at second sight; no brush was ever put to canvas but a great thought preceded it: "In the beginning was the Word. . . . and the Word became flesh and dwelt amongst us."

They are impelled to service by a Stranger—not one of their own, of their race or country or club. The Stranger is all whom they serve. All the slum dwellers who have no place to lay their heads—while birds have nests and foxes their holes—are this Stranger. The Stranger is all those found in highways beaten by thugs and later taken by their helping arms to healing inns. All the wounds on hands, feet, side, and brow they bathe and bind are—to them as one Person—that Stranger.

All the little children separated from parents, meeting elders, asking and answering questions, are as one Child—that Stranger. All the skeptics, agnostics, Communists, beatniks, junkies, delinquents, all crying and weeping and complaining against God and shrieking a Why? for their loneliness, are as one lonely forgotten Man—that Stranger. All their bitterness against the affluence, aggrandizement, and unshared wealth in the face of the world's poverty, all their thrusts against buyers and sellers even in the Temple of God seem to them as the wrath of one Man—that Stranger.

They know not Whom they serve; they only know that they love—these new humanists. One day they will meet the Stranger: Today that vision is opaque; tomorrow it will be transparent. The Stranger will rise out of the slums, the dumps, the hovels, the emptiness of stomachs, the parched tongues, the burning fevers, and the white sores of leprosy. He will stand before all those humanists with scars like stars: "It was I that was hungry! What you did to them, you did to Me."

III

THE WORLD

CHAPTER TEN

The Cultural Differences
of East and West

Missionaries have long been conscious of the East as a dimension to be won for Christ. The West has only recently become conscious of the East—partly because of the East's rebellion against the imperialism of the West, and partly because Communism has wooed the East in order the better to challenge the West.

The East is now stirring like a giant aroused from sleep. The vast difference between the East and the West can be broken down into the elements of a sentence. A sentence is composed of subject, predicate, and the relation of existence between the two. The subject is something which is determinable; the predicate is that which determines it—for example, "The water is cold." "Water," the subject, is determinable; it can be hot or cold, pure or polluted. In this instance, "cold" is the particular determination.

The thought of the East is, to a great extent, based on the subject or the determinable. What is important to it is the great indetermined background of reality like an ocean. Less important is every person born into the world, for he is a small determination of that indetermined mass, a little predicate added to the great subject. He comes into the world from this inchoate soul of the universe, and when he dies, he goes back to it again. This universal, vague, indetermined something is the essence of the Brahman of Hinduism, Taoism, the Nirvana of Buddhism, and to a lesser extent of

Islam in the sense that every person is of little significance before the great Allah. The person has little value; he must be content with his environment and the conditions in which he finds himself; and if he be a Muslim, he must resign himself to God and to His will which is sovereign and absolute. Because freedom is related to the determining principle of life, it follows that the world which emphasizes the undetermined is never very much concerned with the problem of freedom, as such, nor the sacredness of personality.

Now turn to the philosophy of the West with its stress on the individual and his liberty. The laissez-faire of capitalism and the new liberalism stress this freedom to an extreme. When the nations met after World War I, the emphasis was on self-determination; after World War II, the emphasis was on democracy or people's rule. The West puts its emphasis on the predicate, on human freedom, and on progress. While in the East the soul of the universe is all-important, in the West it is the individual who is all-important.

Progress became the soul of the West's religion, as the Brahman and Nirvana, or passive resignation, became the soul of the East's religion. The West acted because persons determined everything; the East contemplated, because the individual was only a sunbeam from the great sun, coming from it in the morning and returning to it at night in the great cyclic spin of the universe.

Neither is right, any more than a philosopher would be right who would define the cycle of twenty-four hours in terms of night exclusively. Each has split the sentence of reality in two. The East has taken the subject or the vague ethereal background of the universe; the West has taken the predicate or the self-determining, free, progressive principle within the individual himself.

Both are incomplete. The future progress of the world is no more to be achieved by making the East imitate our technical progress and follow our democratic patterns, than it is to be purchased by the East's forcing the West to absorb the free individuals into some vague, unconscious Nirvana. From a moral point of view, the East and the West are both sinners, for sin is deordination. Sin consists in taking one aspect of reality and making it stand for the whole; for example, equating prosperity with life (as does the Western view) or equating contemplation with life (as does the Eastern). The great sin of the East is in believing that God does everything and man does nothing. The great sin of the West is in believing that man does everything and God does nothing.

West: Man Does Everything. East: God Does Everything

Each has a lesson to learn: The West, with its almost atheistic humanism, must learn, "Without Me you can do nothing." All free activities of man stem from the original endowment of the Creator. He must acknowledge that source of his energy, as the pendulum acknowledges the clock. Man is independent only because he is dependent on God.

Furthermore, the best of human progress reaches a point of vagueness unless there is a reason for progress. As G. K. Chesterton once said: "There is one thing that never makes any progress, and that is the idea of progress." There must always be a fixed goal or destiny by which progress is measured. Otherwise, one never knows whether he is making any progress. Beyond this, there also comes a point where, to make further progress, the higher must come down to the lower. Before the chemical can enter into the plant, the plant must come down to the chemical and take it up into its system. If man is to live a higher life, the Divine Life must come down to man—and that is the Incarnation. Man then sheds off the old Adam of sin and egotism and selfishness, and enters into the higher life, where he finds his freedom enlarged because there is Spirit "and where the Spirit of the Lord is, there is freedom." He also finds himself more progressive, for he sees that real progress consists in the diminution of the traces of original sin.

The East has a lesson to learn—namely, the opposite one; that man can and must do something in cooperation with the Great Power of the universe. Its lesson is summarized in the words of

Paul: "Nothing is beyond my powers, thanks to the strength God gives me." Man is not just a puppet in the hands of the Almighty. He came naked from his mother's womb but endowed with reason, so that he could build a house for his shelter. God did not make a home for everyone, but He gave men the skill to make tools. God made empty stomachs, and men have to labor to fill their stomachs. The original order given in creation was to "till the garden," and later on, "Work while ye have the light." The man who sits back, passive, on the assumption that God does everything, is to be likened to the man who buried his talents in the ground. God will give him new strength only when he uses up the strength he already has. No one gets a second wind until he has used up the first. No one ever gets a second grace until he has spent the first and particularly in the service of neighbor. Man must be energetic, active, progressive, must take the material things of the universe and make for himself a city—though not lasting, one which will do credit to the mind that God has given him. The West has so much emphasized the material that it has become materialistic; the East has so much despised the material, in its contemplation of the Eternal, that to Western eyes it is reactionary.

The Logic of the East and West

The Eastern world does not have the same respect for Aristotelian logic as does the Western world. The Oriental mentality stresses totality. From one point of view, it seems to come close to what St. Thomas Aquinas describes as the "whole personality, doing the thinking, the willing and the feeling." The entire psyche is at work, though the localization of this total attitude is not in the head but in the center of the body, the heart or the navel. The head is the symbol of Western mentality; the heart or a similar center is the symbol of the Oriental. The Oriental does not so much "think" as we do; he "ponders"—i.e., he fuses all his thinking, loving, feeling experiences into an inseparable unity.

The Westerner knows the world better than man; the Easterner knows man better than the world. The first tames nature; the latter tames himself. The former is an extrovert and thus produces a scientific, technical civilization in which nature is turned into industry; the latter is an introvert and seeks to deepen that inner peace through the fusion of all those human experiences which constitute contemplation.

If for the Oriental not the head but the totality of experience constitutes what we call reason, then what is the Oriental symbol for this centrality and fusion? One Japanese scholar says it is the heart. Writing for the Buddhists, Daisetz Suski explains, "Different though the teachings of Shintoism, of the poetic art, and of Confucius may be, they all aim ultimately at the comprehension of a Single Heart." The Chinese word *sin* and the Japanese word *shin*, though meaning "heart," do not seem to mean exclusively the physical heart. If such were the case, we would not have the "totality," which is so representative of Eastern thought. Rather the heart means "feeling," "consciousness," or "center." Hence the tendency in Asia to speak of "bowels" or "entrails." Here again, this is not to be understood as a definite organ but rather a symbol like the one we use in saying, "My heart bleeds for you." "Thinking and feeling, which in the West exist as separate entities, here operate as a single force," writes the Japanese Kitayania. Yoshiro Nagayo explains that "if we put our whole emphasis on the brain in the sense of the word 'intellect,' the lower portion of the body would float in the air, our feet would become separated from the earth, our ideas would become abstract, and our nerves would break down."

The Western world has a fondness for "The Thinker" of Rodin. Though he is the primitive just having the first idea, he is still a thinker. But in the many statues of Buddha, where does the center of human gravity seem to be, if it is not in the navel? Why do Japanese wrestlers stress the paunch? Why do they stand facing and staring at one another, if it is not to develop a full concentration of body and soul? Why in one of the Chinese books of meditation is it said that one "must first subdue the intellect" and proceed from "conscious action to unconscious inaction?" In India, too, the sentiments of joy, sorrow, and anger in the Tamil language are related to the viscera. Why is there a system as coherent as a cathedral in Thomas Aquinas but no related reflections in Confucius? The Zen contemplations dispense with dogmas, books, and teachings, so as to reach the "confluent experience of universal oneness." A monk once asked the master Ummon, "What is the purest form of truth?" Ummon answered, "The hedge around the closet." This meant that universal truth is beyond all divisions and distinctions of what is pure or filthy.

The Western mind proceeds in reasoning from the major premise to the minor premise to the conclusion. Rationalism is strictly of the head; feeling, sentiment, and desire must necessarily be excluded, if the conclusion is to be logically drawn. The Western mind traditionally has sought to be logical; hence the ultimate in inconsistency is to be accused of contradicting yourself. But with the introduction of Machiavellian politics, the repudiation of ethical norms, the Western mind is no longer so afraid of being illogical. I remember once arguing with an Englishman in Jerusalem, and saying to him, "Sir, you have just contradicted yourself." He answered, "What of it?" For a Western mind, contradiction is intellectual suicide, just as cutting one's throat is physical suicide. The English colonial system was not based on principle but on expediency and, therefore, had a flexibility which defies all logic. American pragmatism, which identifies the true with the useful and the good with the pleasurable, also spurns the Western tradition of rationality. Depite these aberrations, however, the Eastern mind does take pride in consistency. *Think* has become a common sign in our industrial civilization. Western thinking is based on ideas, judgment, and reasoning—all products of the intellect. A judgment is made up of ideas, and syllogistic reasoning is made up of judgments.

Science Is Western

Science is based on the principle of causality, and causality is one of the basic principles of reason. A thing which has not the reason of its being in itself must have it in another. A triangle has within its definition and nature the quality of three-sidedness. But a yellow or red triangle is extrinsic to its nature; hence one must seek the source of yellowness or redness in something else; in other words, it is caused. Science became possible because nature was assumed to be rational, consistent, and universal in its operations. Mind, being logical, could therefore unwrap the laws of nature and bend them to the service of man. Thought was basically reasonable or logical, because behind the universe was the *logos* which is the basic ground of all consistency, both in nature and in man.

The Eastern mind, setting store more on centrality than on rationality, may be illustrated in this fashion: If experiences multiply to a point where, like arrows, they seem to converge to one central point, then the conclusion is "true." At first, all these arrows may fly in different directions, as they do in a mind which cannot decide where to go for a vacation. When a sufficiently large number of reflections or arrows concentrate at a given place, then the conclusion becomes true. The head does not draw the conclusion but the total consciousness, in what we would call thinking, willing, feeling, and living. The Western mind is, therefore, often bewildered by Eastern diplomacy; it seems as unpredictable as a Pearl Harbor. This is because nonhead factors are influencing the thinking. While the Westerner is going from idea to idea, the Oriental is going from mood to mood. Lily Abegg, who has given much enlightenment on these points, says this of the Western mind: Our brains are good for constructing machines but not for understanding human affairs. Witness the inability of the Western mind to understand India, which juggles Communism in one hand, democracy in the other. The Hindu mentality which allows for an indefinite number of gods, regardless of their nature, also allows for political positions which are equally contradictory.

Such a mentality does not produce a highly industrialized civilization or even science. Only Western civilization with its background of intellectual discipline, which Christianity gave it, could produce a logical transformation of the logic of nature. Science and technology can be developed in the Eastern world, but this is only because they are apprentices and imitators of the West. The Eastern mind puts little value on causality. The science of I Ching is not based on causality, but on relationship or coexistence or relative simultaneity or the fact that certain experience began to coalesce or jell. A conclusion is not reached by the head, but perceived by the whole psyche. Feelings affect the mind, resolutions affect sensations in a vast interplay of physical, conscious, unconscious, psychic, volitional elements, and all seem to concentrate in some mysterious center which is not the head. This does not make for science, but it certainly does make for the confusion of Western scientists and politicians.

Western Christian Approach to the East

Missionaries of the Western world seeking to bring Christianity to the Eastern world do not take adequate account of the differences. Apologetics, written in France, Italy, or Germany, are too logical in the Western sense for the Eastern world. A better approach would be to gather up the good religious aspirations of Eastern people and point them as so many arrows converging on Christ, the Savior of the world. God would not be just something "proved" to them but rather a satisfaction of the decent aspirations of the human heart. Confucius is relatively just as good Aristotle for Eastern minds—or even better as a starting point. It must not be forgotten that not even the Western world accepted Aristotle until the Middle Ages, and St. Thomas was rapped on the knuckles for being so "modern" or "reactionary" as to espouse him against Plato. Augustine in his Con-

fessions wrote beautiful pages on Plato and affirmed his superiority over Aristotle, thus influencing the next seven centuries.

It would be well to begin with what is naturally good in any Eastern religion, as Our Lord started with a drink of cold water in converting a Samaritan, as Claudia began with a dream in understanding Christ and which proved more right than her rational husband, and as Paul began with an inscription to a pagan deity in converting the senators of Athens.

In like manner, the concept of Nirvana should not be swept away utterly but purified, as Clement of Alexandria purified the pagan concepts of God held by the men and women of the marketplace. The Nirvana probably does not mean absolute annihilation, but rather the liberation of true personality by the destruction of the ego. Buddhism goes too far in saying that all pain ends with the extinction of desire; but the Western world does not go far enough in teaching that at the point where we extinguish all carnal desires and desire only what Christ desires can we ever attain peace. Was Buddha so far away from seeing that through the death of Christ all men are saved when he said, "Let all the sins that have been committed in this Kali age of the world fall on me, and let the world be delivered"? True, to some Buddhists there is no God, no worship, or sacrificial priesthood, but if Buddha is honored, there is at least one little arrow with which to begin the elevation of the Eastern mind.

The multiple solutions of the Eastern mind for the problem of suffering must not be cleared away as rubbish before one preaches Christ. Rather they already have the horizontal and the vertical bars of the cross to express the contradiction of life and death, Yin and Yang, darkness and light. It is only the person of Christ that can resolve their contradictions by showing that death does lead to life. Mecius was unconsciously pondering the Cross when he said, "When heaven is about to confer a great office on any man, it first exercises his mind with suffering." The Upanishads in the same spirit reflect, "Suffering is the ransom the son of man has to pay if he would attain his glory."

Pope Gregory told Augustine not to destroy the pagan temples of England but to purify them, as his own beloved Rome did in dedicating pagan temples to Our Lady. "I came not to destroy, but to fulfill" has a wider application than to the Jewish Law. It refers to every pagan contemplative who ever groped through the darkness to the light of God. Our Western logic, being so rigid, is apt to concentrate on the fallacies of Eastern thinking, rather than to seek in the language of Pius XI, "to find gold in gold-bearing rocks." Would not a modern Paul see the Unknown God in the inability of the Indian mind to find rest in the abstract idea of the unity of Brahma? Because of this, various Divine workings were gathered up by the Brahmanic teachers and assigned to distinct persons; Vishnu was the Divine Preserver; Siva the Divine Destroyer, and all three—Brahma, Vishnu, and Siva—were regarded in epic poems as constituting a Trinity, three forms or Trimurti. Better still, the Indian name for the Supreme Being is a component of the three names of our transcendentals: *Ens, Verum,* and *Bonum.* Reason cannot know the Trinity, but reason can ask, as Plato did, "If God is one, whom does he love and to be happy one must love?" To liberate their crude religious concepts from the Cross is not easy, nor is the teaching of the Cross easy, but one wonders if there is not a more natural readiness for the Cross in India than there was in Greece. With Browning we may say to them, "How hard it is to be a Christian! Hard for you and me."

One wonders how many missionaries in the Far East ever read Buddha or Confucius or Lao-tse, and how many in India ever read the great epic poems? Yet if our missionaries were courting, they would study poetry to win a poetess and music to win a musician. Then why not, when they go courting for souls, study the traditions and the religious aspirations of the people to win them to Christ? These Oriental hearts have stretched out lame hands of faith and, gropingly, have gathered up both wheat and chaff. The missioner must not see the chaff but the wheat; the wheat is not yet the Bread of Life, but the wheat of any such Eastern religion can be used to point to Christ, as Christ Himself used the wheat to tell the Greeks of His death and resurrection.

It is not well to hate what is good in ancient Eastern thinkers, otherwise we shall find ourselves unhappy in heaven. I expect to find Socrates, Aristotle, and Plato there, and also Buddha, Confucius, Lao-tse, and some of the unknown writers of early Indian hymns. All these and many others are certainly God's gift to the East to keep burning some remnant of Divine Truth. They are not on the level of Isaiah and Jeremiah, but they are certainly what Paul has called witnesses to the pagan world.

What a tragedy, too, that the Indian, Chinese, and Japanese students who study in our Western seminaries have to hear of the errors of Hegel, Kant, and Hume and nothing of the learning of Buddha or Confucius! There is a possibility that we may have occidentalized Christ. Our task as teachers is to do more than make Aristotelians with yellow skins or Platonists with brown skins. This teaching prevails because we do not know Oriental thinking; we have not seen that any of the great national Eastern religions is a *Praeparatio Evangelica.* Paul quoted Greek poets to the Athenians, but if he were in Peking, he would have quoted Buddha or Confucius.

The Oriental philosophers have no supernatural system, but they do have a natural system, and it is a stepping-stone to Christ. The same is true of the dim gropings of the African people for God. These systems are like cedars of Lebanon that can be cut and carved by revelation and compacted into the edifice of charity; they are the quivers from which we can gather arrows to shoot from the bow of Christian revelation, to a target which may not be an Aristotelian head but a Sacred Heart.

CHAPTER ELEVEN

Is Western Civilization Dying?

Rudyard Kipling wrote:

*Oh, East is East, and West is West, and
    never the twain shall meet.*

Since he wrote those lines, the world has moved closer together. Despite cultural divisions mentioned in the previous chapter, the two are drawing closer and closer together. Northrop sought to marry them at a philosophical altar by introducing the scientific philosophy of the West to the aesthetic and contemplative East.

The Indian philosopher Radhakrishnan, starting not from a Western point of view as did Northrop, kept his roots in Eastern religions, but concluded that spiritual Asia and intellectual Europe could one day form one world. Another European thinker, Dr. de Kat Angelino, sought to combine the dynamic or colonializing character of the West with the static East in the hope that both would live happily ever after.

On the other hand, there are those who see no future whatever for the Western world, such as Spengler in his *Decline of the West* who divided all civilizations into the four seasons and pronounced, with a dark fatalism, the senility and inescapable doom of the West.

Toynbee, in a ten-volume study of twenty-one civilizations,

concluded that the vast majority of them had decayed from within, rather than from an attack from without. Western civilization does not seem to have entered yet into that universal state which is necessary for all humanity, but its future depends on whether or not it will rot from within.

The Three Roots of Western Culture

One day there was unfurled a Man on a gibbet at the crossroads of civilization. Over the cross was affixed His Name, His city, and His "crime"—the inscription was in three languages. Three cultures combined in His death: "A proclamation had been written up over him in Greek, Latin and Hebrew, This is the King of the Jews"—Luke 23:38.

Hebrew was the language of the good; Latin the language of the true, and Greek the language of the beautiful. He was crucified in the name of the three cultures of Jerusalem, Rome, and Athens. But the three cultures which ministered to the death of the Crucified were also the instruments for spreading throughout the world the knowledge and love of the Crucified. It is a principle of the Divine economy that the very weapons that are used in defeat are those that are used in victory. In the very beginning, there was a disobedient man, a proud woman, and a tree; later on in re-creating the fallen, there was an obedient Man—Christ—a humble woman—Mary—and a tree of the Cross. These three cultures produce what is known as Western Christian civilization, each contributing one side of the triangle.

THE HEBREW

The Hebrew language on the Cross was the bond between the Old Testament and the New, both of which produced the Hebraic-Christian culture—the value of the human person. Salvation was a history—a history of persons, each one of sovereign worth because made to the image and likeness of God. On the other hand, God is a

Person, encountering man and defining Himself in terms of men: "The God of Abraham, and the God of Isaac, and the God of Jacob." When God came to this earth, He came not as a cloud, but as a Person in the form of man and He taught that a person was more valuable than the cosmos itself: "What doth it profit a man to gain the whole world if he lose his soul?"

On the Cross, He spoke to a repentant thief: "This day thou shalt be with Me in Paradise." This was the proclamation of individual worth, the first stone in the edifice of democracy. The history of Christianity, like a Bible history before it, is a relation between the action of God and the reaction of man. This union of free human will and the light of faith with the power of grace is at the root of the idea of progress which is essentially Western concept.

LATIN

Another characteristic of Western civilization, symbolized by the Latin language, is the drive toward the unity of mankind. It was no historical accident that the Word was made Flesh and all prophecies fulfilled through a decree of Caesar Augustus, Master Bookkeeper of the world seated at his desk by the Tiber: "That the world should be enrolled."

There was only one official language which was Latin, one capital which was Rome, and one emperor who was Caesar. The word used in Gospel Greek for the world was *oikoumene*. At the very end of the Life of Our Blessed Lord, we read that the Gospel of the Kingdom was to be preached throughout the whole *oikoumene*. This was practically a baptism of the decree of Caesar Augustus. The old barrier that existed between Israel and the nations is now transcended. When Paul told the Romans that God's Word of creation and judgment was not limited to any one particular nation or political or cultural order, but was as wide as the world itself, the foundations were laid for a brotherhood and a striving of all nations toward togetherness.

GREEK

As Hebrew was the language of religion and Latin the language of law, so Greek was the language of philosophy and science. The Eastern pre-Christian religions had never separated nature and Divinity. When the two are identified in a pantheistic sense, which is the nature of Oriental philosophy, one can never have science. Technical knowledge is possible only on condition that nature may be studied apart from theology and myth. How study the trees if God is in the trees? How study bugs if God is so much in the bugs that one may not step on them? Science demands isolation from the myths. This was the great pre-Christian contribution of the Greeks to the culture of the world. Thales began to study astronomy without the Eastern myths; Pythagoras became interested in mathematics without the myths; Archimedes interested himself in machines and mechanics without the benefit of myths.

Because Christianity baptized the Grecian culture and continued the idea that God and nature were not fused into one, science arose in Western civilization and not in the Eastern. A. N. Whitehead claims that had it not been for the long discipline of the mind, the schooling, and a sense of order, and a love of research, we would never have had science in the modern form:

> When we compare this tone of thought in Europe with the attitude of other civilizations when left to themselves, there seems but one source for its origin. It must come from a medieval insistence on the rationality of God, conceived as the Personal energy of Jehovah and with the rationality of a Greek philosopher. Every detail was supervised and ordered; the search into nature could only result in the vindication of faith and rationality. . . . In Asia, the conceptions of God were of a Being Who was either too arbitrary or too impersonal for such ideas to have much effect on instinctive habits of mind.

It is not by accident that technology, science, research, industrial development have progressed in Western Christian civilization.

Modern Western Civilization

Our Western civilization is the heir of the three master ideas: the value of the person, born of the Hebraic-Christian theology; the one-world and one-humanity concepts flowing from the baptized law of the Roman culture; and finally, our modern technology, which is the unfolding of the Grecian view of the autonomy of natural sciences.

Western civilization with its Christian roots is not perishing; it is beginning to come into its own. The spread of democracy throughout the world, the formation of new nations rooted in the respect for human persons, the embarrassment of Communist dictatorships at their failure to give free suffrage to their people—all these represent the leavening process of the cult of the value of the individual.

The reverence for the value of person in history is evident in the contrast between the building of pyramids and the building of cathedrals. Pyramids were built on the backs of slave labor, but cathedrals were elevated by persons with master ideas. Instead of the contempt for persons which permeated the works of the ancient cities in the West, the artisan, the architect, the sculptor, and the painter were accorded a dignity and full privilege as free citizens in the service of God. Max Weber has made this basic liberty of persons, which built history in the Name of God, the basic differentiation between the Western and all non-Occidental cultures.

The gradual integration of nations into international bodies, such as the UN, the growing sense of responsibility that we are our brothers' keepers, foreign aid, Peace Corps, missions—all these are the full-blown fruit of the baptized Roman concept of law as the juridical bond of all men. It was ancient Rome that gave law to the world, and it was the Christianized Latin culture which gave it international law. As S. Rosenne put it:

> Public international law, in its historical evolution, is essentially the produce of European Christian civilization, and for the greater part of Western civilization at that.

The same idea has been stressed by J. H. Verzijl—namely, that the international law that stands today

> . . . is not only the product of the conscious activity of the European mind, but has also drawn its vital essence from a common source of European beliefs, and in both of these aspects it is mainly of Western European origin.

Western Civilization Is Not Dying

Western Civilization instead of dying is actually beginning to influence the world more than ever. In a magistral study of the East and the West, Arend Th. Van Leeuwen likens the influence of the non-Western world to a benign virus, which enters into the organism and makes it immune to further disease. It may also be compared to an injection of vitamins which gives strength to the organism. From another point of view, it is like a blood transfusion which strengthens the cells and gives the heart new life. Finally, it may also be compared to a catalyst which precipitates rapid changes and makes new combinations within a stable chemical structure.

This is one of the reasons why Africa, Asia, and elsewhere are undergoing convulsive changes. As Arend Th. Van Leeuwen puts it:

> There are quite a number of signs that the transformation which the non-Western world is undergoing is not a movement in just one particular direction, but it is more like a large scale process of fermentation, in which various extremely diverse and contradic-

tory tendencies are involved. We see the non-Western religions parading as the champions of peace, and yet providing an ideological foundation in the struggle for political power. . . . We see the growth of modern forms of nationalism, of a mark of the progressive type, bent on uplifting and caring for the mass of the people; and side by side with all that—or sometimes cutting right across it —the emergence of violent reactionary modes of nationalism, inspired by an intense yearning to revive the religious pattern of the past. Everywhere modern parliamentary systems are springing up.

Or again:

It is in the West that a human society has been transformed into *the society par excellence*; and it is an extension of the West that has made our world a planetary world, while it is again the West that has achieved the demotion of the earth to the status of a paltry planet.

Secularization

This impact of the roots of Western civilization upon the world has been called secularization. One must distinguish between secularization and secularism. Secularization is a process, a continuing historical *aggiornamento* of the spiritual leaven of the Hebraic-Christian tradition. Secularism, on the contrary, is an ideology or an attempt to find the cause, the origin, and the nature of man within the limitations of space and time. The Kingdom of God and the world are two correlative terms, the latter including the former as the field includes the treasure: "The kingdom of Heaven is like unto a treasure hidden in a field."

As the centuries go on, the Church and the world are in mutual interaction. We leave out the fact of persecution but speak of the Church as an organizing principle of life, like the parable of the leaven and the mustard seed; the leaven in the mass of dough radiates its influence; the mustard seed in the earth absorbs energy from the earth and the air which surrounds it.

These are the two influences of the Kingdom of God in the world—namely, a diffusion of the Divine and the absorption of the cosmic and the human. There is nothing dramatic about the Kingdom of God in the world; it is not a sudden, violent upheaval but a silent, persistent process eventually reaching to the end of the earth. Secularization is nothing else than the two-thousand-year-old influence of Christianity, expressing and manifesting itself in love of neighbor. The flow of laymen and laywomen will go across the world in various kinds of social service, with the deep conviction that God is calling them to witness to Him in every aspect of life. As J. Merle put it:

> Under the comprehensive approach, evangelization is cure of sick bodies, of broken down, inefficient and eroded farms, of illiteracy, of insufficient and unbalanced diet, unsanitary homes, impure drinking water, of a subsistence level of existence, of filthy villages, of the moral, mental and spiritual stagnation of corrupt practices and conditions, every effort upon this wide and comprehensive front of Christian service is a part of the Evangel and is required to enable the individual to reach the fullness of the stature which is in Christ.

CHAPTER TWELVE

The Great Scandal:
The Thirtieth Parallel

The great scandal, however, of Western Christian civilization is that it is prosperous and the non-Christian civilizations, for the most part, are in want. Latin America, while belonging to Western civilization, belongs to the economically poor group. The rough dividing line between the rich and the poor nations on the purely economic level is the thirtieth parallel. If one runs his finger around a globe of the earth, raising it above China, it will be found that almost all the education, health, welfare, and prosperity is found above that line, and almost all the hunger, want, and misery below it.

Dr. David Morley of Nigeria tells of some of the children who come into his hospital: "Some came with swollen legs and faces. . . . Some came with patches of their skin going black and peeling off; they all had one common symptom, that of intense misery. Most of them had not smiled or played for weeks, some not for months; they had sat about in their homes disinterested in everything including food."

In contrast, we in America have so much food we pay farmers not to grow it, and we spend hundreds of millions of dollars a year to store it, in order to keep up the prices, while two thirds of the world starves. This is the challenge. It has been estimated that 10 to 15 percent of the world's population—that is between 300 to 500 million people are hungry—and another 150 million suffer from varying degrees of malnutrition. Never before in the history of the world have so many people been subject to so much undernourishment. Jacquelin Ross writes of Latin America: "The boundaries of human lives are the boundaries of the favelas they seldom leave. They live with the ever-present fear of homelessness and hunger." A bishop in East Africa writes: "I have found children wandering miles in search of food."

A nun from another mission writes: "The people here are really very poor. The majority eat only once a day. Many of the children miss school five months because they have to go to the woods and search for food. Those who attend are restless and inattentive because their 'tummies' are empty. Roots of plants and whatever they are lucky enough to catch when fishing or hunting make up their meager meal."

As *Newsweek* puts it: "First, the belly swells. Then the hair turns gray and the skin cracks crazily. After a while the victim dies in mute misery—and since the victim is always a child his fate seems that much crueler. In Africa the people call it *kwashiorkor*— the disease the old baby gets when the new baby comes, because then there is no mother's milk and hardly any protein for the child."

In another city, 400,000 souls are crowded into one square mile on an old garbage heap; underneath the ground there is nothing but rotted rubbish, old bottles, and rusty tin cans. Children with festering sores or bare legs play in this exposed garbage, adults forage through it for tin to make roofs for their hovels. Water sells at sixteen cents a keg. As one poor man put it, as he moved from the mountain where he hungered to the city slums: "I was once just a man. Now I am many men."

World Hunger

Leonard Hurst writes: "She was a hungry peasant, and she knew she would soon be dead. The truth did not occur to her—that she was yet another victim of conditions that make life a travesty for hundreds of millions of people over large areas of the earth. She was just another bit of humanity, beaten by an intolerable state of affairs that denies human dignity, enthrones squalor, makes daily work a burden instead of a joy, turns sleep into a diseased respite instead of a re-creative function, breeds disease and despair, and finally kills the very will to live. She is the human challenge to the peoples and governments of the world, and to the Christian Church to grapple with one of the greatest problems of the day—the problem of world hunger."

These people are so miserable and hungry that they will accept any kind of government that even promises to give them something to chew on. China became Communist partly because China was hungry, and the Communist promised to give them something to eat. The destitute are neither far-seeing politicians nor undeviating moralists; they are subhuman, and strange as it may seem, so far down in the biological order they become envious of those who have more, and even avaricious in their poverty.

Vow of Poverty

The question is: Have we a right relatively to have so much while they have so little? May we be glutted when they are gutted? Who among those hundreds of millions would not take our vows of poverty if it gave them the right to live as well? The vow of poverty is not poverty as millions and millions know it today. A monk or a nun or a priest or a brother with a vow of poverty can live in communal comfort. He can even be individually detached, while being corporately selfish—that is, attached too much to the material well-being of his community. The question is not: Should those who take the vow of poverty be as destitute and ragged as hundreds of millions on the missions? The question rather is: Does not the vow of poverty imply a greater sharing of corporate wealth with the ragged humanity who have the vow of destitution forced on them?

The twenty thousand who gather around the water faucet that is open three hours a day in one slum in Latin America, four days a week in one city, have no vow of poverty; they have no wish of poverty. They are sunk into that infrahuman condition where there is hardly anything that is voluntary. They become like two men on a raft, floating on the solitude of the ocean, faced by grim starvation, almost despising one another in their isolation. Loneliness spreads among them like a plague. Though they have a common danger, do they embrace one another? Do they plead their love for one another? When poverty reaches those depths, it is not kindly, not paternal, not virtuous—it is deadly, and even the sternest of virtues begins to fail. Involuntary poverty is surly and discontented, because it is forced against its will. Who, with the vow of poverty in the Western Christian civilization, is not rich in comparison to the millions in Hong Kong, Bombay, Delhi, and Rio?

Does this mean there shall be no granite in motherhouses, marble in provincial convents, and imported stained-glass windows in reception halls? No! These things will stay, provided the equivalent of a hundred square feet of that granite, marble, and stained glass is cut out of architectural places, for those who live in dirt and look though paneless windows. Dieting is very common in the United States, fasting is not; the first being for the beauty of the body, the second for the soul. It is unfortunate that the practice of fasting is passing out of the Church, for fasting is not something negative. A beautiful justification of fasting was given by Gandhi, who said: "Prayer attaches us to God; fasting detaches us from creatures." The purpose of prayer, therefore, is to inflate the balloon; the purpose of fasting is to take off the unnecessary ballast that keeps us to the earth.

Just as the vow of poverty must have relation to the millions who are forced into vowless impoverishment, so fasting must mean a little injury to the individual in contrast to the hunger around the world where ten thousand die every day, where in mud huts a wife with six ragged children sits around the fire made of cow dung and once a day eats *chappatties*. What does fasting mean in the light of what Gandhi has called "the eternal compulsory fast" of just 230,-000,000 Indians who live in the state of semistarvation, and of the 50,000,000 children who will die of starvation and malnutrition in the next ten years. Instead of decreasing the laws of fasting, perhaps we should be inspired to fast in order to understand better the emptiness and hunger of our brothers in Christ throughout the world. Fasting should be revived, not to continue an old penitential custom, but experientially to make us enter the empty stomachs, sorrowful hearts, and wasted bodies of our brethren in Christ. What would we think if the Church imposed upon us a law of fasting where we would be allowed a small bowl of rice a day and two inches of fish the day after tomorrow? And yet this not the fasting! *This is the feasting of half of the people of the world.*

The average American consumes 4.66 pounds of food a day. If he ate only half as much a day, he would have 2.33 pounds of food a day, which would be about twice what the average Indian eats a day, though his food is mostly rice (the average Indian has 1.23 pounds of food a day). Experts tell us that there is enough food thrown in the garbage pails of the United States every day to feed China's 686,000,000 every few days.

Sharing

If thou art harvesting the corn in one of thy fields, and a sheaf lies there forgotten, do not go back for it; leave it for the alien, the orphan and the widow; so the Lord thy God will prosper all thy undertakings.

Do not go over thy olive trees again, the fruit once picked, leave to alien, orphan and widow the clusters that hang on thy vines when the vintage is over, still ungathered. Do not forget that thou wast once a slave in Egypt; not without reason I enjoin this upon thee.—Deut. 24:19–22

This law established the portion of the friendless. The poor were to be helped *out of abundance* by the forgotten sheaths in the harvest, by the fruit of the olive tree, and by the gleaning from the vineyard. The stranger, the fatherless, and the widows, were to be remembered by special Providence. The Lord's poor are the Lord's care. Neglecting or despising them is to mock God Himself:

"He who shews contempt to the poor, insults man's Maker; at thy own peril thou wilt take delight in another's ruin."—Prov. 17:5

"Pay the Lord His due with what goods thou hast, letting Him share the first-fruits of every crop."—Prov. 3:9

Because the Jews were strangers and in servitude in Egypt, they should love the stranger when they came into the Promised Land. In the New Testament, Christians once were poor—that is, without grace and a stranger to the Redemption.

"Order your lives in charity, upon that model of that charity which Christ showed to us, when He gave Himself up on our behalf, a sacrifice breathing out fragrance as He offered it to God."—Eph. 5:2

When St. Paul was urging the Corinthian church to liberality, he could think of no stronger argument than this:

"You do not need to be reminded how gracious our Lord Jesus Christ was; how He impoverished Himself for your sakes, when He was so rich, so that you might become rich through His poverty."—II Cor. 8:9

In the Book of Job, Chapter 24, there is an indictment of those who neglect the poor:

"Out of the cities they had made men to groan, and the soul of the wounded had cried out, and God doth not suffer it to pass unrevenged. They have been rebellious to the light, they have not known his ways, neither have they returned by his paths."—Job 24:12–13

If God has made us comfortable, we are not to build a high fence around our house so that no one else may ever see the flowers or smell their perfume nor hear the song of the winged creatures.

Hunger allows no choice to the citizen or the police;
We must love one another or die.

—W. H. AUDEN

The great divorce of the twentieth century is, as we said above, the divorce between those above the thirtieth parallel in the north and those south of the thirtieth parallel. Mankind is split in two. One part is well endowed, well fed, but another part is sunk in wretchedness. Relatively, those above the thirtieth parallel lack little, and those beneath it need everything.

It is over our civilization above the thirtieth parallel which Christ weeps and says, "Would that even today you knew the things that were for thy peace." His tears are being shed over the Cain that is within us; over the unsuspecting, unheeding cities, over the parishes and dioceses of our civilization, over the hammering and pounding, the building of schools and social centers and rich churches, which give the *illusion* of great progress—but they could be only a facade if we overlook the Christ in the poor.

It is almost impossible for us who live above the thirtieth parallel to grasp the horrors, anguish, and emptiness of stomachs and hearts in the slums. Hunger is not just an *economic* problem; it is a *moral and spiritual* problem. It is a greater danger to the future of mankind than is atomic war.

Money to Live

There is no lack of money for killing men, but we have not succeeded in getting enough funds together to keep men *alive*. Fifteen million more Chinese are born every year than there were the year before. The population of India increases six million every year. If this increase throughout the world continues, in forty years, out of every one hundred people in the world more than seventy-six will belong to the underdeveloped nations. Half the children in the world have no chance of education, and far more than half above the age of ten have never been to school. These illiterate people are to be found in Asia, Africa, and Latin America, the hungry lands.

As we see their misery, we hear ringing out, "Where is Abel, your brother?" The amazing thing is that God did not confront Cain in the precincts of the altar but in the fields, in the midst of the world of work—in the midst of gadgets and machinery, universities, split-levels, and refrigerators.

God confronts us above the thirtieth parallel with the *social question,* not about the person we have killed but about the person we have neglected and ignored.

What a staggering thing it is that in Our Lord's great discourse on the Last Judgment, there is no mention whatever of adulterers, murderers, thieves. Rather He speaks of those who neglected something and thus did nothing at all. "I was thirsty and you did not give Me to drink; naked and you did not clothe Me; hungry and you did not give Me to eat." Is not this the more subtle form of murder?

In the parable of the good Samaritan, there is only an incidental reference to the villains who beat up the man. The real indictment was against the priest and the Levite, against the passive, thick-skinned, indifferent people who will be asked at the Last Judgment: "Where is Abel, your brother?"

We can no longer live on crossword puzzles, television, deodorants. We simply cannot! We have had a thousand excuses. We have fiery urges; we say that we must satisfy them. Or we are used to a grand style of living; therefore, we cannot let our wealth go. Is not our Christian world in danger of being stuck with our electric can openers, our Cadillacs, our cocktails before dinner—not because they are bad in themselves, but because they are being used to fill up our emptied and peaceless lives instead of caring for those on the other side of the thirtieth parallel?

We are not going to help these people simply because we are moved by their poverty or shocked by their suffering. We will never arouse ourselves to full responsibility until we see the poor the way Our Lord saw them. When He looked at a guilt-laden person, He saw in him an erring child whom His Father loved and grieved over, simply because he had gone wrong. Our Lord is always looking at people at their best. He saw the Divine Image beneath their apparent worthlessness and ulcerous sores. Should we not say to those who are below the thirtieth parallel:

I do not condemn your resistance. I do not condemn you for listening to the false prophets of the Communists. If Adam and Eve listened to a false promise of a Red from hell in the midst of paradise and plenty, then you, without bread in your pantry, can be excused from hearing those who tell you they will turn stones into bread. You are not the real culprits. *We* are the real culprits—hardened by those sins of omission which are after all the least worthy of forgiveness. We say that you will not listen to the Gospel. But did not Our Lord first feed the hungry before He announced the Eucharist? If your backs are turned toward the sun, have we asked you to turn around? Our religion is the religion of renunciation and the Cross. But you have been *forced* to renounce. Are there not among you hundreds of millions who would willingly take the vow of poverty if you could live as well, dress as well, eat as well, be housed as well, as we who take the vow of poverty or are supposed to live in the spirit of poverty? We throw ourselves on the altar floor to take the vow of poverty. You are thrust upon the cold earth to have it imposed upon you.

Our Lord did not remain at base headquarters in heaven, receiving reports of the world's suffering from below and shouting a few encouraging words to us from a safe distance. He left the headquarters and came down to our dirt and muck, emptiness and futility, suffering and guilt. He crossed the line between innocence and guilt, between the riches with the Father and the poverty of the stable; He went from above the thirtieth parallel of heaven to below the thirtieth parallel of earth. Bethlehem was the spot where the thirtieth parallel was first crossed. From now on, no one can say: "Does God know what it is to have no home, to be denied an inn, to live in a stable? Was God ever a refugee? Did He know what it was to be driven out of one's country into another? Was God ever tempted? He saw foxes with holes, birds with nests, but did He ever know what it was to have nowhere to lay His Head, and then be shoved off the world He made, to die on a gallows?"

As John Donne put it:

No man is an island, entire of itself; every man is a piece of the continent, . . . any man's death diminishes me, because I am involved in mankind; and therefore never send to know for whom the bell tolls; it tolls for thee.

CHAPTER THIRTEEN

Collective Life—Collective Death

The world is the scene not only of cultural differences, economic inequalities, the subjects of previous chapters; here we shall consider the great problem of the survival of the world itself.

According to Teilhard de Chardin, the evolution of the universe through millions of years has seen the gradual unfolding of a protoconsciousness, until man appeared as fully conscious and rational. But within the last thirty thousand years, he holds, there has been no radical change either on the somatic or on the mind level of man. One thing for him is certain: Man's development does not lie in the begetting of some superman; evolution in that direction has practically ceased. From now on, progress, instead of being vertical, will be horizontal—that is, will reach out to the unification of all mankind.

In the earlier phases, the complex atoms entered into new unities and eventually produced a form of life. When one comes to the animal kingdom, one finds socialization, while the higher one goes in the progression of humanity, the more one finds that individuals become less and less isolated, more and more socialized. Psychology reveals also that individuals reach a higher state of perfection in community than they do when separated from a community. As Teilhard puts it: "No evolutionary future awaits man except in association with other men."

Thanks to communications, education, global network of trade and exchange, men and nations are weaving a pattern of greater and greater interdependence. This vast globality of common effort is what Teilhard calls the noosphere. Humanity is now at the crossroads of collective life or collective death. If it is to survive, what energy was to the lower order love must be to the human—namely, the drive to more and more complex social unity. Teilhard opts for collective life. The birth of mankind is a consequence of the birth of man. Borderlines between nations and cultures will gradually be effaced. Peoples will see more and more that they cannot live in isolation and that they must associate with one another.

At this point one can see a slight parallel between the thinking of Karl Marx and Teilhard de Chardin. Both thought the world was developing toward socialization. Marx believed that the socialization would be a kind of ant heap in which the individual lives only for the mass, resulting in a complete loss and submerging of personality. Teilhard de Chardin felt that the socialization would result in an increase of freedom for personality. As he put it: "A tremendous spiritual power is slumbering in the depths of our multitude, which will manifest itself only when we have learned to break down the barriers of our egoisms."

This is possible, because both at the beginning and at the end of the whole evolutionary process, there is Love. The Love-point at the beginning which makes everything turn from complexity to unity is the Alpha; the goal toward which all tends is the perfect Love or the Omega. As he wrote:

> One day the Gospel tells us, the tension gradually accumulating between humanity and God will touch the limits prescribed by the possibilities of the world. And then will come the end. Then the Presence of Christ, which has been silently accruing in things will suddenly be revealed—like a flash of light from pole to pole.
> —*The Divine Milieu*

Collective Death

An opposite view to Chardin's is that there will be a socialization which will produce a Superman and eventually end in the destruction of humanity. The mass society which will be formed will destroy personality. As Lenin wrote: "The whole society will be one office and one factory with the same work and the same wages." Lenin called the leader of this mass society the "dictatorship of the proletariat." Friedrich von Preen, in the same spirit, held that the great future authority was developing toward an absolute center of power. Our Blessed Lord spoke of such a one as the "Prince of this world," St. Paul called him "the god of this world" (II Cor. 4:4). St. John called him "an other" and said, "If an other come in his own name, him will you receive" (John 5:43). It is to be noted that when Satan in the temptations offers Christ all of the kingdoms of the world and the glory thereof, saying, "For to me they have been delivered, and whomever I will I give them" (Luke 4:6), Christ does not correct him.

Christopher Dawson, sees the world as entering "into a new phase of our culture in which the most amazing perfection of scientific technique is being devoted to purely ephemeral objects . . . it is obvious that a civilization of this kind holds no promise for the future, save that of social disintegration."

The Spaniard, Donoso Cortes, in 1849 wrote: "Mankind is hastening with great strides towards the certain fate of despotism . . . this despotism will evolve a power of destruction greater and mightier than anything we have hitherto experienced."

Dostoyevsky makes Ivan Karamazov say:

"As soon as men have, all of them, pronounced that God is dead, man will be lifted up with a spirit of the divine, titanic pride, and the man-god will appear. . . . Man will unite to take from life all that it can give for nothing else but for the joy and happiness in the present world."

The new collectivity, effected through a depersonalization, will beget an authority which would be to all people their will and their collective center of consciousness. No person will think for himself. This kind of collectivity was forecast by Hobbes, by Hegel, and by Marx. Dostoyevsky, looking back on all the states which made themselves absolutes, said that they were only embryos of the new collectivity, which would be destructive:

> Underworld man refuses any organization based on harmony. I shall not be surprised if in the midst of this Universal Reason that is to be there will appear, all of a sudden, and unexpectedly, some common face, or rather cynical and sneering gentleman who with his arms akimbo will say to us: "Now then, you fellows, what about smashing all this reason to bits, sending their logarithms to the devil, and living as we like according to our own silly will." That might not be much, but the annoying thing is that he would immediately get plenty of fellows—men are made like that. And the cause of all this is so that it would scarcely seem worth speaking of: man.

It will be recalled that Dostoyevsky also said: "There are two ages of man—one from the gorilla to the death of God and one from the death of God to the annihilation of man."

It was his constant prediction that a Godless humanity must eventually destroy man. He pictures the Antichrist as a humanitarian and a sociologist who reverses the three temptations of Christ on the Mount and glorifies man without God. This dictator publishes a book on "Peace and Prosperity"; he has seemingly all the compassion of Christ, except that he is evil—or better, he had no scars from suffering for mankind. Cardinal Newman was asked in 1871 who he thought would be the future Goths and Vandals of the next century and he answered: "The lowest class, which is very great in numbers and, unbelieving, will rise up out of the depths of modern cities and be the new scourge of God."

Thomas Aquinas in the thirteenth century said that a socialization and control of personal lives would one day be directed by a "secular city," a *potentia secularis* based on the death of God. The historian Gibbon earlier had said that if dominion of mankind fell into the hands of one individual, the world would become a "prison for his adversaries."

Nietzsche taught the Superman who would bring chaos: "I teach you the Superman. Man is something to be surpassed. What have you done to surpass man? All beings hitherto have created something beyond themselves. . . . Would you rather go back to the beast than surpass man? Lo! I teach you the Superman! Let your will say: The Superman *shall be* the meaning of the earth. . . . The self-chosen elect will grow into a chosen people and out of this will grow the Superman. But he must first appear as an atheist—*Thus Spake Zarathustra.*

In the end there will be the "Chaos of the All" which is the exclusion of all purposiveness. "Where are the barbarians of the 20th century? Evidently, they will become consolidated themselves only after enormous socialistic crises." The method by which these barbarians will be created will be by a "transvaluation of values." Evil must be multiplied to a point where there is no remorse. Then the superman can say, "Evil be thou my good; good be thou my evil."

Instruments of Collective Death

The new order introduced by the "Death of God" will be the secular city. The secular city will be the new Bethlehem, and to that new Bethlehem without the Child the Wise Men will bring three gifts: gold, frankincense, and myrrh:

Gold, the symbol of the primacy of profit; the yellow stuff with which one buys pleasure; the status symbol of power in a world where one can buy anything with money.

Frankincense, or the modern science of scent; chemistry and biochemistry which will completely control the genes of man and produce the superman.

Myrrh. It was once used for burial; now it will be the new science of collective death—namely, nuclear weapons.

What more could the secular city ask for than gold which is power over pleasure, frankincense which is power over life, myrrh which is power over death?

The destruction of man will thus be as easy as *A,B,C*: the *A* for Atomic energy; the *B* for Biological transmutations of the human species; and *C* for Chemical nuclear energy.

For this reason, the Vatican Council did not speak of nuclear weapons but of "scientific" weapons, to embrace all three phases of atomic, biological, and chemical warfare.

There is no need to mention the importance of gold in the new collectivity, because everyone experiences round about him the love of affluence. But a word might be said about the new frankincense of chemistry and biochemistry in the way of the transmutation of man. One Nobel prize winner in the United States hopes that we can develop through chemistry and biology "a new man with a super brain." Another Nobel prize winner in the United States looks to the day when chemistry can increase brain cells' intensity to the tenth degree. Still another Nobel prize winner suggests enormous deep freezes to keep the sperm cells of men most suited for the human race. Corresponding to this, an English biologist recommends the sterilization of all women by contraceptive hormones, in order to leave fertile only those capable of producing the master race. A French biologist says, "Man is the weakest link in evolution, a blunder in construction, and should be replaced by the superman scientifically engendered." At a conference of Nobel prize winners, W. M. Stanley suggested placing all the embryo plasm of the world in the hands of the chemist; thus the power of the world would be transferred from the nuclear physicist to the chemist. Sir Julian Huxley foresees the day when "electric currents stimulating certain bases of the brain will make all men 'feel happiness.' "

The new myrrh, or the scientific embalmer of collective death, is nuclear warheads. Presently there are sufficient numbers of nuclear weapons in the world to explode over every single person on earth ten tons of nuclear destruction. A few years ago the United States had an overkill of 1,250. This means: Assume the maximum number of enemies the United States might conceivably have in the future, there is sufficient nuclear energy to kill them over again 1,250 times. At a recent conference of nuclear scientists it was said that, if there was nuclear warfare, the United States would lose in the first thirty minutes between 80 and 125 million people.

Armaments in the world are costing $140 billion a year. The United States and the Soviet Union account for 70 percent of the total. In the United States our expenditure is $63 billion a year. Fifteen other nations are already preparing nuclear energy, for today an atomic bomb has become a status symbol. Nations stockpiling atomic weapons are like misers hiding money under carpets. What is regrettable is that the money spent every year on arms could have raised the per capita income of the underdeveloped countries three times.

Arms and Men

The historical background of nuclear arms shows a progression toward collective death. The first war weapon was a club, used by Cain to shed his brother's blood. This caused him to fall into despair as he became a vagabond on the earth: "Going out from the presence of the Lord," that is, to a God-forsaken life. His descendants built the first city; inasmuch as he had left the Divine Presence, it was the first secular city. Because he was constantly living under anxiety and dread, and because the red thread of another's life had been woven into the fabric of this new civilization, there was constant fear. The first secular city was built in the spirit of cruel egotism, and Cain's red finger marks are on it still.

Among the descendants of Cain was Lamech, the first man to

have two wives. One of his sons, Tubalcain, was a smith who worked in brass and iron for service in war. He became the first swordmaker. Lamech, proud of this new war weapon, dedicated a song to his two wives, chanting proudly that if God avenged Cain sevenfold, he with his new sword, would not need nor ask the Divine Avenger; he would act himself on the principle: "Vengeance is mine and I will repay, and not merely sevenfold, but seventy and seven times."

His song ran:

"Adah and Zillah, hear my voice,
O wives of Lamech, give ear to my speech:
I have killed a man for wounding me,
A boy was injuring me.
If Cain be avenged seven-fold,
Then Lamech seventy-seven fold."

Setting at naught vengeance which belongs to heaven, he denied judgment and made light of sin's recompense. Such is the thought behind the invention of his sword. He is far ahead of Cain. No longer need he look to God for protection; he can provide more amply for it himself than God did for Cain with a brand on his forehead.

As time went on, weapons became more complicated such as the bow, catapults, and ballistas. The Second Lateran Council in 1139 outlawed the crossbow. It was about five or six feet in length, and the arrow discharged was about a yard and a half long, made of metal.

It is sometimes said that Roger Bacon knew of gunpowder in the thirteenth century, but it is more certain that Berthold Schwarz, a German monk of the fourteenth centry, also knew of it. In 1892 Maxim invented the silencer, and the press proclaimed, "There will be no more wars, for men will not fight if they cannot hear the explosion of gun." Dynamite, in its modern form, was invented by

Nobel. Then journalists wrote: "There will be no more wars, for they will be too destructive. Dynamite is a deterrent." Having made $40 million from his dynamite factories and from explosive nitro-glycerin, in an attempt to ease his conscience, he then established the Nobel Prizes for Peace.

Thus the sword of Lamech became longer and longer, more fratricidal, more destructive until at 3:25 P.M. on December 2, 1942, some scientists standing on a squash court gave a signal for a reactor to start working; it began the chain reaction for producing plutonium. The machine worked twenty-eight minutes. This date was the birthday of atomic energy. The scientists opened a bottle of Italian wine and drank, to celebrate the New Age.

Within two months after that birthday, and despite all the secrecy involved, a warning came from another part of the world. At the opening of the session of the Pontifical Academy of Science on February 11, 1943, two years before the bomb dropped on Hiroshima, Pius XII spoke as follows:

> Since atoms are extremely small, it is not thought seriously that they might also acquire practical importance. Today, instead, such a question has taken an unexpected form following the results of artificial radio-activity.
>
> It was, in fact, established that in the disintegration which the atom of uranium undergoes when bombarded by neutrons, two or three neutrons are freed, each launching itself—one being able to meet and smash another uranium atom.
>
> From special calculation, it is then ascertained that in such a way in one cubic meter of oxide powder of uranium, in less than one-hundredth of a second, there develops enough energy to elevate a weight of a billion tons sixteen miles into the air—a sum of energy which would substitute for many years the action of all the great power plants of the world.
>
> Above all, it should be of utmost importance that the energy originated by such a machine should not be left to explode—but a

means found to control such power with suitable chemical means. Otherwise, there could result not only in a single place, but also for our entire universe a dangerous catastrophe.

His second warning was given in 1954.

On the sixteenth day of July, 1945, in an isolated area of mountain-ribbed desert in New Mexico, at 5:30 A.M., a group of nuclear scientists began a countdown beginning at fifty. At zero, an explosion vomited a boiling, surging cloud forty thousand feet into the air, leaving a crater twenty-five feet deep and four hundred feet wide. The secret operation was blasphemously called Trinity.

One of the observers wrote afterward: "It warned us of dooms-day and made us feel that we puny things were blasphemous to dare tamper with forces hitherto reserved for the Almighty." President Truman was at the Potsdam conference when his secretary handed him a cable reading, *Babies born.*

On the sixth day of August, 1945, at 9:15 A.M. Japanese time, a plane banked in a sharp turn; a button was pushed, and a mush-room of nuclear destruction rose over Hiroshima. *Babies dead.*

In 1949 Einstein was asked: "What is the future of atomic energy?" He answered: "Come back and see me in *1969.*"

During a dinner conversation in Paris in 1869 recorded in the *Journal* of the Goncourt brothers, Pierre Bethelot predicted that in one hundred years—that is, 1969—"man would know of what the atom was constituted, and would be able, at will, to moderate, extinguish, and light up the sun as if it were a gas lamp."

The Goncourt brothers answered, "We have a feeling that when this time comes to science, God with His white beard will come down to earth, swinging a bunch of keys, and will say to humanity: 'Closing time, gentlemen.'"

It is a coincidence that at that very period when "God is dead," when there is formed the secular city without religion, when Sartre calls "life . . . meaningless and absurd," and Camus writes that "suicide is the only true philosophical problem"—is it a coincidence we invented the atomic bomb to blow the earth into meaninglessness?

This is our choice: Collective life through the amorization of humanity or collective death through pride. The moral has been told in the story of two trees growing in a forest. One is a giant tree; the other beneath it is a shriveled tree which engages it in conversation, heaps ridicule upon it not only for climbing so high but also for wasting its strength on roots which cannot be seen. The healthy tree says, "But I grow toward the sun, toward light. And I am dependent on the past for much of my strength."

"There is no sun," says the little shriveled tree. "I cannot see it. Neither can you, and what cannot be verified is void of meaning."

"But I feel the sun. It opens its warmth to me as if it were love; its truth enters into my fibers, and whatever it touches becomes sprouting bud and fruit."

"I feel the warmth of the sun just as much as you do, but this is merely a scientific fact which we cannot verify. It is a condition that is known as spring. It is something that is within us, has no other source than ourselves, and is of our own making. You are wasting your energy and sap with fruit and branches and climbing to the sun and deep roots. I keep all of my sap for my own inner strength."

And the little shriveled tree continued to grow only in egotism as the days went by, until one day the gardener came and cut it down.

CHAPTER FOURTEEN

Hopes for Peace

Granted the dangers of nuclear warfare, there are nevertheless hopes for peace. Some who have seen the Meditation Room of the United Nations building have been disappointed with its size, its somberness, and its simplicity—a symbol of modern confusion. It nevertheless represented to Dag Hammarskjöld, who designed it, a place dedicated to silence in the outward sense and stillness in the inner sense. The block of iron which was made into the altar was one of sixty chunks wrested from the earth by a Swedish mining company, before the right one was found. It was polished until it shimmered as a solitary light shone on it from above. Hammarskjöld explained it as follows:

> In this house, we are trying to turn swords into plowshares, and we thought we could bless by our thoughts the very material out of which arms are made. For that reason we felt that it was appropriate that the material to represent the earth on which we stand, as seen by the light of the sky, should be iron ore, the material out of which swords have been made, and the material out of which homes are built. It is a material which represents the very paradox of human life; the basic material offered by God to us may be used either for construction or destruction. This leads our thoughts to the necessity of choice between two alternatives.
>
> The original idea was one which I think you will all recog-

nize; you will find it in many great religions; it is the empty altar, empty not because there is no God, but empty because God is worshipped in so many forms. The stone in the center is the altar to the God of all. . . . In this house with its dynamic, modern architecture, there are few things that give you the feeling of weight, solidity, and permanence; in this case we want this massive altar to give the impression of something more than the temporary. . . . We wanted a room of stillness with perhaps one or two very simple symbols, light and light striking on stone. It is for that reason that in the center of the Room there is a block of iron ore, glimmering like ice in the shaft of light from above. That is the only symbol in the Room—a meeting of the light, of the sky and the earth.

Passing from the Meditation Room to the United Nations itself, does this body offer any hope for peace, and what other hopes are there? The United Nations; the rectification of the imbalance between the rich and poor nations of the world; and Russia.

1. *The United Nations*

The United Nations embraces almost all of the governments of the world. Its greatest contribution has been to make the giants the dwarfs and the dwarfs the giants. A song has come out of Brazil:

But one day the giant awoke,
He ceased being a sleeping giant,
And lo! A dwarf arose;
He was an underdeveloped country!

The underdeveloped countries of the world, like Asia, Africa, and Latin America, are giants and dwarfs. They are giants not only because they are conscious of a rich cultural and spiritual heritage, but also because they constitute the vast proportion of the population of the earth. Asia alone contains one half of humanity. But these giants are also dwarfs economically, because they are poor; technologically, because they are underdeveloped; scientifically, because the masses are uneducated; physically, because the people are underfed.

But these underdeveloped nations are an emergent force for developing peace and for even determining international relationships, for two reasons:

The underdeveloped nations represent a new revolutionary force in the world—new because their revolution is not so much political, as it was when seeking freedom from colonial powers, it is rather an economic revolution, or the right of the poorest state to live like the richest state. This prompted the London *Economist* to say, "The underprivileged nations have been winning votes by losing heads." They raised such a stir by their protest at meetings that they may have been said to have lost their heads; they won votes in their claim to have a share in the world's wealth.

That brings us to the United Nations as the basis of peace. This international body has taken over a principle of rights which was written into our own Declaration of Independence—namely, that every man has a right to life, liberty, and the pursuit of happiness. This basic recognition of the worth of human personality has been carried over to the United Nations. The old principle that dominated politics was that right is might, but with the formation of the United Nations something new has been introduced—namely, that there must be another standard of measurement than the power to subjugate a neighbor. The Christian principle has always been that a single soul is worth more than the entire universe.

In the United States, the principle of self-determination of all nations, which was introduced by President Wilson, has now been applied to the voting system of the General Assembly of the United Nations. Mauritania with 780,000 people has the same vote as the United States with 200,000,000 people. Here, at least, a big nation cannot dominate a little nation. In a similar way, the Soviet Union and Jamaica each have one vote. The underdeveloped nations represent a numerical superiority at international gatherings. So long as the meetings continue to be democratic and each has its own voice, these underdeveloped nations will break down the distinction between affluence and intolerable poverty.

By giving every constituent member of the General Assembly a vote, the distinction between might and right is to a great extent destroyed. There has been developing in democracy through the years a sense of personal worth and dignity; now this right of the individual has moved into the realm of nations. Not only in the field of religion has there been a development of the ecumenical spirit, but also in the field of politics there has been a deepening sense of what unites, rather than what divides the communities of the world. Pope Paul said, when he visited the United Nations, it was the first time in human record that all the peoples of the world shared in some measure in a common jurisdiction.

LIMITATIONS OF THE UNITED NATIONS

There are, however, certain cautions that must be kept in mind, lest too much hope be placed in an international body. This touches the effectiveness of guarantees and treaties. One needs only to go back to the League of Nations, which was formed after World War I, to recall that it sought to bind men together under the principle so popularly enunciated at the time, "The War to End All Wars." During the nineteen years of the League of Nations, 4,568 treaties of peace were signed by the constituent members. All were broken at the outbreak of World War II. It must also be recalled that Russia entered into a nonaggression pact with every independent nation in eastern Europe, but within the course of a year or more the Soviets had destroyed the independence of every single nation by aggression.

What is to be thought of treaties banning nuclear weapons? It is generally agreed that a nuclear war would be suicidal. There is, however, a limit to the deterrent value of nuclear warfare. Every city has education in fire prevention and a fire department. No one of the home owners wishes to set fire to his home; at the same time, every fire department hopes that no fire will ever break out. But human nature being what it is, there always remains the possibility of a fire. Furthermore, arsonists delight in setting fires. They are rare in a population, but they are of sufficient number to cause alarm.

If our society can produce madmen who with guns will wipe out whole families or groups, for no apparent reason whatever, what is there to prevent a madman with nuclear weapons from wiping out civilization? The humanity, which a few decades ago could produce a Hitler and a Stalin, could produce two or ten more men with equal determination to destroy the world, particularly as the moral decline of civilization continues. There is always the possibility of international arsonists who would like to set fire to the world, and who would fulfill that rapid transition from "the death of God to the annihilation of man," as Dostoyevsky expressed it.

What makes peace more fragile is the erosion of moral principles. Two principles were invoked in any discussion of a "just war": One was the distinction between weapons of war and methods of extermination; the second, the distinction between the military and civilian population. Both of these principles have been destroyed in modern times in the following manner:

The distinction between weapons of war and extermination was to some extent destroyed by the use of gas in World War I.

The second principle of the distinction between the military and the civilian was blurred by the sinking of the *Lusitania,* the bombing of cities in World War II, and particularly the use of the atomic bomb on Japan.

The new wars do not place so much emphasis on men and heroism as upon technology and the ability to manufacture weapons of destruction. One notices this absence of ethical restraint in the tendency toward total destruction through war. There is now no difference between a soldier and mothers and children. In World War I, ten million were killed of whom 5 percent were civilians. In World War II, fifty million were killed of whom 50 percent were civilian, 50 percent military. In the Korean War, nine million were killed of whom 84 percent were civilian and 16 percent soldiers. This latter figure indicates that the soldier in modern warfare has a better chance of survival than the civilian. This brings up the question as to whether or not there is any chance of survival.

COMMON HUMANITY

Despite these limitations and dangers, what chance has love?

Stalin has given a negative proof of the need of love binding men together. His problem was how to unite men in a classless society in which everyone was the comrade of another. Negatively, he did this by keeping out Western ideas, persecuting religion, and by living up to a name that was given him in school, when one day a boy in back of him wrote on his back the word "steel" or in Russian stalin—a word that became prophetic. The only way to bind Communists into a compact, monolithic structure was by "steel." Since *agape,* or love, was missing, unity could come only from riveting people together; or, to change the figure, citizens who were individual straws had to be baled together by wire lest they confusedly should fall apart. Once that steel passed out of Communism, it failed to have a true center. It is this want of center which will destroy Communism, unless it finds another bond of keeping men together. The false assumption of Communism was that men who share the same things are brothers. This is a fallacy; because one divides an apple with another, one does not necessarily make him a brother. It may create the basis of a quarrel as to whose piece is the larger. If, however, men are really brothers and love one another, then they will divide. Sheep who will not be united by the leadership of the Shepherd will have to be herded into the sheepfold by a dog barking at their heels. Fundamentally, the brotherhood of man alone is not enough. Brotherhood without Fatherhood makes us all illegitimate children.

Second Hope: Remedying the Imbalance Between Nations

There has always been poverty in the world, but there is a difference today. In other generations, people accepted their poverty; today they do not. In the past, they did not know they were poor; today they *know* it; they feel it; they insist that the poorest of them has the same right to be as rich as the rich nations.

The tropic of Cancer is a kind of dividing line of the earth. About 25 percent of the population of the earth above that line enjoys 75 percent of the world's trade, investments, resources, and wealth. The 75 percent below enjoy only 25 percent of the wealth. From another point of view, the United States is 6 percent of the population of the earth and yet controls 46 percent of the world's wealth.

Furthermore, the gap between the rich and the poor nations is becoming greater. As Barbara Ward has expressed it: "The rich are becoming richer, the poor are becoming poorer. The gross national income of the United States in one single year increased more than all of Africa's and 50 percent more than Latin America. . . . The joint income of the developing countries with two thirds of the world's population is only about one tenth of the industrialized countries." It is no wonder the world is in revolt and that there is what has been called "the revolution of rising expectation."

One of the conditions of peace is that the gap between the rich and poor nations must not continue to polarize and to widen. Otherwise the certain outcome will be war. The problem then arises: What kind of war? A nuclear war no one will win, but in limited warfare, the poorer nations in a prolonged war could bring the richer nations down to the level of their own poverty, thus destroying for years any prospect of either prosperity or peace.

The answer to this is not merely organizations which strive to reduce poverty through voluntary contributions of the people; there must be also a shift from the notion of rights to the notion of responsibility. Otherwise the poor nations will feel they must unite against the rich nations. In 1964 this happened in the United Nations Trade and Development Council, where seventy-four poor nations consistently opposed the richer ones.

It is quite wrong to think that Christianity demands a passive submission to poverty. One is apt to fall into this view because Our Blessed Lord said, "Blessed are the poor." We have already explained that this does not mean economic poverty; it means humility of spirit. But even where it is generally understood, Our Blessed Lord overbalanced it with another statement, "Woe to you who are rich, for you already have received your reward" (Luke 6:20-24). It is rather difficult to take the sting out of the words, "It is easier for a camel to pass through the eye of a needle, than for a rich man to enter the Kingdom of God" (Matt. 19:24).

One of the complaints made against Christianity by the East is that we have not lived out our Christian obligation. As one Hindu put it, as he plucked up a rose and looked toward it with a smile of anguish on his face: "In my judgment the Christian faith does not lend itself to much preaching or talking. It is best propagated by *living* it and *applying* it. Does the rose preach about the particular merits of its fragrance? When will you Christians really crown Him as the Prince of Peace and proclaim Him through your deeds as the Champion of the poor and the oppressed?"

What is there in affluence, either individual, corporate, or national, which makes one forget the poor? A remarkable illustration of this was a woman in Brazil who a few years ago wrote a best seller which was translated into twenty-two languages (*Child of the Dark* by Carolina Maria de Jesus, translated from the Portuguese by David St. Clair). It was the story of how, with several illegitimate children in her shack, she tried to support them in the worst of all slums, by gathering papers and selling them or by rummaging through garbage pails. Every night, in sorrow, hunger, and agony of soul, she would write down a few notes on scraps of paper, which later were gathered into this book which sold ninety thousand copies in six months in Brazil alone. One afternoon she autographed six hundred copies in a bookstore. Some of the passages were moving beyond the description of any novelist who never lived in poverty. Reflecting on a dream she had of living near palm trees, she said, "How good God is; He lets us see beautiful things in our dreams."

Her book sold so well that she moved out of her slum with her money, and bought a home and a farm. Gone were the days which she described: "I would lie on the bed and start to worry about the next day. I knew there was no bread in the house and that Vera needed a pair of shoes. Then I would get up, light the lamp and write."

How bitterly she complained in this book about the rich merchants who dumped their rotten fruit in the slums to poison the children. Where is the woman today? Back again in the slums! She could not stand prosperity. There is no record that she ever gave any of that money to the poor people with whom she suffered.

Though private charity makes it difficult to handle adequately all of the poverty of the world, one of the great missions of the Church in an affluent society is to arouse men to a sense of responsibility in the midst of their prosperity. There may be instances when poverty in individual cases is due to laziness. But on the scale that it exists in the world today, it is an offense against both God and man.

Arnold Toynbee, speaking of our affluent civilization, wrote concerning the money wasted on advertising in the face of the world's need:

It has made a fine art of taking advantage of human silliness. It rams unwanted material goods down surfeited throats when two-thirds of all human beings now alive are in desperate need of the bare necessities of life. This is an ugly aspect of the affluent society; and, if I am told that advertising is the price of affluence, I reply without hesitation that affluence has been bought too dear.
—"Why I Dislike Civilization,"
The New York Times Magazine, May 10, 1964

Despite the affluence in civilization, there are nevertheless many indications of hope. First of all the Churches are becoming uncomfortable in their comfort and are beginning to revive poverty in their lives. Secondly, the youth of this country are anxious to serve the underdeveloped nations of the world. Thirdly, the United Nations is making aid one of its primary objects and a condition of world peace.

The Good Lord has put a thermostat into the human body, with the result that though the mouth tastes and the stomach receives food, nevertheless, all of the vitamin value of the food is distributed throughout the entire organism. Otherwise the right ear would be the size of the foot; the left arm might become five times the size of the right arm. This regulator inside of the human organism should be paralleled by a regulator inside the social organism, the basis of which is love, and love prompts a sharing.

Third Hope: Russia

This may come as a surprise to many, but it is well to keep in mind the distinction between an ideology and a people. An ideology may be intrinsically evil, but the people may be good. Furthermore, it is possible for an ideology to change, because no revolution ever attains the end for which it was created. The Western world has been going on the assumption that because Communism is evil, therefore the Russian people should be destroyed. One does not find this in St. Paul who lived in an empire that deprived him and others of freedom, and eventually beheaded him. There is no record that he ever once planned or incited to the destruction of the Roman Empire. He did not organize a Christian party but began to remake men as a leaven in a mass.

But this is not our reason for finding hope in the Soviet Union. The hope is rather to be found in the words of the Gospel:

There was a man with two sons. He went to the first and said, "Go and work in my vineyard today, my son." He said, "All right, sir"— but he never went near it. Then the father approached the second son with the same request. He said, "I won't." But afterward he changed his mind and went. Which of these two did what their father wanted?

"The second one," they replied.

—Matt. 21:28-31

The one son who said that he would not go was rebellious and disobedient. The other son said that he would go. He had the swift tongue and the slow foot. He represented the lukewarm Christian, so often found in Western civilization, who takes out religion once a week for an airing. Such faith is temporary and occasional, like fountains of water that are turned on on holidays and turned off at other times.

How many refuse who later repent, and how many repent who refuse later on. Maybe the son who would not work in his father's vineyard did not really know or love his father. He liked the imaginary independence in being his own master outside of the vineyard. But later he changed; the vineyard appeared in a happier aspect, and the sentiments toward the father changed. The first son began by saying, "I will go, I am religious," but ended up by saying, "God is dead." The second one began by saying, "I will kill God," and ended up by saying, "God is life."

It could be that the two sons are symbols of Western civilization and Russian civilization. As Berdyayev and Gide have said, the "truth" of Communism comes from the betrayal of Christianity by Christendom. The one who said, "I will not go," is the one who may possibly go into the vineyard.

Two points are to be noted about the Russian people: first, their prophetic forebodings in the nineteenth century of twentieth-century godlessness, and secondly, their spiritual traits which are a basis of hope for world peace.

NINETEENTH-CENTURY PROPHECIES
ABOUT COMMUNISM

There has been a deep-seated tradition in Russia that it would one day become very wicked before it would ever become very good. Nineteenth-century Russia, which might be called the twilight of Communism, foresaw the terrible upheaval. Unlike the Western writers who were babbling "inevitable progress," the Russian writers were full of warning about bourgeois, materialistic civilization. Not shackled by standardized conventions, they saw more deeply the mystery of life and death. Leontyev believed the mission of the Russian people was to beget the Antichrist. He foresaw the revolution as a tyrannical and bloody one, attracting the people of the East and then going on to annihilate the bourgeois world of the West, bringing not the end of the world but the end of the epoch of materialism, nationalism, and liberalism. Pecherin believed that Russia would bring "its own annihilation" for which one would hate his country for a time, but in the end it would inaugurate a new cycle of world history. Pushkin foresaw the possibility "of a Russian revolt senseless and merciless," but in the end freedom rising on "her light-shedding wings." Lermontov in his poem "Prediction," written in 1830, foretold the revolution given in Gorodetsky's treatise:

> The day will come, for Russia that dark day
> When the Tsar's diadem will fall, and they,
> Rabble who loved him once, will love no more,
> And many will subsist on death and gore.
> Downtrodden law no shelter will provide
> For child or guiltless woman. Plague will ride
> From stinking corpses through the grief-stricken land
> Where fluttering rags from cottages demand
> Help none can give. A famine's gnawing pangs

Will grip the countryside with ruthless fangs.
Dawn on the streams will shed a crimson light.
And then will be revealed the Man of might
Whom thou wilt know; and thou wilt understand
Wherefore a shining blade is in his hand.
Sorrow will be thy lot, grief melt thine eyes
And he will laugh at all thy tears and sighs.

Tyutchev feared the dark, irrational elements in Russia would bring a catastrophe and foresaw Christianity as its saving power:

A homeless orphan, man, bereft of power
And naked, stands before the dread abyss,
Stands face to face in this his direful hour
With its dark emptiness: and all that quickens,
Glad things and light seem now a dream long past;
'T is familiar things, unsolved, as darkness thickens
Reveal his fated heritage at last.

Chaadayev foresaw the triumph of barbarism in Russia, saying: "It will triumph not because it is right, but because we are wrong." Dostoyevsky, in *The Possessed*, studied all the phases of man's rebellion against his Creator, concluding that the denial of God meant the deification of man. Evil degenerates into arbitrary self-will and finally to the setting up of oneself as arbitrary law. "Boundless liberty leads to a boundless tyranny." Atheism brings man face to face with dark, irrational forces and finally suicide. Kirillov reaches this conclusion: "The whole of history is divided into two parts; the first from the gorilla to the destruction of God, the second from the destruction of God to the change of the earth and of man. Everyone who wants to attain complete freedom must be daring enough to kill himself. Who dares to kill himself becomes God."

The revolution that Dostoyevsky saw coming was to him not a result of external forces, but an indication of a fracture of man's original relationship with God and His creatures. It would take on the form of socialism which is "concerned with atheism, a modern incarnation of godlessness, the tower of Babel built without God, not to raise earth to heaven, but to bring heaven to earth." Dostoyevsky makes the devil tell how socialism will organize everything: "We shall make them work, but in their spare time we shall organize their life like a children's game. . . . We shall allow them even sin, knowing they are so weak and helpless." Socialism was the escape from the burden of responsibility. Dostoyevsky predicted that Russia would undergo the "temptation of bread and power" of a godless social teaching. It would almost seem that he was writing in the twentieth century as he describes how the godless regime would work:

> Every member of society spies on the others, and it is his duty to inform against them . . . all are slaves, and equal in their slavery. Cicero will have his tongue cut out, Copernicus will have his eyes put out, Shakespeare will be stoned . . . slaves are bound to be equal. . . . A teacher who laughs with children at their God, and at their cradle is on our side; the lawyer who defends an educated murderer because he is more cultured than his victims and could not help murdering them to get money is one of us; the school boys who murder a peasant for the sake of sensation are ours; the juries who acquit every criminal are ours; the prosecutor who trembles in court because he fears he shall not be liberal enough is ours; among officials and literary men we have many adherents, and they don't know it themselves. . . . We will proclaim destruction, we will set fires going, we will set legends going, every scurvy group will be of use. Well there will be an upheaval; there's going to be such an upset as the world has never seen before. Russia will be overwhelmed with darkness, and the earth will weep for its gods.

But he never saw Communism as the final master of his country. In the *Journal of an Author,* published in 1881, he wrote:

Not in Communism, not in its mechanical forms is contained the socialism of the Russian people. They believe that the final salvation and the all-illuminating unity is in Christ and in Him alone. . . . The Russian people bear the image of Christ, and love Him alone.

Another Russian writer of the nineteenth century who saw both tragedy and hope ahead for Russia was Aleksey Khomyakov. The triumph of individualism in the Western world meant for him not progress but degradation. "Modern society in its decay releases every individual to the freedom of his own impotence." Russia was taking too many lessons from the Western world which had forgotten its God and was becoming "like a ship, on board of which only German words of command are heard." After a phase in which a godless fanaticism would possess Russia, he saw a dawn when Russia would give the Faith to Europe and be the medium of uniting Europe and Asia. He did not expect to see that day but believed it would come:

We must remember that not one of us will survive until the time of the harvest, but that our spiritual and ascetic labors of plowing, sowing, and weeding are not for Russia's sake alone, but for the sake of the whole world. This thought alone can give permanence to our efforts. Russian life holds many treasures not for her own people, but for many others, if not for all nations.

Solovyov, who died at the close of the last century, contended that the godless man had his origin in the rationalism and secularism of the Western world. Under its impact the Eastern people would degenerate into passive resignation to dictatorship. The Western people would become arrogant and proud. Despite the fact that he saw a vision of catastrophe ahead for the world because of its godlessness, he nevertheless believed that "Russia has a religious calling of worldwide significance. In the poverty and humiliation of her people are the signs of her special vocation."

Dostoyevsky best expressed the evil and the goodness in Russia in the terms of a young man in the land of the Gerasenes.

All the sores, all the foul contagions, all the impurities, all the devils great and small, have multiplied in that great invalid our beloved Russia. [But recalling that as the devil was cast out of the young man into the swine, which then plunged themselves into the sea, so the devils of Russia] will cast themselves down, possessed and raving from the rocks into the sea, and we shall all be drowned—and a good thing too, for that is all we are fit for, but Russia will be healed and will sit at the feet of Jesus and will look upon Him with astonishment. . . . Sin is a stench, but stench will pass when the sun rises. Sin is transient; Christ is eternal; our people are subject to many sins, but they have only one idea, only one true love, and that is Christ.

RUSSIAN SOUL

There are three great qualities of the Russian soul which warrant optimism as to the future brilliance of Russia: deep religious feeling, capacity for pain and suffering, and fellowship.

First, the deep religious feeling. Atheism is not natural to the Russian people; rather, it has been an importation from the Western world. The Russian people have never been concerned with the problem of atheism but only the problem of God's dealing with men in a sinful world. Russian writers and philosophers have seen in their country's persecution of religion only its attempt to ignore the truth. What is it that gives substance to the violence of their atheism if it be not the reality of the object which is attacked? Could men espouse prohibition unless there was something to prohibit; could there be anti-Christians unless there were Christians? How could there be atheists unless there were something to "atheate"? All atheists would be fools fighting against imaginary windmills if God did not exist. They are capable of denouncing sacred ideals, of blaspheming and deriding the truth they have worshiped, only because, fundamentally, they believe in God. Men cannot be so violent against myths. Only the reality of the Christ Whom they hate saves them from being fools fighting a figment of the imagination. Whence comes their idea of the communion of all men in one body, which is so foreign to Western individualism, if it be not from the very religion they attack?

Whence comes the idea of the brotherhood of men, of equal worth of all classes, so foreign to pagan Greece and liberal Europe, if it be not from Christianity whose fundamental doctrine they stole only to caricature? Dostoyevsky tells the story of a Russian peasant who fires a shot at the Host in the Eucharist. This reveals not only how little Christ's followers could expect mercy at the hands of that kind of an enemy, but it also reveals the astonishing power of faith in the persecutors. They believe in God, but being unable to love Him, they want to attack Him and destroy all those who dare worship Him, like a man who cannot love a woman whom he knows to be good, so he begins to hate her.

The basic reason why Communism appealed to Russia was religious. Deeply imbedded in the Russian soul were passionate religious convictions: the universal vocation of Russia to call all men to brotherhood, the need of sacrifice and pain to accomplish this mission, and the supreme need of resigning oneself to God's Will. Communism, in the face of a declining Church, promised the people the realization of these three ideals but without clearly telling them that they would be emptied of God. Brotherhood became a revolutionary proletariat; sacrifice became violence; and the Will of God became the will of the dictator. Communism is a religion, a surrender to an absolute. That is why it appeals to those who are without faith, and why *Soviet Russia is today regarded as the last hope of the Western man who lives without God.* As Communism fills up the void in the Western world created by a loss of faith, so it filled up the void in Russia made by a secularized or state Church. The Russian mind will not long remain satisfied with either atheism or a Church that becomes the instrument of a Communist ideology. As Khomyakov said, "We Russians do not belong to this doomed world," and their failure to become atheistic after thirty years of persecution proves that they possess a power for spiritual resistance which makes them the natural allies of their suffering brethren in the eastern part of Europe. Did but the Western democracies think less of political categories and more about spiritual realities, they would see a great bond existing between themselves and the Russian people. Not in the realm of war but of the spirit the solution of the problem is to be found.

Russia's capacity for pain and suffering is insatiable. It is a paradox but nevertheless true that the Russian soul is never completely happy unless its cup contains a few drops of the bitter draught of pain. While the Western Christian world emphasized the glory of the ascended Christ, Russia in its history has rather stressed the emptied Christ. As Nekrasov put it:

But only a Crown of Thorns
suited thy sullen beauty. . . .
Thou lovest the sufferer, O Russian folk,
the sufferings made us one.

The Western world has stressed the Glorified Christ, but the Russian Church has stressed the Suffering Christ, or the Christ of the Transfiguration, Who in the midst of His anticipated glory spoke to Moses and Elias of His Death. Many of the Russian churches in the north are dedicated to the Transfiguration, bearing witness to the need of sacrifice as the condition of betterment. Their word for ugliness, violence, and disorder is *besobrazie,* meaning "that which lost its image."

Even the very endurance, readiness for sacrifice, and power of faith that are revealed in the Russian Communists are a proof that they come from a dynamism of a soul far more intense than that of the dechristianized and disillusioned modern man of the Western world. Turgenev in the *Living Relic* tells of Kukera, the village beauty and best singer, who fell by accident from a staircase. Withered and paralyzed, left alone in a remote hut, hardly ever visited by anyone, she is all love and praise of God. Refusing to pray to be healed, she asks, "Why should I worry the Lord God? What can I ask of Him? He knows better than I do what I need. He sent me a cross which signifies that He loves me. We are commanded to understand it so." Asked if she wanted anything she answered, "I want nothing. I am content with everything, thank God, but you ought to persuade your mother to reduce the rent of the peasants."

It is no great mystery where the self-sacrifice of Russian Communism has its font and origin. Although it is hostile to Christianity, Communism is using the thousand-year-old Christian training of the Russian soul in the spirit of self-sacrifice and self-discipline. It is only because the shadow of Christ's Cross still falls across Russia that men are inspired to self-denial for a suprapersonal cause. Whether it knows it or not, Communism is living on Calvary's heritage, still so deep in the souls of the peasants—the very word in Russian meaning "Christian." If the impossible ever came to pass, that Christianity should be blotted out of the world, even Communism would lose its inspiration for sacrifice. No transfiguration of the soul or society is possible without descent into the abyss, where sin is purged away, as the Cross becomes the prelude to the crown. Thus while Communism attacks Christianity, it does so only by utilizing the very forces which Christianity has supplied. It was this that Soloviev had in mind when he said that "poverty and humiliation are the signs of its special preelection to a religious calling of worldwide significance." As the Christ by the example of His Love transformed the blasphemies of a suffering thief into a request for a heavenly kingdom, so too a day may dawn when another blasphemer with a capacity for pain will be lifted up by that same Christ, to hear the blessed words: "This day . . . Paradise."

There may then be verified the truth contained in the poem of Aleksandr Blok, who the very year after the Bolshevik revolution pictures the soldiers of the Red Army going through the country, chanting: "Freedom, Freedom, hey, hey! Freedom without a Cross."

They shoot a bourgeois girl who happens to be unfaithful. A little noise disturbs them, and a half-vision moves in front of them; they can see nobody distinctly, and they receive no answer, so they fire in the dark. The poet continues:

So they go with sovereign tread . . .
Behind them a hungry cur,
And at their head, with a bloodstained banner
Invisible in the raging snow,
Unwounded midst the bullets' flight,
With gentle gait above the storm,
Scattered o'er with pearls of snow,
With a white aureaole of roses,
At their head goes Jesus Christ.

SOLIDARITY

The third characteristic of the Russian people is a deep sense of fellowship and solidarity with their fellowman. The Western world is inclined to be individualistic in religion. A society begins to decay when it "releases every individual to the freedom of his own impotence." One of the most common words of the Russian language is *sobornost,* which means the transcendence of all petty categories, races, and classes for the sake of humanity. It was natural for Communism, with its emphasis on the collectivity, to arise as an ersatz substitute for the Christian spirit of fraternity which possessed the Russian soul for centuries. One finds something of this symphonic spirit, in which all work together, in the Russian writer Gogol. In his work *The Cloak,* he tells of a stupid clerk who, when teased in his office, used to ask, "Am I not your brother?" One meets it also in Tolstoy's reflections as he wandered about the poor quarters of Moscow:

I beheld the misery, cold, hunger, humiliation of thousands of my fellow men. . . . I feel, and can never cease to feel, myself a partaker in a crime which is constantly being committed, so long as I have superfluous food while others have none, so long as I have two coats while there exists one man without any. . . . I must seek in my heart at every moment, with meekness and humility, some opportunity for doing the job Christ wants done. Can I not be of some use to stop up a hole? To wipe something with? Can I not be used as an example of meanness, of vice and sin?

This deep sense of solidarity with one's brother is a perfect, natural medium on which Divine Grace can work, and just as the Savior once praised the Roman sergeant who built a synagogue for the Jews out of a deep sense of the oneness of humanity, so too there may be reserved for a future day praise for the Russians, who, though presently delayed in the totalitarian drive of Communism, are nevertheless on the way to that Communionism where Christ is the Brother of all men and God their heavenly Father.

Though these writers of the nineteenth century knew that the revolt against God was coming and that Russia would be at the head of it, enslaving men under the guise of liberation, they nevertheless were convinced that the deep-rooted faith of the Russian people would one day be a light and beacon to the world. There are about 200 million people in Russia, and it must be repeated that less than 6 million of them are members of the Communist Party. Hidden underneath the tatters of their crucifixion is the promise of a resurrection. As one of their modern poets, Andrey Bely, wrote of Russia's mystical expectation, in her present agony of being nailed to the cross:

Russia—you are today the bride.
Receive the message of spring.

TRANSFIGURATION

What is true of individuals is true of nations; it is their transfiguration, not their defeat, for which we must yearn. Magdalen the sinner was not crushed but transformed, so that the passion that once burned for the flesh now burned for the spirit. God did not raise up a saint to battle the Manicheanism of Augustine; Augustine the saint answers Augustine the rhetorician: "As I live, saith the Lord God, I desire not the death of the wicked, but that the wicked turn from his way, and live" (Ezek. 33:11). Those who mock may one day pray; those who ignore may one day acknowledge; but those of the Western world who know God and yet ignore may be cast out. The patronizing indifference to religion of our Western bourgeois would never suit the passion of the Russian soul. One of two things had to happen: either radical denial with persecution or integral acceptance.

Russia is now in the first stage of persecution, but through our prayers and charities we can hasten the day when the Lord's words will be fulfilled: "Behold I do new things, and now they shall spring forth, verily you shall know them" (Isa. 43:19). It would be wrong for those who remain in the Father's house to complain like the elder son against the return of the prodigal son, for he who would resent the return of a sinner thereby makes himself unworthy of the Kingdom of God. Not in war but in prayer must we trust that the land which once was known as Holy Russia may become again the wellspring whence a pure stream of Christianity may flow. Then shall we see fulfilled the words of the Russian poet Khomyakov, who was conscious first of Russia's great sins:

But now, alas, what sins lie heavy,
Many and awful on thy soul!
Thou art black with black injustice,
And slavery's yoke has branded thee,
And godless flattery and baneful lying
And sloth that's shameful, life-denying,
And every hateful thing in thee I see.

But then he saw in his land a vessel of election summoning souls to penance:

For all that cries for consolation,
For every law that we have spurned,
For sins that stain our generation,
For evil deeds our Fathers learned,
For all our country's bitter passion,
Pray ye with tears the while we live.
O God of Might, of Thy compassion
May'st Thou forgive! May'st Thou forgive!

There are other indications of hope such as the dialogue that is being developed between Communists and Christians. This is due in part to the fact that the Marxists have begun to discuss freedom and man in a larger context than that of Marx, while Christians on the other hand are attempting to rescue what is good in Marx from the Stalinists, dogmatists, and party leaders. A Yugoslavic writer, Dobrica Cosič wrote:

> Man is not only healthy, positive, good, reasonable. Man is also sick, dark, unreliable, insincere, evil, and dangerous. He will remain so for so long as he inhabits this earth. Communism will not be a paradise of angels without God. It will not be the "happy society of happy people." We cannot believe in such an end to history; that would be apocalyptic error, that would be theology, naïveté, conscious deceit, the negation of freedom.

The new human nature promised by Communism is not arriving and it is not going to arrive.

NEW ATTITUDE TOWARD CHRIST

In a higher realm there has been very significant change among Soviet historians about the Person of Christ. The Communist position has been, up to the present time, that Christ did not exist; He is a myth, a legendary figure. This was in accordance with the theory of Engels that Christianity had originated outside of Palestine.

But the change began in February, 1966, when the principal atheistic journal of the Soviet Union, called *Science and Religion,* contained two articles, one by the historian Sergei Skazkin of the Academy of Sciences of the USSR. This historian lent his authority to an article by another historian, A. Kazhdan. The point of the article was to overthrow the atheistic pamphlets such as "The Legend of Jesus Christ" and also the myth that Christ was invented in order to aid exploiters. Kazhdan used the following arguments to prove that Christ was an historical figure. One, there is a strong tradition to the effect that the Gospel of Matthew existed originally in Aramaic and then later on was translated into Greek. Two, it is unlikely that a myth-forming process could have developed a mythical Christ so quickly, for in the whole history of Rome there is not a single instance of a god becoming a man; it was rather the reverse process which was common. Three, the theory that Christianity is an assemblage of mythical elements of other religions such as the Virgin Birth, Resurrection is rejected:

> If Christianity did not fall from Heaven (and a good atheistic historian is bound to deny precisely such a notion!), it must have had a founder. This religious reformer might well have been named by his followers Messiah, the Christ.

Four, Kazhdan is not very much impressed by the argument that there are not many historical records of the first century. He quotes the following example from Russian history; "In 907 Prince Oleg sacked Constantinople. This was an event of primary importance for all his contemporaries and for history. Yet, not a single Byzantine historian notes that fact." Five, "the Gospels are evidently based on different versions of oral tradition. For instance, had the authors of the Gospels invented the date of Christ's birth, they would have been unanimous about it."

Another writer in the same issue, Nevgod, goes a step further and argues that the sayings ascribed to Christ reflect a living, oral speech addressed to fishermen, peasants, tradesmen, and these are to be ascribed to the Person of Christ Himself. This brings up the question which Nevgod formulates: "Having acknowledged the historical existence of Christ, where do we go from here?" At this point the Soviets go on to say that they must deny the Resurrection and therefore the Divinity of Christ. Because this radical change has taken place in Russia, and because whenever Russia sneezes, the Marxists outside of Russia blow their noses, the French Communists—who had published a month before an article saying that the existence of Christ was a myth—in the following issue reflected the idea of Moscow that He was an historical character.

This rejection of the myth theory is already making its impact on the lower levels of Russian life. Within a few months after the article of Kazhdan appeared, the Moscow publishing house issued a book called *Biblical Stories* which retold incidents which happened to Moses and other Old Testament characters. Up to this point Moses and others were considered myths. Here there is an acknowledgment that they really existed. But in order to minimize this sudden change in Soviet.policies there were commentaries written ridiculing the stories. Some of them authored by Alexander Osipof, an ex-priest turned atheist. Despite the attempt to minimize the effect of biblical stories on readers, within a very few hours the first edition of 100,000 copies was completely sold out.

Though the son who said to his father, "I will not go into the vineyard," has not yet returned to the vineyard, evidently he is thinking about it.

The High Cost of Peace

We live in an age of violence. But the kind we are using is wrong. Presently violence is understood only in relation to others, such as wars, mugging and assassination, rioting. This violence may be literary as well as physical. We live in an age of judges, in which the best of motives of others is impugned. Many articles in contemporary magazines are born of an uneasy conscience. When David heard of a man who stole a lamb from another, he decreed that his punishment should be death. It took Nathan to remind him that he had already stolen another man's wife; it was the uneasy conscience within that made him warlike against others.

Analyze some of the peace lovers of today, and it will be found that at bottom they are cowards. Psychologically, the man who uses violence toward others is often a coward turned tough. Violence and cowardice are related in somewhat the same way as a bow that is taut and a bow that is relaxed. Peter, who drew his sword to hack off the ear of the high priest's servant, was later on the coward who denied that he knew his Master. On the other hand, He whose soul was all love refused to draw the sword. He was not afraid of the Cross.

Some are afraid of making enemies against themselves; others believe in letting evil conquer as they let sleeping dogs lie; others flatter themselves that they are good-natured, benevolent, tolerant, when actually they are cowards. Their longing for peace is often an indifference to good and evil. It was against this mediocrity and temporizing with evil that Christ said, "I came not to bring peace but the sword." But did not Christ also say to Peter, "Put your sword back into the scabbard"? There are two kinds of swords, because violence is of two kinds: violence to others and violence to ourselves. He who is not at war with himself is at war with others. Violence to ourselves means nonviolence to neighbor. This is the high price of peace.

Christian nonviolence is no more related to cowardice than chastity is related to impotency. Christian nonviolence means not only nonviolence to our neighbor but a violence to ourselves. One turns the sword inward to cut out one's own egotism and selfishness, in order that the sword will not be directed against the neighbor. The peacemakers, the last group mentioned in the Beatitudes, are those who have already passed through the other Beatitudes— namely, have known poverty of spirit, have wept tears for their own sins, and have been humbled.

Nonviolence to Gandhi, who was the greatest exponent of it in our contemporary civilization, meant two things: first of all, truth, and secondly, love of neighbor. (1)Truth (*satya*), which for him was the voice of conscience; one must first determine what is morally right before heaven. (2) *Ahimsa; ahimsa* was not negative but was a love of neighbor; it was not passivity but a love force; not a weak submission to the will of the evildoer, but the putting of the whole force of one's soul against the will of a tyrant. As Gandhi put it: "It is not nonviolence when we love those who hate us. Nonviolence implies a complete self-purification."

There is no doubt that Gandhi derived this notion from Christianity, for he said, "One seeks to convert his opponent by sheer force of character and suffering. . . . I saw that nations, like individuals, could only be made through the agony of the Cross."

This kind of nonviolence, therefore, costs something. First of all, it costs self-purification of all egotism and pride. It never antagonizes the neighbor, provokes him to a fight, but loves him. It is much easier to carry a placard than to carry a cross; to shout a hymn of hate than to give a drink of cold water to a neighbor or to mortify our anger. The great defect in many of our peace demonstrators is that, while they are opposed to war, they wage no war—that is, they wage no war against themselves. This kind of a peace lover is at bottom a coward. As Gandhi said, "If the only choice was between violence and cowardice, I should not hesitate to choose violence."

If he who, in answer to evil, answers violence by violence, there will be multiplication of violence. If there are ten men in the line, and hatred is preached to them, the first one in hatred strikes his neighbor, the second one strikes his neighbor, the third his neighbor, and so forth; there is only one way to stop it, and that is for someone to turn the other cheek and absorb the violence. Then it will not be communicated to another. But is not this absorption of violence, and this digestion of evil from another, a form of suffering? Precisely this. Simone Weil said, "He who will not take up the sword must perish by the cross."

Cup and Sword

In the Garden of Gethsemane there was a contrast between Peter's violence in using the sword and Our Lord's submission in drinking what He called the cup of the Passion. What we have here is the contrast of the cup and the sword. The sword is the physical sign of violence and resistance either for attack or for defense, the symbol of secular authority and carnal power. When Peter unsheathed his sword, Our Blessed Lord told him to put it back into its scabbard, for he who takes the sword will perish by the sword; Blood begets blood. As Napoleon said, "There is one thing you cannot do with bayonets, and that is sit on them." It is, however, to the credit of St. Peter that just a short time before his death, when Nero was emperor and was butchering and killing the Christians and using them as Roman candles to illumine his chariot course, Peter wrote and said, "Obey the emperor." While Our Lord was telling Peter to put down the sword, He was prepared to drink the Chalice saying, "If it be possible, let this Chalice pass from Me, but not My Will but Thine be done."

This submission of Our Blessed Lord to violence was for higher spiritual ends. John the Baptist had sent from prison ambassadors to Our Lord asking: "Are You the One or shall we look for another?" Probably the reason that John had doubts was because Our Lord was not using His power to release him from prison. Our Lord answered, "Blessed are they who shall not be scandalized in Me." John was learning that Our Blessed Lord brought a Cross, and it must be sufficient even unto death. John must submit to Herod as Our Blessed Lord would submit to Pilate. As John the Baptist was looking for some show of power, so Peter was manifesting that power by the sword. The prayer offered by Our Blessed Lord accepting the cup touches everything in human life from the center to the circumference.

There is something of this mystery hidden in the Russian story of the *Yurodivy*, which means "born poor." These people in concentration camps take on the punishment that is directed to others. They know that many, when they are punished by the guards, will return hate and thus multiply the evil in the world. The *Yurodivy*, however, take the violence and forgive, thus diminishing the content of evil in the world. Our Lord in the Garden is powerless Goodness. This is His Cup. He gives no certitude of victory to comparatively righteous causes, for conflict is between apparently righteous causes. The cup must be drunk in the face of the sword.

We have this queer combination of Divine powerlessness in two verses of the Creed: "I believe in God, the Father Almighty" and then "in Jesus Christ Who suffered under Pontius Pilate and was crucified." In the first instance, we have power; in the second instance, we have apparent powerlessness. The powerlessness of the Cup and the Cross is no bogus promise to historical success. Therefore, on the Cross His enemies sneered, "Come down, and we will believe." The test of power was the overcoming of the enemy who had nailed Him. If He came down, He never would have saved us.

The Goodness of Christ can be emulated only by the disavowal of power, or the putting of Peter's sword back again into its scabbard. Gustave Thibon has said, "There is a vast gulf between the man who is so weak that he is incapable of taking his revenge, and who therefore puffs himself up with pride, assiduously fostering his deficiency in a sort of travesty of religious virtue, and the man who knows with all the bitterness of self-knowledge that he is strong, and yet avoids taking his revenge because he has enough supernatural love to acquiesce in such a humiliation of his nature." The Christian doctrine is not too weak for our times; it is too strong for our times. Most of us are too good to succeed in the world, but not good enough to overcome it.

IV

ALPHA AND OMEGA:
THE BEGINNING AND THE END

CHAPTER FIFTEEN

The Death of God

When Mark Twain was in Europe, he heard that an America newspaper had printed an obituary notice of his death. He immediately sent a cablegram reading: "The reports of my death are greatly exaggerated." It has now been eighty years since Nietzsche (1844–1900) announced the death of God. But as some popularizers pick up Nietzsche's theme, others with Shakespeare ask:

Say from whence
You owe this strange intelligence.

PASSIVE ATHEISM

The Name "God" Is Dead

Here the problem is one of communication—namely, how to make the reality of God clear to our age. Pope John expressed this concern in saying that the deposit of truth remains always the same, but the manner of describing and explaining that truth differs from age to age. St. Paul had to face this difficulty in translating the Hebrew idioms of religion into Greek. In the Middle Ages, St. Thomas Aquinas had to lift philosophy out of its Platonic mold into that of Aristotle.

Some say that the name "God" is dead, on the basis of a philosophy called Linguistic Analysis or Analytic Philosophy or the Philosophy of Analysis. Actually, it has been refuted by many thinkers, but the God-is-dead group ignore the refutation. Their argument is this: We live in a technological, scientific civilization, in which it is possible to verify any kind of knowledge experimentally. No name is valid unless one can apply to it the "verification principle," such as was proposed by A. J. Ayer in his *Truth and Logic*. According to him, all statements about metaphysics, philosophy, and theology are not true or false; they are meaningful or meaningless. Have they any sense in our technological context? Do they fit into our secular city, where man is capable of doing everything from flying to the moon to changing genes? This language philosophy, as Ludwig Wittgenstein stated, demands that every name or word be subject to "logical atomism"—that is, be split into parts and analyzed scientifically, to see if it makes sense for our highly technical, experimental world.

Applying the scientific tests of whether or not a word is meaningful, these philosophers conclude that any biblical thought or philosophical thought, such as "There is a God" or "God is a Father" or "God loves us as a Father loves children," is meaningless. Such ideas fitted into an ancient context of civilization but not into our secularized mold. The word "God" conveys to them no information whatever; neither does "religion." The word "God" is what might be called a *blik*, which is a Dutch word for "view," and in this particular case, it means a word where no reality is visible All talk about God and religion and the Heavenly Father is just a *blik*—void of knowledge.

Failure of Analytic Philosophy

What is to be thought of this linguistic school? The first difficulty is that it is too unmodern, too unsecular, not sufficiently contemporary; it is behind the times and out of keeping with our technological civilization. Everything our modern linguistic philosophers say has been said before by Roscellinus of the eleventh century; for him names were meaningless and without reference to reality; they were alien to the world in which he lived.

One of the pupils of Roscellinus was Peter Abelard, whom everyone remembers in connection with Héloïse. But he was more famous still for combating his teacher. Abelard traveled about Europe on his donkey, arguing against the linguistic school of Roscellinus. In his own lifetime he convinced all thinking men "Roscellinus is dead" and that we were not talking in circles when we use names. It is surprising that in this country we should be so medieval as to revise this antiquated theology. It is no wonder that the philosopher G. E. Moore, after hearing Dr. Tillich read a paper describing linguistic analysis, said to him, "No, really, Dr. Tillich, I don't think I've been able to understand a single sentence of your paper. Won't you please try to state one sentence, or even one word, so that we can all understand it?"

A second difficulty with linguistic analysis is that it assumes that the only knowledge we have is scientific knowledge. It forgets that we have knowledge of two different types of things: objects and persons. Persons are not subject to computers as are objects. God does not belong in the category of objects; God belongs in a category of persons. The two are known in entirely different ways. Suppose that the wife of one of the linguistic philosophers asks her husband, "Do you love me?" He answers, "Well, don't I let you use my credit card? Don't I allow your mother—and I hate it—to spend two months with us every year? Don't I pay for twelve permanents a year? Haven't I fixed fourteen fenders and paid six traffic tickets? Why do you ask, 'Do you love me'?" Now this linguistic philosopher has given an answer to his wife in terms of verification. He has pointed to certain behavioral patterns that can be added up and counted, but he has not answered the question of his wife, "Do you love me?" That kind of knowledge is not communicated by an IBM machine.

One linguistic philosopher of the United States has a pet name for his wife, and she has one for him. This very well-known God-is-deader calls his wife Sugar, and she calls him Diabetes. He calls her Sugar because she is so sweet. She calls him Diabetes because he is so fond of Sugar as to be in danger of being diabetic. Logically "atomize" these two words. Do they refer to anything that is verifiable? Are they not *bliks*? If we say that words are meaningless unless they can be scientifically verifiable, then one would have to say that both the wife and the husband were nonexistent or, better, that the "wife is dead" and the "husband is dead." St. Paul says something of the same kind when he puts love beyond all verifiable behavior, even what seems so meaningful.

"If I should give all my goods to the poor and deliver my body to be burned, and have not love, it profits me nothing." As it has been well said, "Physics may one day find the answer to all physical questions, but not all the questions are physical questions."

Persons and the love of persons are beyond scientific technological knowledge. Suppose that all the linguistic philosophers were challenged to prove that they were legitimate children of their father and mother. How many could prove it? They might become very angry, but what scientifically verifiable information could they give then and there? They might answer, "I have been loved since earlier memories. I not only know my parents, but I have been known by them, and nothing constitutes a greater certitude for me than being known and being loved." Others say, "I have a certitude, quite beyond any proof that I can give you, that I am a child of God. I only know that I've been known by God and that I've been loved by God." Are we to insist that either our parents or God should use hard-sell or soft-sell arguments to prove their love daily or that God should use cosmic commercials in order to break down our cosmic resistance? In a certain sense, we do not prove God; it is God Who proves us. "Lord, Thou hast searched me out and hast known me," wrote Bonhoeffer in prison. Man does not really ask so much if God is a person, but: "Am I a person? Am I all that I ought to be? Have I realized the full potentiality of my personality?"

Linguistic or analytic philosophy arises because we are so far away from the reality of things. We rarely see a sunset in the city. Many a city boy has never seen a cow. Through advertising we think that milk comes from Mr. Borden instead of Mrs. Cow. Kant once said that there were two things that filled his heart with wonder: one was the starry heavens above his head; the other, the moral law within his breast. The moral law has vanished, inasmuch as the psychiatrist has told him there is no guilt. The starry heavens he cannot see. Neon lights do not make one think of the Giver of Light but rather: "Look, Ma, see what we have done!"

Besides *problems*, there are *mysteries*. Problems are outside of me, mysteries are inside of me. Man who is face to face with a mystery is not up against something of which he is ignorant and cannot find words to express; he is up against something which strikes him with awe. Straining to make a language meaningful, analytic philosophy has ignored the mystery of life. When a biologist has completely dissected the frog and analyzed all of its parts and given each of them names, does he understand the frog any better than before he cut it? When one unwraps layer after layer of an onion, what is left besides the odor? Analysis of water in a sinking ship does not prove that the ship itself is not sinking. We are very apt to ignore the nature of birds if all of our study is made upon the redbird that always flies backward to see where it came from.

God Himself Is Dead

Now we come to the other side of the God-Is-Dead movement in which the Reality of God is denied, not just the name we give Him. This demands explanation. Man has two faculties: the intellect and the will. One by which he knows the truth, and the other by which he loves it. It is possible for a man to darken his intellect, and it is also possible for him to blind his will. Modern atheists give no arguments against the existence of God. Their originality lies in the fact that they *will* that there be no God. A good principle to go on in judging any intellectual position is to consider not only *what* is said, but *why* it is said. What is important is not the reasons they give against God, but the motives behind their denial.

In days when photographs of Presidents were very rare, Lincoln was entering a hospital in Alexandria. A young man running out of the hospital knocked Lincoln over, sent him sprawling on the floor. Over his prostrate form, he said, "Get out of the way, you long, lean, lanky stiff." Lincoln looked up at him and said, "Young man, what is troubling you on the inside?" There is an intimate correlation between a philosophy of life and the way one lives. If one does not live according to a philosophy of life, one will soon be making a philosophy of life to suit one's behavior.

The old Socratic error was that all evil was due to ignorance. It was then assumed that if everyone was given a sufficient education, character would result. But character is not in the intellect but in the will. Education can make clever devils out of what would ordinarily have been very stupid devils. Even in the Church, there is a tendency sometimes to reduce a religious life to a thoroughgoing knowledge of catechism. Judas had very good catechetical instruction, and yet he turned out badly. Our Blessed Lord said, "If you do My Will, you will know My doctrine." He did not say, "If you know My doctrine, you will do My will." The reason why a man believes is to be found in his right moral state and the cause, very often, of a wrong belief is a wrong moral state.

There are different kinds of truths: Some are speculative and addressed wholly to the intellect as truths of mathematics, physics, and astronomy. Some are aesthetic and are addressed to the taste and the sense of the beautiful. Some are moral and suppose a moral sense for their apprehension. Some are religious and spiritual and suppose a religious or spiritual state of mind for their understanding. Speculative truths imply understanding; aesthetic truths presume cultivation; and Scripture says that, as an animal cannot know what is going on in the mind of man, so man cannot understand what is going on in one who has the spirit of God in him. Hence, St. Paul says: "If our Gospel be hid, it is hid to them that are lost." A marriage counselor who beats his wife is hardly equipped to instruct others on how to be happy though married.

This is not to say that a particular atheist must necessarily be a particularly bad man, but it is to say that one must, in dealing with beliefs, see the correlation between *willing, doing,* and *knowing.* It would seem that one should know first, then later on would follow the willing and the doing. One might object, "I must know a theory before I can put it into practice." In some instances theory does precede practice, but practice in other instances precedes theory. Did men never sow and reap until they had analyzed soil and developed a Department of Agriculture? Did they never use wheat until chemistry had taught them how much gluten, starch, and phosphate there was in the grain, and taught them how essential it was to the physiology of the human body? Did men never lay four walls of a building until they had mastered the entire science of architecture? Do children study grammar, or do they first learn to talk? Did men wait until Aristotle had constructed his logic before they reasoned?

How many theologians there are who are not saints, and how many saints there are who are not theologians! The Lord thanked the Heavenly Father that He had hidden the great truths from university professors and revealed them to little ones. Granting then that there is a certain reasonableness in saying that doing may precede knowledge, where does the willing come in? The willing here means a moral determination toward God, a submission of affections and desires to do His Will. It means a receptivity and an openness to the truth that is revealed. When one does not act on a truth already given, very often no new truth is revealed. Pascal has said, "The reception of truth is a moral act," and Fichte stated, "If the will be steadfastly and sincerely fixed on what is good, the understanding will of itself discover what is true." The nineteenth-century professor T. H. Huxley stated, "The great deeds of philosophers have been less the fruit of their intellect than that of the direction of that intellect by an eminently religious tone of mind. Truth has yielded herself rather to their patience, their love, their logical acumen." Uprightness of heart is one of the indispensable conditions for ever understanding religious truth.

I, who taught philosophy for twenty-five years, look back upon a great defect in teaching history of philosophy. Almost every textbook gives the dates of each philosopher's birth and death, but tells practically nothing about his life. It was not just his brain or his intellect which wove out certain theories by which he later became known; there were at work all of his emotions, decisions, faults, jealousies, hopes, and aberrations. Is not the dialectical materialism of Marx better understood when one realizes that Marx himself never worked? Why did Lenin and Dostoyevsky turn out so differently, from an intellectual point of view, when there was common in the lives of both incidents which would break a human spirit?

Beliefs Are Affected by Morals

Behavior affects one's beliefs. Why is it, when a strong argument for morality is presented to A and to B, that A will accept and B will not? Since the cause is the same, the effect ought to be the same—but it is not. There must be some other factor present which makes one man embrace and the other reject. There is an X factor, which is not intellectual, but which belongs in the will or conduct. As Thomas Aquinas put it in his own finely chiseled way: "Divine things are known in different ways by men according to the diversity of their attitudes. Those who have good will perceive Divine things according to truth; those who have not good will perceive them in a confused way which makes them doubt and feel they are mistaken." The message of the angels on Christmas night was that only men of goodwill would become God's friends.

There may be intellectual atheism, but there is more often an atheism of the will; that is why the Psalmist places atheism not in the mind but in the heart: "The fool said in his heart, there is no God." Escapist minds take refuge in the use of scientific truths as a basis, because scientific truths are impersonal and nonethical, and create no personal demands. Even psychological statements rarely demand moral amendment; we can remain as spectators to the truth. But moral and religious truths do involve *me* uniquely and with an urgency that is at first frightening. The woman at the well was very willing to discuss with Our Blessed Lord the geographical or theological problem of whether one should worship in Jerusalem or Mt. Gerazim, but when Our Blessed Lord brought the theological problem down to the concrete order and told her that she had five husbands—then she changed the subject. A woman in an audience heard a preacher go through the Commandments, and after each Commandment, as he gave them in order, she shouted out, "Amen! Amen!" When finally he came to the Commandment "Thou shalt not commit adultery," she said, "Now he is beginning to meddle."

Atheism and agnosticism can be moral positions rather than intellectual. They are ways of making oneself invulnerable to Divine Truth, responsibility, and upright ordering of life. "Anyone who acts shamefully hates the light, will not come into the light, for fear that his doings will be found out. Whereas the man whose life is true comes to the light, so that his deeds may be seen for what they are, deeds done in God" (John 3:20–21). "You pore over the scriptures, thinking to find eternal life in them (and indeed, it is of these I speak as bearing witness to me): but you will not come to me, to find life. I do not mean that I look for honour from men, but that I can see you have no love of God in your hearts" (John 5:39–42). "They profess recognition of God but their practice contradicts it; it is they who are abominable, who are disloyal, who are ill qualified for the practice of any virtue" (Titus 1:16).

It is not always possible to investigate the behavior or conduct of irreligious, atheistic writers, and there may be some who lead fairly decent lives. Sometimes this could be not because they have abandoned passions but because passions have abandoned them. But it could also be because they have stolen some splinters from the cross of self-discipline and found a bit of peace. Three kinds of dirt can accumulate on the windows of the soul to keep God's light from coming in. There is a carnal dirt or sexual excesses; money dirt or lust for possessions, and egocentric dirt or selfishness and vanity. "Blessed are the clean of heart, for they shall see God."

The Will to Deny God

Study the great atheists of literature, and it will be found that they rejected God—they pushed Him away. "We will not have Him reign over us."

Such atheism is more properly antitheism; it is less godlessness than anti-God. As Nietzsche puts it in one of his works: "I have killed God because He separates me from men, and now His death isolates me more than ever. I will not allow this great Cadaver to poison my human friendships." There can hardly be a denial of God when one is constantly accusing Him of injustice. Fists are not lifted against high Heaven in revolt, unless there be One against Whom one takes up the cudgels. The very sentences in which they declare God nonexistent, they reproach Him for diminishing their godlikeness; the very phrase in which they call Him dead, they charge Him with being a living devil. The heavens cannot be so empty if the atheists are angry at its emptiness.

Camus revolted against the human condition of man, but the revolt against the mortal condition of man has no sense if it is addressed to no one and if there is no one responsible for the condition. Why is death a problem? Why is the existence of conscience a problem, and the desire of happiness and immortality? Why this dynamism of my being which rejects all limitations and seeks to get beyond limit, if it be not a prayer to God turned upside down.

The new existential atheism starts with a kind of atheistic egotism. Its argument in part is moral and in part philosophical. The moral argument is, as one of the atheists in the novel of Dostoyevsky put it, "Without God all things are possible." A popular God-is-dead book in the United States argues that homosexuality will become normal in a humanistic society where there is no restriction of morals which come from religion. St. Paul declared homosexuality and atheism were related to one another as effect to cause. Nietzsche argued precisely for this point in his "transformation of values"—namely, sin and crime should be multiplied to a point where one cay say, "Evil, be thou my good; good, be thou my evil." In upsetting the world and its Christian values, night will become day, and day will become night.

The philosophical argument is closely related to this—namely, the existence of God restricts liberty. As a German philosopher put it: "If it could be absolutely proved that God existed, I should still deny His existence because He set limits to my independence." Madame Simone de Beauvoir, at the age of fourteen, said that she deliberately gave up her faith and did so with tears. But, she added, she had to give up God in order to affirm her freedom.

NIETZSCHE

Nietzsche, the son of a minister, began with a profound love of God, then rejected it to avoid all limits to his self-will. André Gide said of him, "In the presence of the Gospel, Nietzsche's immediate and profound reaction—which must be admitted—was jealousy." In his last work, Nietzsche keeps Christ in the background. So much was the Gospel and the Light of Christ before him that he parodied the Last Supper, the Mount of Olives, the Death on the Cross, the Beatitudes. Nothing reveals the inner loneliness of such a one better than a letter that Nietzsche wrote to his sister: "A man of spiritual depth needs friends, unless he still has God as a Friend. But I have neither God nor friends." About the same time he wrote: "Doubt devours me. I have killed the Law, and now it haunts me as a cadaver haunts a living person. If I am not *more* than the Law, then I am among the damned souls, the most damned."

But as atheism is not just a positive conclusion but rather a negation of reality, he is as one who wandered among men and ideas like Adam outside of Paradise. As a young man, he asked of God in a poem:

What dost Thou ask of me, Thou Thief of the great highways?
Thou wantest me—all of me?

Later he wrote:

I want to know You, Unknown One,
You who are reaching deep into my soul
And ravaging my life, a savage gale.
You Inconceivable yet Related One!
I want to know You—even serve.

He also jotted down in his notebook in Latin: "Life, thou art my cross; cross, thou art my life." Later on, after willing to negate God, he wrote that his world was based on illusions: Thus the cycle began, and it goes on, but where will it end? After having run a full course, whither are we to turn? Perhaps we will have to make a new start with faith? Perhaps . . ."

At the age of forty-three he wrote: "I have now lived for forty-three years, and I am just as lonely as I was in the years of my childhood."

After he had finished *Zarathustra*, he fell into a melancholic depression. Meeting an astronomer near Florence, he said to a companion about the visit, "I wish this man had not read my books. He is too good. My influence on him could be very disastrous." Just a few years before he died, he wrote to his friend, Peter Gast: "I live constantly under the cynicism of danger without an answer to the question of life." Nietzsche's life could very much be like the story of the angels, who lived with God on probation and then shouted, *"Non serviam,"* and rebelled to a place prepared for them. Nietzsche at the age of twelve wrote: "I saw God in His Splendour in a vision." Now in his last years he was like one of the fallen angels, not able to leave alone the Flame of Divine Love.

ANDRÉ GIDE

André Gide's atheism was also willed. He felt that if he could kill conscience, then he could kill God. When Paul Claudel tried to arouse his conscience at the end of his life, Gide answered, "I have ceased to worry about my soul, conscience, and salvation." But he did continue to worry. In his work *Strait Is the Gate* there is a satire about God and conscience. God is pictured as a wealthy banker who at one moment hands out wealth to every passerby and the next moment boxes the ears of those to whom He gives wealth. God would not let Gide alone, so Gide would not let God alone. In *Prometheus Illbound,* there is again the theme of conscience in which Prometheus, full of gratitude and guilt in regard to the Divine Lover, is devoured by the eagle, which is his conscience. Then he hits upon the idea of devouring the eagle; from that point on lives in "peace."

The point is that through the denial of conscience, Gide seeks to arrive at the denial of God, which is necessary in order to avoid responsibility and judgment. The theme of religion and conscience appear again in the form of a Protestant minister who takes a young girl into his home to educate. Under the spell of his love, he makes her believe there is no such thing as sin. She later on realizes her sin and drowns herself. The pastor revolts against religion, which made a sin of what was a sweet experience in his life. The denial of God is forged not out of thought but out of an evil life.

Still using religious themes to defend irreligion, antireligion in his *The Return of the Prodigal,* Gide pictures himself returning again to the Father's house, but before entering, being seized with a nostalgia for those sinful wastes from which he had fled. This is the tragic secret of his life. Writing about that work in *Morceaux choisis,* he said, "Christ's words blazed out before me like the pillar of fire which led the chosen people through the night and amid the thick darkness into which I *determined* to plunge." In what appears to be atheism there is a terrible frightening consciousness of Christ. In his fragments of a spiritual diary entitled, *Numquid et Tu,* Christ frightens him out of his false peace, His words standing out like pillars of fire, as he writes: "Terrible filth, the filth of sin. Ashes left by an impure flame, dross—canst Thou cleanse me from it all, O Lord? that with pure voice I may sing Thy praise."

A few months later appear in his diary frightening words about the devil:

> If I could at least relate this drama, could depict Satan as he is when he has taken possession of a man, could relate how he makes use of him to influence others! An absurd notion, you may think. But I have lately come to understand it for the first time. You are not merely taken prisoner, but the evil which is an active power demands from you an activity in its service. You are compelled to fight in a false and perverse cause.

Why is it that a man whose first principle is, "There are no fairies," spends his life writing about them, fighting them off, spitting at them, and scratching to get them out of his hair? Such writers remind one of a poem of the young Soviet writer, Aleksandr Blok, which pictured atheistic Russian soldiers shooting at a Host carried by a priest. Would they shoot at bread? Sane men can endure the sight of virtue. Versilov, the atheist in Dostoyevsky, could not; it made him mad. The older torment of writers comes from not living up to the meaning of life; the new torment, the new hate, comes from refusing to *ask the question*—they do not want to hear the answer.

They who have boasted that man achieves perfection when he alienates himself from God, produce in their poetry and in their writings the saddest, most frustrated of characters of all men. Sartre, in his work *The Flies*, has a character, Oreste, who is the perfect free man because "emancipated from all slavery and all beliefs, without religion, without profession, free for all commitments and yet knowing that he must never commit himself." But what does his freedom bring him, since he is liberated from nothing and is bound to nothing? He kills his mother and her lover in order to rise above anxiety and remorse. But what is this anxiety and remorse in the soul of an atheist but the panting of the lungs for the very air which one has denied it?

There is no love of neighbor, for in the discussion among souls in hell in Sartre's work, *No Exit*, each of the speakers talks only about his aches, pains, worries, frustrations. No one else listens, for no one else cares. They are just waiting their own chance to mouth and vomit their own discontent. Because each man is a god, he will tolerate no false gods before him. When the curtain goes down, the last line of the play is: "Hell is my neighbor." Thus, even when the love of God passes out of the world, so also passes out love of neighbor. As in a collective state the exile of God ends in the tyrannization of man.

In that same play, the characters are asking about their toothbrushes. Then it suddenly dawns on them that their whole philosophy of life is that life is meaningless. There must, therefore, be no meaning in having a toothbrush. In an endless corridor of meaningless, brushing one's teeth, or taking a rest, is absolutely senseless. None of the existentialists are happy, and all the characters they create are miserable.

The New Idol: The Man-God

No one ever gives up God without substituting an idol. There must always be a Golden Calf, and the reasons given for adoring it are as irrational as the one Aaron gave: "I put gold in the furnace, and it came out a Golden Calf." In the eighteenth century, the "calf" was Nature; in the nineteenth century, it was Humanity; in the twentieth century it is the Ego. Now it is each man making himself the god-man. As Camus said, "It is not true, after all, that I have never loved. I conceived at least one great love in my life of which I was always the object. I was bursting with a longing to be immortal; I was too much in love with myself not to want the precious object of my love never to disappear." In a novel boasting of atheism, one man writes on the mirror of the bathroom: "This is the face of God you see." Max Stirner in his *The Ego and His Own* writes: "All things are nothing to me. Nothing is more to me than myself. I no longer do anything for man's sake; but what I do, I do for my own sake."

Thus the question, "Do you believe in God?" as Robert Elliot Fitch said, is now: "Do you believe in your ego?" Do you believe that you are your own creator, your own savior, that you transcend all your darkness and fears and dreads, and that there is something greater in you than your own importance and littleness? It was in the face of all such atheism of this kind that George Bernard Shaw wrote: "I am an atheist, because I cannot believe in such atheists who make themselves god."

What will the God-is-dead, willed by man, eventually produce? The very God-is-dead-ers say it will produce a double effect: titanic spirit of pride and the ultimate destruction of the world. As Ivan Karamazov says: "As soon as men have, all of them, denied God, man will be lifted up with a spirit of divine Titanic pride and the man-God will appear." As Nietzsche proclaims: "The dead are all gods. Now we desire the Superman to *live*."

A common spirit will eventually bind all atheists together to produce the man-god, as there is a common spirit which unites those who live by Christ. In *Crime and Punishment* of Dostoyevsky, two characters gaze into each other's souls, full of loathing at the bottom for each other, and they perceive that Lucifer dwells in them as a common spirit. The devil says to them, "Men will unite to take from life all that it can give, for nothing else but for joy and happiness in the present world."

The will-to-have-no-god becomes clear in Nietzsche's "transvaluation of values." He begs man to go on sinning so very much that he will upset all the values, so that night will be day, day will be night, virtue will be vice, and vice will be virtue. One can go on sinning with impunity without that terrible remorse which drives men to suicide. Nietzsche "considered crime as necessary to human greatness."

Dostoyevsky makes some of his characters live out this side of Nietzche's transvaluation of values. There is a world of difference between a mother who robs an old woman and kills her in order to buy dope, and the one who kills in order to kill remorse. Thus, the philosophy of Nietzsche and some of the characters of Dostoyevsky are one and the same, though the Russian chose the bankruptcy of the philosophy itself. Take, for example, the character Kirilov whose Luciferian cry leads him to suicide. Even this theorist and impractical atheistic humanist cannot leave Christ alone, though he says he will kill himself and thus complete the Sacrifice of Christ: "I shall manifest my will; I am required to believe firmly that I do not believe. I shall begin, I shall make an end, and I shall open the door. And I shall be a saviour. This is the only thing that will save all men and will transform them physically from the next generation onward for in their present physical state, it seems to me that it is impossible for man to do without the old God."

Kirilov decides to kill himself not only to imitate or to pervert the Sacrifice of Christ, but also to prove that his will is higher than God's. If there is a God, our life is in his hands. If there is no God, then life is in the hands of Kirilov. To prove, therefore, that no one has control over him except himself, he kills himself—or, better, his divinity devours him. Just as the stem of a rose cannot stand the burden of a marble bust upon its frail base, so neither can poor, weak man stand the burden of his own so-called God-likeness. Like the monsters of the deep, he preys upon himself. Something that is not to be forgotten in the character of Kirilov is what is found in some of the writings defending the atheism of the existentialists— namely, his kindness toward his neighbors and his mystical fervor for humanity.

The mere denial of God is not emptiness and a negation but the affirmation of man as God. It does not take a gift of prophecy to see that humanity is presently polarizing and that all men are beginning to fall into the ranks of accepting either the man-god or the God-Man.

Dostoyevsky, who understood atheism better than Nietzsche and who saw it coming in his own beloved land, knew that atheism had to be associated with the destruction of the old society. There was some suggestion that an overplanned or socialistic society had to be the prelude of an atheistic society. As he made one of his characters say: "If Aloysha had not believed in God, he would have become a socialist." For the man-god to grow in age and wisdom, two conditions must be fulfilled. The heavens must be emptied, and man must be secularized. Both will be achieved by turning freedom into license. Men will be asked to give up God because His Commandments "enslave" and because our will often runs counter to His. When finally everyone has his own will and does whatever he pleases, then there will be a chaos due to the conflict of egotisms. It will then be necessary for Big Brother, or the state, to organize this chaos into a closed socialist society and the formulas given by the character, Shigalev, the theorist of the Communism to come: "Having set out from unlimited freedom, I have ended up with unlimited despotism."

What Dostoyevsky was predicting through his characters, Nietzsche was saying through his philosophy. As he put it: "I heralded the coming of the tragic era. We must be prepared for a long succession of demolitions, devastations, and upheavals. . . . There will be wars such as the world has never seen. Europe will soon be

enveloped in darkness. We shall watch the rising of the black tide."
And in another work, he wrote: "A catastrophe is at hand. A catastrophe whose name I know, whose name I shall not tell. . . . Then
all the earth will writhe in convulsions."

CHAPTER SIXTEEN

The Absence of God

Nietzsche felt the terrible loneliness of his atheism, saying, "The very eternality of the individual is but a damnation." He saw no home to which he could return as a prodigal, for his loneliness had no home, and in desperation he cries out about Russian music, "I would exchange the happiness of the entire Occident for the Russian manner of being melancholic." The wounds of his godlessness never healed.

He wrote once to his sister: "Do not think that we atheists are without our cares, our anxieties. When life becomes meaningless, it becomes a burden that few can bear, for anyone can bear the *how* of life so long as he knows the *why*."

As Gustave Thibon has said, "The absence of God moves about with the intimacy of a Presence." One may deny air, but one breathes it. One may deny water, but one thirsts for it. One may negate food, but one hungers for it. One may despise love, but one was made for it, and to be without it is hell.

The modern man is not going to God through the order in the universe; he is going to God through the disorder inside himself. He is less impressed by the necessity of a watchmaker for the watch of the universe, but more impressed about a Father's House to which he may return after living with swine and feeding on husks. The modern soul is restless, anxious, and fearful, and this can be the *normal* movement of a soul that is naturally Christian. As Hölderlin put it:

That which thou seekest is near and
Already [*it is*] *running to meet thee.*

This thought is something like that of Pascal who makes God say, "Thou wouldst not be seeking Me, hadst thou not already found Me." It is because we are kings in exile that we are restless to return again to our kingdom. St. Augustine had the same thought of restlessness: "How, then do I seek Thee, Lord? For when I seek Thee, my God, I seek a happy life. . . . But how do I seek it? Is it by a remembrance, as though I had forgotten it, knowing too that I had forgotten it? . . . Truly we have it, but how I know not. . . . For did we not know it, we should not love it."

God to the modern soul is not "way out there" in infinite space, which the Soviet cosmonauts failed to see. He is rather moving within the soul, as Augustine put it: "Behold, Thou wert within, and I without, and there I did seek Thee: I, unlovely, rushed heedlessly among the things of beauty Thou didst make. Thou wert with me, but I was not with Thee."

It could very well be that the age in which we are living might be described as the age of the absence of God, and the age through which we have just passed the presence of God. An interval seems to be ticking away between a burial and a resurrection—a period of time like a lovers' quarrel in which love preexisted and now seems dead and yet is destined to be reborn. Anyone who has dealt intimately with souls, and their griefs, woes, wounds, and burdens, never despairs at their despair, is never restless with their restlessness and never without hope at their hopelessness. They may boast that they have severed the umbilical cord that bound them to the Ground of their being, but the Healer sees but two broken ends and binds them together in the oneness which is peace. Just as in the Creed the words, "He descended into Hell," precede the words,

"He ascended into Heaven," so, too, the modern man is going into the temporary hell of his own soul, and it will not be long until there will be an ascent to heaven.

No Despair Without Eternity

Granted that there is despair, man is the only creature who can experience it, and as Kierkegaard has so well said, "It takes eternity to make a man despair." Chickens never have any complexes, roosters no psychoses. No pigs have ever had an Oedipus complex and no hippopotamus an Electra complex. Even the best of Christians have a sense of "the absence of God," particularly when they sin. It is not the consciousness of breaking the law that disturbs their soul and gives them something of this uneasiness well described by modern poets; rather it comes from having wounded Someone we love. This is why St. Paul repeatedly states: "Grieve not the Spirit," because the one who lives in the presence of God has an intimate sense of communion with Him, and anything wrong disturbs that communion. In fact, it creates a far greater uneasiness than any atheist could ever know, simply because the Christian has had a greater love.

Picture two men marrying two old shrews. One of the men had been married before to a beautiful young wife who had died. The other had been unmarried. Which of the two suffered more? Evidently the one who knew the better love. Thus there is a despair, an unhappiness, an uneasiness in the soul of a Christian as well as in the soul of an atheist, but the uneasiness in the soul of the Christian is greater, for he had the greater love. Every atheist who walks from the tomb as the undertaker of God makes a path of tears over which he can find his way back. In the older myths it often happened that dragons were turned into princesses, and so, in this Age-Between, it could very well be that they who are feeling the absence of God in restlessness will feel the Presence later in peace.

God in Search of Man

Fallen man is not so much in search of God as God is in search of man. When one opens the first page of Genesis, he may be seeking the answer to the question, "What is the first thought God has in Scripture?" One would surmise it would be God's thought about Himself: His eternal Life, His all-embracing Truth, and His ecstatic Love. But we do not find this in Genesis. God is not carrying on a monologue about Himself. His first thought is about man: "Let Us make man." After man had disordered his soul through an abuse of freedom, the first question of God is: "Man, where art thou?" And the second question of God is: "Where is thy brother?" It was not Adam who sought God, but God Who sought Adam, and this has been the order ever since: "No one seeks for God."

It was God Who sought Jacob at Bethel, fleeing from the consequences of his wrongdoing; it was God Who sought out Moses while a fugitive at Madian; it was Christ Who sought out the Apostles while engaged in fishing so that He could say, "You have not chosen Me, but I have chosen you." It was the same God-Man Who called Himself the Good Shepherd, Who came to seek the sheep that was lost: "We love Him because He first loved us." It was Christ Who sought out the persecuting Saul: "The light shineth in darkness." The biblical story is made up of the progressive chapters in which the evil that came into the world through sin is ever being pushed back and back.

Some Meet God in Their Hatred

Every atheist has an idol lodged inside of his human psyche which is a quasidivine character and is experienced as such. There is never rejection without substitution of one kind of God or another. This conflict between two "deities" ignites hate for one. The urge to affirm the idol implies of necessity a negative attitude toward

God. Nietzsche did that then when he said that God was experienced as "a robber behind clouds"—that is, an envious tyrant Who tries to steal man's dearest possessions and Who demands detachment from the things to which one clings.

Atheists encounter God in hatred, just as He is encountered in the lives of saints by love. In ancient times the idols were outside of man, on pedestals. In modern times they are inside man. The first commandment is no less valid now against idolatry than it was when Moses received it from God. When this hatred of God becomes intense and desperate, the temptation to suicide arises as a possibility of escape. One wishes to skirt this encounter with God and idols, and death seems to give promise of tranquillity and oblivion.

Atheism is not a denial of God; it is rather an aggression against God. It is the setting up of the Golden Calf as an object of worship. Once the tortured soul is made to see that it is the idolatry of the idol that has blocked the vision of God, then he begins to see that He Whom he hated was real. Once the heart is free from fixation, then there comes the true liberation. It was probably this dark moment of psychological death which the Lord felt on the Cross when He said, "My God, My God, why hast Thou forsaken Me?" Then He took upon Himself the sum total of satanic aggressions, the volcanic hates of a Nietzsche, and the militant emptiness of the Communists. Christ, at that moment, felt the emptiness, the darkness, the loneliness of all idolators. It is to be noted that, in His death for mankind, He never contemplated atheism as something from which men had to be redeemed, for atheism is the emptiness of idolatry. It was this descent into hell of the terrible void which makes possible until the end of time the encounter of atheists with God.

Overtness toward God is possible even in the moments when the idol-absolute is exercising its tyranny. Those who have not delivered themselves over completely to the idol will sometimes confess, "I hope that God does not demand more of me than I am able to give." Such a person is only half an atheist, for he feels that God to Whom he gives his finger may also take his hand. The striving of the person toward God—even in its deviant forms—is never totally extinguished. The idol in the end always proves disappointing.

This hatred of God may exist in a lesser degree in all believers in God. One of the profoundest insights into this hatred of God comes from the pen of the psychiatrist Wilfred Daim in *Death, Psychology and Salvation,* in which he holds that every idol is affirmed out of hatred for God. Nietzsche called God an envious tyrant, the rival of man. This hatred of God can be almost as deep as the love of God. We read in Scripture of the hatred of David's wife for him. "The hate with which she hated him was greater than the love with which she loved him." And the same can be true of God. Atheistic hate is a sign of the reality of God—not a sign of the nonexistence of God.

The hatred of God is in every human being to the extent that there is resistance to His Will or a temptation to break with Him. Bent on evil, the person has the feeling of being hemmed in by His tantalizing Presence. A conflict arises between the consciously experienced "ought" and the inability to "break loose." This causes a torment bordering on despair. When there is a break with God, the soul always comes out wounded. But when there is a total resistance to God, the soul undergoes a *rigor mortis,* just as the body does. The *rigor mortis* is a fixation in sin.

The hatred of God thus grows out of the realization that every human being owes his existence to Him, even at the same time that He is denied or a new false idol is set up, such as sex, money, or the ego. The soul's inferno is created by the rebellious mind and the perverted will of man. From this there comes torment—greater or less, depending on how much the pendulum is separated from the clock, the carbon from the original, the creature from the Creator.

Hell Begins Here

Hell does not begin in the next life as Heaven does not begin in the next life. St. Thomas says that there is relationship between grace and glory, like to that of the acorn to the oak. There is less difference between a soul on this earth in the state of grace and a soul in heaven than there is between two persons on earth, one in the state of grace, the other not. It is quite wrong to think of heaven or hell beginning when we die: "You go to Heaven or you go to Hell." We are already there! Unbelievers are close to the truth when they say, "We have our Heaven and Hell in this life." True! It begins here! It does not end here. Everyone is carrying about the Light of Heaven in his heart or a burning sensation on the inside which is a spark from the fire of hell. As Rimbeau wrote: "I feel I am in hell; therefore I am."

The God they hate must be shown to the God they love. I have been the instrument of God in the conversion of three atheistic Communists, all high in the party. In no single instance did I even speak of Communism. I began by talking about how unhappiness was common to both of us, down deep in our heart was a yearning for something we did not possess. Douglas Hyde, the former editor of the Communist *Daily Worker* of London, told me that this was the *only* approach to Communists. One night, he and his wife were listening to a speech by Molotov. His wife challenged a statement, and he challenged her fidelity to the party. Words became stronger, and finally he said, "You talk as if you were about to become a Catholic." She said, "I am." He answered, "Shake hands—so am I." Grace touched each of them separately; the human fuel, which made their hearts combustible, was their craving for inner happiness which they had never discussed together.

After all, what proves the inner discontent of Communists more than their passion to destroy? They are not at ease in their philosophy, as the sinner is not at ease in his sin. Hate is nothing but love upside down. Hell is the other side of heaven. The Saul who hated was the Paul who could love. And one wonders whether the Church again will have a large measure of zeal until it converts its persecutors. God is in the soul of each of them, buried under the ashes of Marx, the clinkers of Lenin, and the smoldering putrefaction of a Stalin. Why do we assume that atheists are unconvertible? Is not the image and likeness of God in each of them? Was not Sartre redeemed? If we approach them with hate, do we not receive hate in return? If we love the Communists (while hating Communism), we fan the embers of love that are already there.

Religion Today Is in the Subconscious

When treating the bourgeois atheism, its followers must not be judged by what they say with their lips. Their arguments are often blind alleys to lead us astray. Their conscious, superficial mind is atheistic, but do they ever think about religion? They say they do not. They even claim they have no need of it. Is this true? Yes! On the surface. *But religion in the modern mind has moved down into the subconsciousness.* Its disgusts, its remorses, its escapes from responsibility, its battered conscience have been thrown down into the basement, kept out of view, out of sight. But the good in them can be brought out as Our Lord brought it out gradually from the woman at the well.

All skeptics and atheists are *voluntary* atheists, not *intellectual* atheists. They *will* the nonexistence of God. They are like a man who will not open a letter because it contains bad news. Belief in God, then, in them has a depth and an inwardness covered by a hard crust of rationality—i.e., presumptive reasons for doubt. Too often we spend time on the crust which to them is very satisfying, because it makes religion a subject of *discussion* rather than a matter for *decision*. These souls, so filled with anxiety, silent nothingness, and the dreadful lawlessness of a fatherless world, are more like lost sheep than ravening wolves. They are caught in the thickets of an endless void; but where are the shepherds who seek them out?

The new Commandment is, "Thou shalt love thyself with thy whole heart, with thy whole soul and thy whole mind." This is the first and greatest Commandment. The second is like unto this: "Hell is my neighbor"—Sartre. Jean Jacques Rousseau once wrote: "I cannot conceive anyone in the world greater than myself." Walt Whitman, in his "Song of Myself" wrote:

I dote on myself, there is that lot of me and all so luscious, . . .
And nothing, not God, is greater to one than one's self is. . . .
Nor do I understand who there can be more wonderful than myself.

Albert Camus in his work, *The Fall,* writes: "It is not true after all that I have never loved. I conceived at least one great love in my life of which I was always the object." Thus the alternatives presented to man are those of the God-man and the man-god.

Because there is nothing beyond the Self, life is *absurd.* Defenders of this new kind of god are more interested in the problem of evil and human depravity than any theologian. Why? Because self-love expressed itself in a quest for pleasure and power, and both are doomed to disappointment in the face of evil and war. That is why there is so much pessimism in modern literature.

Loneliness

It is only an anthropomorphic way of saying it, but Rilke, in one of his poems, expressed the loneliness for God by comparing it to a child sleeping in a room above his parents. During the night the child awakens, is frightened by the darkness, and because he is alone, he drops a book from the table, shakes his bed, and kicks his foot against the wall. The parents hear and bring the child a glass of water. Reassured, he falls asleep. That child is man in his loneliness. He may rebel against God, shake his fists against heaven, write books embalming His Divinity, and yet all the time he is lonely.

And in his exile and homeless heart God will come with the waters of life.

Everywhere in denial, restlessness, anxiety, fear, and dread, one is coming up against God negatively. The hatred in one instance, and the flight in another, would not be so intense if it were not from the infinity of the One from Whom they have recoiled. As it takes an explosive thrust of power to send a rocket to the moon, it also takes the thrust of God to explain the flight from Him. Wherever the flight takes us from God, there the absence pierces, as the Psalmist said, "If I descend into hell, Thou art present." As Max Picard has put it:

> They are being hunted by God and they can move so swiftly only because He hunts them. Even this is God's Love, that He and no other wills to pursue the fleeing, so that He the Swiftest may always be the nearest to those in flight. He goes after them; in the pursuit He anticipates them. They arrive and He is already there; in every place He is there before them. *They* follow after *Him*. No one in the flight knows the Pursuer from the pursued. This too is God's Love.

> —*The Flight from God*

Modern man, having uprooted himself from the past, from his fellowman, and God, is lonely. That is one of the reasons why he loves the city, the crowd, the mob, and Communism, each of which gives him an opportunity into which he may steal into an anonymity with his restless soul. As Kierkegaard put it:

> In contradistinction to the Middle Ages and those periods with all their discussions of possession, particular men giving themselves to evil, I should like to write a book on diabolical possession in modern times, and show how mankind en masse gives itself up to evil, how nowadays it happens en masse.
> It is for this reason that people gather into flocks, in order that natural, animal hysteria should take hold of them, in order to feel

themselves stimulated, inflamed and *beside themselves* . . . for being outside of oneself, one hardly knows what one is doing or saying, or who or what is speaking through one, while the blood courses faster, the eyes turn bright and staring, the passions and lust seething.

As Miguel de Unumuno put it: "Man must be thrown into the ocean, deprived of every anchorage, so that he may learn again what it means to live as a human being."

The despair and the loneliness of those who walk upon thin ice and above the dismal depths still can raise their eyes up any moment to a beacon of light. There is creative despair as well as pessimistic despair. Peter and Judas were both told that they would fall. The Lord implied that they both were devils in their fall. They both denied Him, and yet the remorse of one led to a tree where each branch was like a pointing finger at his conscience. The other led to One Who was to be on a tree and Who would leave it alive. Despair then can also be creative as it was in the case of Peter. Maybe it is from such doubts, which the modern world is going through, that we will come to the insight of Pascal: "We would not have sought Thee, O God, if we had not already found Thee."

CHAPTER SEVENTEEN

Morticians of God and the Future of Humanity

The advance of technology, space travel, and atomic energy is apt to blind us to the other side of the picture, in which the same man who boasts of his future shrinks in terror from what it may bring. The team of scientists who worked in Chicago during World War II were thrilled at the fact that they had produced a new energy like to that with which the sun lights the world. While their work imposed upon them the greatest secrecy, they nevertheless were stricken with terror at the monstrous evil that might result from their discovery. They wrote to President Truman urging that the bomb should be used only in some desert place, but their letter was never answered. And yet, they lived to see the horrors of Hiroshima and Nagasaki. Could the production of nuclear reaction, which was capable of bringing so much benefit to man, be also the demon which might destroy him?

Is there not also a parallel in the fact that, as medicine has succeeded in conquering many organic and functional diseases, there has been an increase in mental diseases? Never before has there been so much power, and never before have men so prepared to use it for the destruction of life. Never before has there been so much education and never before so little coming to the knowledge of the truth. The new technological inventions in growing secularism must be viewed from two sides: that of giving great freedom to man and also that of possibly increasing his slavery and his destruction. What makes the problem all the more poignant is that technology has no place for the word "I."

None of the new secularist philosophies, whatever they be, have any place for the personal man. They propose to make him absolutely responsible for his own history and for everything that happens in the world. But at the very moment that they are glorifying him, the individual man, the existing human personality is being swallowed up by collectivism, the omnipotent state, the Organization Man. A classic description of this is to be found in George Orwell's *1984*.

Once the reality of God has been eliminated from society, what safeguard have we for the human person? What is to prevent planners in a technologically advanced civilization from treating human beings as functions rather than as persons? During World War II, Hitler sent men to the famous Bethel Hospital to inform Pastor Bodelschwing, its director, that the state could no longer afford to keep hundreds of epileptics who were useless to society and who constituted a drain on its resources, and that they had better be destroyed. Bodelschwing finally won the battle with no other weapon than the simple affirmation that they were men and women, made to the image and likeness of God, and to destroy them would be to sin against God.

When the Communists swept from northern to southern China, one of our large leper colonies in charge of sisters was seized by the Communists. The Communists called them all together, told them that they had been poorly cared for by the sisters and not well fed. From now on, under the Communist regime, they would have a banquet every day. They were all told to go into the common dining room. They went in, the doors were locked, the Communists set fire to the building, and all were burned. If there is no authority beyond public authority, then there is no one to whom I can appeal against its pressure. The authority then becomes the one who is strongest. This idea has been developed by Arthur Koestler in his book, *Darkness at Noon*. This is one of the reasons why a purely secular society produces martyrdom, which witnesses to the existence of authority. Once this authority is denied, nothing can prevent the secular state from affirming with Pilate, "Dost thou not know that I have power to crucify thee?"

What Will the World Be Like in Which God Is Dead?

One of the most shattering expressions of the death of God is to be found in a novel by Jean Paul (Jean Paul Friedrich Richter), *Siebenkäs*, which appeared in 1796. The author was one of the early romantic writers in Germany, and he interrupts his story to recount a "speech of the dead Christ from the top of the structure of the universe, that there is no God." It is not that Jean Paul does not believe in God. It is rather that he has a dream—a macabre dream —of a world without God. A man falls asleep on a hillside and dreams that he awakes in a cemetery, finding himself alone in a world in which there is no God. In the preface to this speech, Jean Paul speaks of how "no one is so much alone in the universe as one who denies God—he mourns with an orphaned heart which has lost the Supreme Father":

Once on a summer evening I was lying upon a quiet hillside in the sun. I fell asleep, and dreamed that I awoke in a churchyard. The rattle of the wheels of the clock running down as it was striking eleven had awakened me. I looked for the sun in the dark and void night sky, for I supposed that some eclipse was hiding it with the moon. And all the graves were open, and the iron doors of the charnel-house kept opening and shutting, moved by invisible hands. Athwart the walls shadows went flitting; but no bodies cast those shadows; and there were others, too, moving about out in the open air. Within the open coffins there were none now asleep, except the children. Nothing was in the sky but sultry fog, heavy and gray, hanging there in great clammy folds; and some gigantic shadow closed and closed this fog as in a net, and drew it ever nearer, closer and hotter.

Up overhead I heard the thunder of distant avalanches, and beneath my feet the first footfalls of a boundless earthquake. The church was heaved and shaken to and fro by two terrific discords striving in it, beating in stormy effort to attain harmonious resolution. Now and then a grayish glimmer passed with rapid gleam fittering athwart the windows; but, whenever this glimmer came, the lead and iron of the frames always melted and ran rolling down. . . .

There was but one of the dead still lying on his pillow, and he was one who had but just been buried in the church; he lay at peace, his breast without a throb, a happy dream upon his smiling face. But now, as I came in (I, one of the living), his sleep broke; he awoke, and smiled no more; with painful effort he raised his heavy eyelids—and there was no eye beneath—and in his beating breast there was no heart, but a deep wound instead. He raised his hands, folded as if for prayer; but then his arms shot out and came apart from his poor trunk, the folded hands came off and fell away. Upon the dome above there was inscribed the dial of eternity; but figures there were none, and the dial itself was its own gnomon; a great black finger was pointing at it, and the dead strove hard to read the time upon it.

And at this point a lofty, noble form, bearing the impress of eternal sorrow, came sinking down toward our group, and rested on the altar; whereupon all the dead cried out, "Christ! is there no God?"

He answered, "There is none."

At this the dead quivered and trembled; but now it was not their breasts alone that throbbed; the quivering ran all through the shadows, so that one by one the shudder shook them into nothingness. And Christ spake on, saying, "I have traversed the worlds, I have risen to the suns, with the milky-ways I have passed athwart the great waste spaces of the sky; there is no God. And I descended to where the very shadow cast by Being dies out and ends, and I gazed out into the gulf beyond, and cried, 'Father, where art thou?' But answer came there none, save the eternal storm which rages on, controlled by none; and toward the west, above the chasm a gleaming rainbow hung, but there was no sun to give it birth, and so it sank and fell by drops into the gulf. And when I looked up to the boundless universe for the Divine eye, behold, it glared at me from out a socket, empty and bottomless. Over the face of chaos brooded eternity, chewing it forever, again and yet again. Shriek on, then, discords, shatter the shadows with your shrieking din, for He is not!"

The pale and colorless shades flickered away to nothingness, as frosty fog dissolves before warm breath, and all grew void. Ah! then the dead children, who had been asleep out in the graves, awoke, and came into the temple, and fell down before the noble form (a sight to rend one's heart), and cried, "Jesus, have we no Father?" He made answer, with streaming tears, "We are orphans all, both I and ye. We have no Father."

Then the discords clashed and clanged more harshly yet; the shivering walls of the temple parted asunder, and the temple and the children sank—the earth and sun sank with them—and the boundless fabric of the universe sank down before us, while high on the summit of immeasurable nature Jesus stood and gazed upon the sinking universe, besprent with thousand suns, and like a mine dug in the face of black eternal night; the suns being miners' lamps and the milky way the veins of silvery ore.

And as he gazed upon the grinding mass of worlds, the wild torch-dance of starry will-o-the-wisps, and all the coral banks of throbbing hearts—and saw how world by world shook forth its glimmering souls on to the Ocean of Death—then He, sublime, loftiest of finite beings, raised his eyes toward the nothingness and boundless void, saying, "Oh, dead, dumb nothingness! necessity endless and chill! Oh, mad, unreasoning Chance! When will ye dash this fabric into atoms, and me too? Chance, knowest thou—thou knowest not—when thou dost march, hurricane-winged, amid the whirling snow of stars, extinguishing sun after sun upon thy onward way, and when the sparkling dew of constellations ceases to gleam, as thou dost pass them by? How every soul in this great corpse-trench of a universe is utterly alone? I am alone—none but me—O Father! Father! Where is that boundless breast of thine, that I may rest upon it? Alas! if every soul be its own creator and father, why shall it not be its own destroying angel, too? . . ."

And I fell down and peered into the shining mass of worlds, and beheld the coils of the great serpent of eternity all twined about those worlds; these mighty coils began to writhe and rise, and then again they tightened and contracted, folding round the universe twice as closely as before; they wound about all nature in thousand folds, and crashed the worlds together, and crushed down the boundless temple to the little churchyard chapel. And all grew narrow, and dark, and terrible. And then a great immeasurable bell began to swing in act to toll the last hour of Time, and shatter the fabric of the universe to countless atoms—when my sleep broke up, and I awoke.

And my soul wept for joy that it could still worship God—my gladness, and my weeping and my faith—these were my prayer!

Wit, Wisdom and Philosophy of Jean Paul Frederick Richter

Nietzsche's Vision of the Antichrist

Jean Paul's vision of the death of God was that of one who believed in God and His kind of world. Nietzsche, however, was one who really chose to believe that God was dead, in order to make room for his ego and the Superman. Fittingly, he makes a madman make this declaration. Nietzsche himself became mad. One day seated at his piano, he stopped touching the keys with his fingers and began thumping them with his elbows, shouting and shrieking against the Person of Christ. The madman speaks in his *Die Fröhliche Wissenschaft*, and tells of the effect of atheism on modern consciousness.

Have you not heard of the madman who lit a lantern at noonday, ran to the market place and cried unceasingly, "I am looking for God! I am looking for God!" Since there happened to be many standing there who did not believe in God, he roused great laughter. "Is He lost?" said one. "Or gone astray like a child?" said another. "Or has He hidden Himself?" "Is He afraid of us? Has He gone on a voyage? Or emigrated?" So they shouted and laughed. The madman leaped in their midst and pierced them with his glance. "Where has God gone?" he cried. "I will tell you. *We have slain Him—you and I.* We are all His murderers. But how did we do it? How could we drink up the sea? Who gave us the sponge to wipe out the whole horizon? What did we do, when we unchained this earth from its sun? Where is it moving to now? And where are we moving to now? Away from all the suns? Backwards, sideways, forward, in every direction? Is there an above and a below anymore? Are we not wandering as through infinite nothingness? Is empty space not breathed upon us now? Is it not colder now? Is not night coming, and evermore night? Must we not light lanterns at noon? Do we not hear the noise of the gravediggers as they bury God? Do we not smell God decaying?—God too decays!

"God is dead. God stays dead. *And we have slain Him.* How shall we console ourselves, chief of all murderers? The holiest and most powerful that the world has ever possessed, has ebbed its blood away beneath our knives. Who will wipe this blood from our fingers? What water can make us clean? What propitiations and sacred rites will we have to invent? Is not the greatness of this deed too great for us? Must we not ourselves become gods, in order to seem worthy of it? There was never a greater deed, and because of it all who are born after us are part of a higher history than ever before!"

The madman fell silent, and I looked at his hearers again. They too were silent, and I looked at him with shocked eyes. At last he threw his lantern on the ground, so that it broke in pieces and went out. "I come too early," he said. "It is not yet my time. This monstrous event is still on the way—it has not yet penetrated men's ears. Lightning and thunder need time, the light of the stars needs time, deeds need time, even after they've been done, in order to be seen and heard. This deed is still further from men than the remotest stars—and yet they have done it."

Has it been noted that our age is one in which there is a conjunction of two mental planets: one in which we affirm God is dead, with its consequent philosophy of Nothingness and the Absurdity of Life; the other, one in which we discovered the atomic bomb which is capable of annihilating the earth. Could any other age which believed in God have conceived a weapon to destroy man? Was one of the characters of Dostoyevsky right when he said there are two ages of humanity: one from the gorilla to the death of God, the other from the death of God to the annihilation of man? Was Nietzsche right in saying it demands a little time yet to bring out this catastrophe too awful to contemplate, the name of which he knew? There is one thing I know: These God-Is-dead-ers have not convinced us there is no God. They have convinced us there is a devil.

CHAPTER EIGHTEEN

Modern Saints

Amorization, or love of humanity, is a form of sanctity. But who are modern saints? We are here not asking about Church saints, canonized saints, plaster saints, book saints—saints who never seem to have had any kind of human weakness—but rather those whom the modern world regards as saints. There may be something about their politics, their economics, their social background which may prejudice many people. But on the whole, they have come to the surface of modern approval and have been "canonized" by popular esteem.

The four whom we have chosen as representatives of modern saints are: Gandhi, John F. Kennedy, John XXIII, and Hammarskjöld.

Three characteristics are common to these:

1. Modern saints are *nonconformist,* in the sense that none of them followed the crowd or the masses. Despite the emphasis on individual liberty, there is increasing tendency on the part of the masses to be "other-directed." For example, youths conform to the mores of the crowd to which they belong; leaders of labor unions determine to a great extent the decisions of the members; homes are other-directed when they are the passive recipients of a TV program made in Hollywood or in New York; women become slaves of anonymous directors of fashion, bowing down in veneration, saying, "They are wearing green this year," without ever inquiring who are the

"they." The result is an apathy and a passivity which makes it difficult to participate in the reconstruction of society. Citizens then ask, "What can I do about it?"

The masses are always uncreative. The leader must be one who will snap his fingers at the conformist device, "Everybody's doing it"; he is governed by some master idea which is not taken from the group or the way society is presently acting. When all of the people are converging or running to an abyss, it sometimes seems that he who is going in the opposite direction is out of his mind. But maybe he is a leader. A log will float downstream; it takes a man to resist the current, to stand up against the way everyone is going even when it is hard and unpleasant, and to be dominated by an ideal is the mark of a leader.

2. Modern saints have a *dedication to a cause which creates a readiness to die for it.* While the rest of men are governed by safety-first principles, saints seem to be governed by safety last. While others drink life as men drink water, they drink the danger of death as other men drink wine. It is not that they seek martyrdom, because martyrdom is a gift of God; rather they are so lost in their cause, as instruments of God, that they desire nothing for themselves. As Boris Pasternak put it in *Doctor Zhivago*: "It was not until after the coming of Christ that men began to live toward the future. Man does not die in a ditch like a dog—but at home in history, while the work toward the conquest of death is in full swing; he dies sharing in this work." Or, as Arthur Koestler put it in his *Dialogue with Death*: "They believe that it was good and necessary to live, and even to fight in order to live, and even to die so that others might live. They believed in all this, and because they believed truly in it, because their lives depended on this belief they were not afraid of death." It is to be noted that three of the modern saints died violently—Gandhi, Kennedy, and Hammarskjöld—while Pope John lived in that prospect for he said, "Any day is a good day to die; my baggage is always packed."

that prayer united us to God, while fasting separated us from an excessive love of creatures. The fast, he claimed, was a means of reaching men's hearts and minds: "I fasted to reform those who loved me. You cannot fast against a tyrant, for a tyrant is incapable of love." His fasting was often for the sake of the Untouchables, who were not permitted to enter a Hindu temple and inhabited the worst of the slums and villages. His fasting, which identified him with the starving, helped to win equality for the Untouchables.

Gandhi embraced Christ, but rejected Christianity. He had a black-and-white print of Christ hanging in his little hut, on which was written: "He is our Peace." "If I had to face only the Sermon on the Mount in my own interpretation of it, I should unhesitatingly say, 'Yes, I am a Christian.'"

Anyone in public life has burdens. St. Paul spoke of bearing on his shoulders the burden of all the churches. Gandhi bore the emptiness of India's starving millions. Edna St. Vincent Millay expressed in poetry the cross that lies on such a man in public life:

All sin was of my sinning, all
Atoning mine, and mine the gall
Of all regret. Mine was the weight
Of every brooded wrong, the hate
That stood behind each envious thrust,
Mine every greed, mine every lust.
　　　　—"Renascence,"
　　　　Collected Poems

John F. Kennedy

The dominant idea in his life, or the *contemplata* or the Come-Come inspiration hidden to others, was the *occult cross*. It was almost as if the Christ had laid His Hand upon him for destiny, but left the imprint of His Scars. According to his brother, "At least one half of the days that he spent on this earth, pain was always with

3. Modern saints *avoid the extremes of excessive detachment from humanity and excessive attachment to it*. Souls with deep spiritual vision are apt to regard the world as evil; they then withdraw from it and leave it to its dissolution, as did a certain type of hermit and ascetic. Others go to the opposite extreme and become immersed in humanity as a drowning man is immersed in water, forming a brotherhood without tears, a humanism which lacks the depth of man's frustration as a sinner and also the height of man's potentiality for holiness.

Go-Go—Come-Come

The two extremes which one finds in the modern world are the Go-Go group and the Come-Come group. The Go-Go's are the new breed; the Come-Come's are the old breed. The Go-Go's believe that man has only a horizontal relationship with other men; the Come-Come's that man has only a vertical relationship with God. The Go-Go's know only one side of the Commandment— namely, the love of neighbor. The others know only the love of God but not the love of neighbor. The Go-Go's would build a secular city, because God is dead. The Come-Come's would build only a city of God, because the world is evil. The Go-Go's are flowing rivers with no beds; the Come-Come's are all bed and no flowing waters of life.

The first are all action and no contemplation; the second all theory and no practice. The Go-Go's are pendulums without clocks, and the Come-Come's clocks without pendulums; the Go-Go's love for the present, the Come-Come's for the past. The Go-Go group insists that sociology be the new theology, that Christianity is humanism, that spirituality is pragmatism, and that if religion is not wholly in the world and for the world, it should perish. The Come-Come group refuse to budge from where they are. To them, change is decay, a protest is rebellion, and in their minds the greatest contribution one can bring to the world is by remaining in the sanctuary, keeping the *status quo*, and observing the minutiae of liturgical protocol.

The real leaders are those who avoid these extremes—or better, combine both, for both were united in the Life of Christ. Almost the first word of Our Lord's public Life was "come" (John 1:39, Mark 1:17, Matt. 4:18). The final word of His public Life was "go" into the world (John 20:21, Matt. 28:19, Acts 1:8). First one must come to Him to learn, to be inspired, to find the ultimate goal of life, to discover meaning, purposes, the significance of justice and liberty. Then go among the nations, go to accomplish, go to serve, to wash feet, to feed the hungry, to establish equality, to pick up the wounded men like good Samaritans.

A leader must begin with "abide with Me," receive My Truth, My Life; then "go," accomplish, mingle in the world with Jews, Greeks, barbarians; go to the hill of the Areopagus and in the barracks of Caesar. "He appointed twelve to be with Him and to be sent out" (Mark 3:14). They who identify Christ's mission with secularization are torches without flame; they who identify Christ's mission with isolation from the problems of our day are those who would pass by wounded men to hurry to temple services; the Go-Go's lack the love of God, the Come-Come's lack love of neighbor.

The true vision is that of the rock and the river, for both are side by side in Scripture. On one side there is the rock: "Upon this rock I will build my Church" (Matt. 16:18). But out of the rock came rivers of living water, "and all drank the same prophetic drink, watered by the same prophetic rock which bore them company, the rock that was Christ" (I Cor. 10:4). The rock is that which stands for stability and solidity; the waters that flow from it are dynamism and action and secularization. One can summarize all three principles in a Latin expression *contemplata aliis tradere*—"Give to others those things upon which there has been meditation." First the idea, then the action. Begin with the love of God, then spread that love to neighbor.

The four modern saints mentioned above had somet[ ] common: First, there was a dominant or master idea which [ ] as the mainspring of their activity. For Gandhi it was viol[ ] self, nonviolence to others. For President John F. Kenned[ ] the occult cross. For Pope John XXIII it was love of God and [ ] neighbor. For Hammarskjöld it was interiority.

Gandhi

For Gandhi, the *contemplata* was nonviolence to oth[ ] violence to self. When asked to take part in a war of indepe[ ] he answered, "I decline to take part in it; today I am teach[ ] people how to meet a national crisis by nonviolent means." [ ] sword that he refused to swing against others, he thrust into [ ] flesh.

Christianity and Hinduism have something in con[ ] namely, the value of asceticism, self-denial and renunciatio[ ] ther of them glorify self-renunciation as such. St. Paul said t[ ] should deliver his body to be burned and have no love, it [ ] less. Gandhi also, in the same spirit, said, "A mother wou[ ] by choice sleep in a wet bed; but she would gladly do so, in [ ] spare the dry bed for her child." Renunciation was never t[ ] its own sake but for the sake of others.

One of the first steps toward the crushing of the ego, [ ] to make himself available to others, was the taking of the [ ] celibacy when he was thirty-seven years old, which vow [ ] until his death in 1948. Celibacy in the Hindu lore was ca[ ] *macharya*, which is a complete self-control that ruled out [ ] ness, lying, hate, and anger, and made one like to God bec[ ] self-centered. This abandonment of the pleasures of the [ ] believed, would make his love for his fellowmen more free [ ] reaching.

Another form of self-renunciation which helped him [ ] himself with others through de-egotism was fasting. Gandhi [ ]

him. Those who knew him well would know he was suffering only because his face was a little whiter, the lines around his eyes were a little deeper, his words a little sharper. Those who did not know him well detected nothing."

It was midnight on August 2, 1943, when the P T boat which he was commanding was struck by a Japanese destroyer, broke in two, and sank. Two of the men were killed instantly; Lieutenant Kennedy was thrown violently on his back across the deck. With those who were saved, he swam miles to an island, being in the sea fifteen hours. Back at the squadron's base, it was believed all were lost; memorial services were held for all thirteen of the men. From that moment on, his life was to become as one risen from the dead. Finally, three of the group of survivors made their way to another island and to safety, and all sang a song of thanks to God.

The old back injury, which began with a ruptured disk while Kennedy was at Harvard, became aggravated at the ramming of the P T boat and began to give constant pain. The metal plate that surgeons had attached to the spine failed to do the job completely. One of his friends said, "Some days during the 1958 campaign he could not move without crutches, and he hated to be seen by the public using them. When he would come to the door of a hall where he was going to give a speech, he would hand the crutches to one of us at the door, throw his shoulders back, and walk down the aisle, with his back as straight as a West Point cadet—I never knew how he did it."

In 1954 a team of surgeons operated on the back, seeking a double fusion of disks. The last rites of the Church were twice administered to him, but once again there was a kind of a resurrection from the dead. While lying on the sickbed, he began writing material which he and others had collected concerning the courageous political decisions made by early American statesmen. The spirit which prompted his own life inspired him to give it the title *Profiles in Courage*.

Midway during his Presidential term, he said in a news conference, "There is always inequity in life. Some men are killed in war, and some are wounded, and some men never leave the country. . . . It is very hard in military or in personal life to assure complete equality. Life is unfair. Some people are sick; others are well."

He never spoke of this occult cross, but it was that to which he abandoned himself without complaining. The night before he was killed he quoted St. Peter's address on Pentecost: "Your young men shall see visions, and your old men shall dream dreams," little knowing that he was about to be ushered into the Vision of visions. But what he left behind was the truth that politics may be a sublime vocation, for "here on earth God's work must truly be our own."

In his inaugural address he revealed the action which came from his *contemplata*:

> In the long history of the world, only a few generations have been granted the role of defending freedom in its hour of maximum danger. I do not shrink from this responsibility—I welcome it. I do not believe that any of us would exchange places with any other people, or any other generation. The energy, the faith, and the devotion which we bring to this endeavor will light our country and all who serve it—and the glow from that fire can truly light the world.
>
> And so, my fellow Americans: Ask not what your country will do for you—ask what you can do for your country.
>
> My fellow citizens of the world: Ask not what America will do for you, but what together we can do for the freedom of man.
>
> Finally, whether you are citizens of America or of the world, ask of us the same high standards of strength and sacrifice that we shall ask of you. With a good conscience our only sure reward, with history the final judge of our deeds, let us go forth to lead the land we love, asking His blessing and His help, but knowing that here on earth God's work must truly be our own.

Pope John

The mystique of Pope John XXIII was the love of God and the love of neighbor. There are some who love neighbor without loving God, but such love reaches limits beyond which it refuses to humble itself for another. One soldier, during the last war, boasted, "I am glad I am an atheist. If I were a Christian, I would have to help those dysentery patients." Those who love God without loving neighbor have a heart which keeps all the blood for itself, refusing to send it to the extremities. Pope John's deep and all-encompassing love of mankind came from his love of God: "I am like every other man in the world. I have been blessed with a disposition to love mankind, which keeps me faithful to the teachings of the Gospel, makes me respectful of my rights and the rights of others, and which prevents me from doing evil to anyone. In fact, it encourages me to do good to everyone."

This accounted for his perpetual good humor. When he was Patriarch of Venice, a high tide flooded the Piazza di San Marco; to escape the rising waters he went into a small wineshop. The man behind the counter recognized him and stammered out, "Dry throat, Eminence?" He shook his head and said, "No, wet feet." I visited with him in company with Karsh, the famous photographer. Pope John said, "God knew from all eternity that I was destined to be Pope. He also knew that I would live for over eighty years. Having all eternity to work on, and also eighty years, wouldn't you think He would have made me better looking?"

This love of humanity also begot in him a profound humility and a resistance to ever considering himself above others. Though he was a Cardinal before he was named Pope, he refused to be a Cardinal in the sense of being an Eminence, for "eminence" is taken from the Latin word *eminens* which means "far off." The origin of this elevation began in 1244 when Margaret, Countess of Flanders, visited Pope Innocent IV in Rome who had just been elected the previous year. She was the daughter of Baldwin II, the Latin emperor of Constantinople. She was gently chided in the course of the visit to the Pontiff, because she seemed to address everyone alike, justifying herself, "How is it possible to tell an abbot from a cardinal? They all dress in black." The Pontiff asked her, "Well, what would you suggest?" She said, "I would suggest giving them red hats."

The red hat John never took very seriously, for immediately after his elevation he made a retreat in which he wrote in his notebook: "It costs me nothing to acknowledge and repeat that I am nothing and worth precisely nothing."

That love of humanity also came out in his famous encyclical, *Mater et Magistra*, in which he pleaded for a socialization of mankind but not socialism. Socialism, he said, destroys the work of personality by absorption into the mass, but socialization "is at one and the same time an effect and a cause of growing intervention of public authorities in even the most crucial matters, such as those concerning the care of health, the instruction and edification of the younger generation, and the controlling of professional careers and the methods of care and rehabilitation of those variously handicapped. But it is also the fruit and expression of a natural tendency, almost irrepressible in human beings—the tendency to join together to attain objectives which are beyond the capacity and the means of single individuals."

This love of humanity had its even greater expression in the opening of the doors of the Church to let in the world and also to let the Church out. The purpose was to end the division in Christendom that has lasted in one instance over four hundred years and in another instance over seven hundred. On the day of his coronation, when he stood outside the doors of St. Peter's and bade the whole world to come to him, his great arms were like fleshy columns of Bernini, embracing all humanity and forever reminding the children of the heavenly Father that all men are brothers.

Hammarskjöld

The spiritual motif of Hammarskjöld was interiority as the condition of peace. Peace is something that must be on the inside of a heart before it can be projected outside. A man who is at war with himself will be at war with others. Interiority was the *contemplata* of his life for he was a very difficult man to know. There was only one person in whom he confided, one whom he knew from his youth. Outside of him, it was only his diary, with its acute self-analysis, that revealed his character: "What do I have to forgive myself today?" . . . "Whom have I offended?" . . . "Am I overbearing?"

Almost all of the great saints of the past have left their records describing their own personal encounters with God, such as Juliana of Norwich in her mysterious *The Cloud of Unknowing*. Lancelot Andrewes wrote his *Devotions* that others might follow them. St. Teresa dictated her *Castle of the Soul* and the Little Flower, *The Story of a Soul*. Most of these were members of religious communities apart from the world, writing mostly to those, who like themselves, were unworldly in not doing worldly things.

Dag Hammarskjöld had the same hiddenness and interiority, but he allowed it to come into the open in his quest for peace. His spirituality was like a hidden river which appears on the surface from time to time. Giving the clue to the sanctity of the future he wrote: "In our era the road to holiness necessarily passes through the world of action."

The man who knew him best was Sven Stolpe, who wrote a "spiritual portrait" of Hammarskjöld in which he brought out the central theme of his life. As a boy he had seen that his father had suffered unjustly in public life. This made him turn his thoughts to Christ, Who in a greater measure was without guilt and yet was slain for His love and steadfastness. In order to cultivate this interiority, Hammarskjöld resolved to give himself to a life of purity. In a lighter vein he once wrote: "I have the impression that most married men devote 90 percent of their energies to coping with the neuroses of their wives; and this can hardly produce good work."

Sven Stolpe says of him: "From the beginning I felt very strongly that this young man was purer than perhaps anyone I had ever met." Speaking of dedication to other things than to women, he wrote, Hammarskjöld wrote in his diary:

The ultimate surrender to the creative act—it is the destiny of some to be brought to the threshold of this in the act of sacrifice rather than the sexual act; and they experience a thunderclap of the same dazzling power.

Delicately, he portrayed how the energy that otherwise would be lost sexually is transmuted into higher purposes: "Denied any outlet the heat transmuted the coal into diamonds."

Markings, Hammarskjöld's own book, represents the record and the profile of a man who was unworldly in the midst of worldly success, who had a preoccupation with death in the midst of life, and who strove for peace among warring nations.

Markings covered a number of years. In 1956 he said of them: "These notes?—They were signposts you began to set up after you had reached a point where you needed them, a fixed point that was on no account to be lost sight of."

Presumably, the fixed point was on Pentecost, 1961: "But at some moment I did answer *Yes* to Someone—or Something—and from that hour I was certain that existence is meaningful and that, therefore, my life, in self-surrender, had a goal."

His fixed point was one also in which he seemed to gather up his whole life. In one of the poems that he wrote he said, "He must be ready at any moment to gather everything into one single sacrifice." This brought him to the concept of the Cross: "The cross should not separate those of Christian faith from others. It should, instead, be that element in their lives that enables them to stretch out their hands to peoples of other Creeds in the feeling of universal brotherhood."—T. S. Settle, *The Light and the Rock.*

In 1958 he visited the Basilica of St. Peter and had an audience with Pope Pius XII, who amazed him by knowing every detail of the knotty problem of disarmament. He said afterward, "Isn't it odd that I had to come to Rome to learn about disarmament." During the interview Pope Pius said to him, *"Vous êtes mon homologue laïque"*—"You are my lay counterpart." W. H. Auden, the poet, wrote that Hammarskjöld told him that he regarded himself a kind of a secular Pope seeking the peace of the world.

It was Hammarskjöld who was responsible for a Meditation Room in the United Nations to which he not only gave much attention, but also directed its symbolism. He visited the chapel two or three times a week and never went anywhere without dropping in for a few moments of quiet. On the south wall of the room before the entrance, there is a bronze plaque commemorating the death of Count Bernadotte who was assassinated on September 17, 1948—a plaque which Hammarskjöld himself unveiled.

The day before he was to leave for his mission in the Congo in which he would be killed, he visited the Meditation Room and ordered that another plaque of black marble be put on the west wall. This was one of his last official acts. He wrote out how it should read: "This is a room devoted to peace and those who are giving their lives for peace." Thirteen years to the day on which he unveiled the plaque to Count Bernadotte, he was killed.

Emery Kelen said that ten months before Hammarskjöld died, he wrote a poem in which he pictured himself in a forest on a mystic night under the moon, fearful and yet submissive to God's Will, calling out to those who cannot hear; knowing well that he stood at the dawn of judgment day, when the love he had fostered in his heart for others would have its weighing. As he had already written, "He who fears God need fear no man."

On September 26, 1957, he wrote: " 'The best and most wonderful thing that can happen to you in this life is that you should be silent and let God work and speak.' Long ago you gripped me, Slinger. *Now* into the storm. *Now* towards your target."

His whole life was summed up in a poem which he wrote in *Markings*:

The road,
You shall follow it.

The fun,
You shall forget it.

The cup,
You shall empty it.

The pain,
You shall conceal it.

The truth,
You shall be told it.

The end,
You shall endure it.

Divine and Secular

We too often think of God as one item in the universe, as one object among other objects; of service of Him as distinct and apart from any service to humanity. Once we do this, we make religion a department, a task among other tasks. Then, those who hear that God is one object among other objects begin to choose other objects in preference to Him. St. Paul says that if one should speak with the tongues of men and angels, and have prophecy and faith to remove all mountains, and give all one's goods to the poor, but lack love, one would have nothing. In other words, theory without practice is vain.

These four men all had the quality of vulnerability; they took on the hurts and wounds of others. Love is a process of feeling others' hunger, thirst, want, and injustices. But their vulnerability came from their vision of the ultimate.

Such was an Abraham who turned from all that he owned for the sake of a promise; a Moses who infected a whole people with his dream to give them political freedom; an Amos who faced the economic and social realities of his day with breathtaking utopian vision; a Jeremiah who, scandalized that a temple had been ossified and had condemned itself to death, believed that only a new vision could revive it. All of these sought to wrest a blessing from the actual human situation. This is the prophetic spirit, which makes a man responsible, persuades him that he can overcome overwhelming odds, and continues to hope against hope.

Our error has been to separate the sacred and the secular, the natural and the supernatural, the redeemed and the unredeemed, the church and the world. We have a tendency to divide men into good and bad, forgetful that man was made from the dust and at the same time was made an image of God. Every man, therefore, has to discover in himself that there is something good, there is something bad. Only then does he begin to know himself—and only then does he begin to know others. One might also say that only then does he begin to understand the world. It is not wholly evil. It is not wholly good. Man is a bruised, strong creature, running one moment, crawling another, leaping one moment, creeping another. The modern saint is one who lives for the world, not for the secular city; for humanity and for Christ's sake.

Sanctity never shows, but it is necessary. Sanctity has a hiddenness about it. When among human need, the hands are never folded, the voice is not cultivated, the head is not cocked to one side. It is hidden as the Gospel said, "When you give alms let not your left hand know what your right hand does and when you fast anoint your head and wash your face and appear then not to fast." The essence of sanctity is the external love of mankind as sons of God, because of the interior love of the Father—*it does not take much time to make us saints—it takes only much love.*

CHAPTER NINETEEN

Flight

Modern man is in flight; he wants to live his own life, be his own judge, his own creator, his own savior, but the more he makes himself absolute and independent, the more lonely and frightened he becomes. For a poetic and literary description of this flight, perhaps no one excels Francis Thompson. His was a life crowned more with thorn than with laurel. Though he was a Victorian, he stood outside of the Age of Victorian literature, but his poetry fitted all centuries. As it has been said: "No one has ever waved a torch with so fitful splendor over the gulfs of darkness."

"The Hound of Heaven," which is the title of his greatest poem, is the Divine in pursuit of the escapist, the long struggle before the resisting soul acknowledges its final defeat. The everlasting Arms are around the fugitive from the start to the finish. An escapist can use many trap doors to evade the Hound of Heaven, but out of them all Francis Thompson has chosen about five, of which we mention three: drugs in the flight into the subconscious; sex in the flight into momentary intensity; children in the flight into vicarious innocence.

We learned to fly in an age of flight. It is the one clear psychological characteristic of our times. A child wakes up frightened—he was chased by a dog perhaps. We say, "It was only a dream." When adults become uneasy and frightened, and drown their conscious-ness, they too are in flight. But instead of analyzing it, we avoid it, saying, "It is only a dream."

Flight is not the same as fear, such as of growing old, of being poor, or of being alone. Fear looks to the future danger or something which may happen. Flight has reference to something which has already happened; it has something to do with our origin, something that lies behind and around us. Something pursues us.

In the morning, a man in flight feels that he has not so much passed a night as passed through a tunnel. Flight occupies his whole world; it is in every drink, every sleeping tablet, every orgy, every distraction. If now and then it seems to disappear, it is because it has gone underground, only to reappear as a geyser of flight.

Flight drives men to cities, where it is hoped that personality will be lost in the anonymous mass. Just as gypsy tribes who are always on the move need once a year to prove they belong to the same tribe, so frightened souls need to affirm their loyalty to the Tribe of Flight. One out of every four Americans move every year; their mobility is lack of stability, their fluidity is flight.

We fly from the city to the country, hoping the open arms of nature will embrace us:

In vain my tears were wet on Heaven's grey cheek.
For ah! we know not what each other says,
   These things and I; . . .

A false mysticism makes it appear that man is seeking God. True, he is equipped with the radar of conscience which will guide him to perfect Love, but in many instances man is fleeing from God. He wants to forget Him. It is when one finds God and accepts the encounter that the flight is reversed: The soul becomes like the man who found a treasure in the field. He leaves all else to follow Him. But the vast majority of men try to avoid the encounter.

The first question in Scripture is: "Man! Where are you?"

What are you running from? Why are you naked and ashamed? Why did you feel naked? Why do you feel over *against* something?

The second question in the Bible is: "Where is your brother?" Why have you fallen from fellowship, brotherhood, true togetherness? Why do you keep looking back, as if you had deserted or even annihilated someone? What makes you feel declassé, a refugee, a vagabond on the face of the earth.

The Psalmist reiterates that theme in Psalm 139:7-12 (JB):

Where could I go to escape your spirit?
Where could I flee from your presence?
If I climb the heavens, you are there,
there too, if I lie in Sheol.

If I flew to the point of sunrise,
or westward across the sea,
your hand would still be guiding me,
your right hand holding me.

If I asked darkness to cover me,
and light to become night around me,
that darkness would not be dark to you,
night would be as light as day.

If there is a flight, is there not also a Pursuer? If we are running away, is there not a chase?

There was bound to appear in literature someone who would articulate flight in poetic form. Such was Francis Thompson, who lived through it all in his "The Hound of Heaven." "Hound" suggests speed, grace, and instancy. It perhaps is not a new way to describe God, for Papini states that there was found a Punic inscription in northern Africa which means "Hound of Divinity." There is a possibility, too, that Thompson, who had such a fondness for Shelley, may have derived the title from an expression in *Prometheus Unbound*, "Heaven's Winged Hound." St. Augustine in his *Con-*

fessions speaks of God "at the heels of those fleeing from Him." Hammarskjöld has written, "I am the cup. God is the draught; He is the thirsty One."

This poem was begun when Thompson was thirty-two years of age, having been born on December 16, 1859, in Preston, Lancashire, England. It is an authentic description of the soul of Everyman—not as the hound in pursuit of God, but the far more terrible truth, namely, the relentless pursuit of the soul by God. When we pursue, we can do it leisurely or break off the engagement; when He pursues, there is nothing leisurely but a relentlessness which makes some men hate Him and others deny Him, to give a momentary peace. The Bible, as stated above, pictures man in flight, and God in pursuit.

Drugs: The Flight Into the Subconscious

Dante, in keeping with biblical and philosophical insights, divided the universe into three levels: heaven, earth, and hell. Spatially imagined, heaven was above, hell was below, and earth in between was on the present plane of life.

Our modern age has moved the levels of existence within man himself. The three new stages are: the super ego, or the world of totems, taboos, and morals; the second stage, consciousness; the third level, subconsciousness or the storage house of primitive instincts.

One of the most popular ways of modern youth to explore the subterranean caverns is by drugs, opium, LSD, marijuana, and dope in general. The flight from whatever one is fleeing from is heightened by colored images, kaleidoscopic imaginings and confused mental rumblings. The victim seems monstrously great, for his giddiness and dizziness make him forget for the moment that he is in flight. Because of the crazy, mixed-up images which opiates create, their victims often seek an outlet in literature and art which are equally crazy and mixed-up.

Francis Thompson was like any beatnik of our day, in the sense that he too was an addict, a dreamer, and a poet. The first escape which he mentions—that is, the first escape from God—is the new world of images that is opened up by drugs.

How did Thompson fall into the habit? His father was a doctor, so it was rather natural that he would wish his son to follow in the same profession. This was particularly so because he was the kind of practitioner who not only treated diseases, he treated sick people. In addition, he deliberately sought out the destitute, the poor, and those who could not pay. It was not just a career that he would have his son follow; it was rather a vocation to serve humanity. Francis' schooling was directed toward medicine, but his major interest was Latin and Greek, which he loved much more than the sciences. Ill health made him indolent and of that laziness he wrote:

Thou wilt not lie abed when the last trumpet blows.
Thy sleep with the worm will be long enough.

Ill at ease in the lecture rooms of medicine, instead of following a scientific textbook, he devoured Thomas De Quincey's *Confessions of an English Opium Eater*. Later on, he became anxious to emulate de Quincey and to share his experiences. At the age of twenty-six he was a dope fiend, an addict.

Coming to London, he earned money to buy drugs by selling matches and newspapers, carrying signs sandwiched on his thin body, holding horses' heads as patrons went into expensive theaters and restaurants; his chief concern was to avoid any other company or any other contact with men like himself: the bums, the derelicts, and the wrecks of humanity.

One night when he had taken opium, he was lying among the trucks, baskets, and vegetable carts at Covent Garden where he was wont to take his worried sleep. He had intended to take, in the morning, a dose sufficient to kill himself. During that night before the contemplated suicide, he had a dream of a man who had a laced ruffle on his arm. As he was about to reach for another dose of drugs, that arm stopped him. He looked up at the face and recognized it as the poet Thomas Chatterton, the poet who had poisoned himself in a garret on the very eve of what would have been his rescue. Thompson was later asked how he knew it was Chatterton, and he said that he had seen his picture and recognized him. This ghost from the past made him resolve to live for a few more days.

Like many dope victims he wrote, and one of his articles he sent to Wilfrid Meynell, the editor of a review *Merry England*. The essay was on "Paganism." With little hope of its acceptance, he had marked on the manuscript, "Kindly send your rejection to the Charing Cross post office." It was the morning after the dream that he received a note from Wilfrid Meynell to call at his office, and Meynell sent him to a monastery to try to break him of the dope habit.

Partly cured, he returned later to London where he always had to fight against the habit, and looking back on the number of victims that the drug had produced, he wrote in one of his poems:

Thou hast sucked down
How many Ninevehs!
Hast not thy fill?

Nursed back to health by the Meynells, he began to write poetry that was a kind of Easter Sunday crowning a Good Friday; phoenixlike his poems came from ashes:

Most wretched men
Are cradled into poetry by wrong
They learn in suffering what
They teach in song.

The first escape from the Hound of Heaven, which naturally he recorded at the very beginning of his poem, was the use of drugs, which excavated so many subterranean caverns in his mind, made him sad, then glad, full of hope and then despair. But unlike many beatniks during that long sojourn in the cavernous ground of the subconsciousness, he could hear the footfall and the slow beat of the Hound of Heaven:

I fled Him, down the nights and down the days;
 I fled Him, down the arches of the years;
I fled Him, down the labyrinthine ways
 Of my own mind; and in the mist of tears
I hid from Him, and under running laughter.
  Up vistaed hopes I sped;
  And shot, precipitated,
Adown Titanic glooms of chasmèd fears,
 From those strong Feet that followed, followed after.
  But with unhurrying chase,
  And unperturbèd pace,
Deliberate speed, majestic instancy,
  They beat—and a Voice beat
  More instant than the Feet—
"All things betray thee, who betrayest Me."

Sex: The Flight Into Carnal Intensity

Drugs failing to halt the Voice and the Footfall of the Hound of Heaven, he now turns in his flight to the flesh. Sex is another means of escape of man living a meaningless existence, for therein one hopes to make the intensity of an experience satisfy for the want and goal of life. It would not be in comfortable parlors that he would find his escape, but in the gutters and dives of the city. They offered little hope, but once he found in them a gold florin, and at another time Lord Rothschild bought a paper from him and gave him a gold florin. What strange twists Providence takes in making the Rothschild unknown, but Thompson known wherever men sing!

But gold was no substitute for the flesh until one day a woman of the streets, whom he calls a "natural sister of charity," saw him as an outcast and a derelict, and brought him to her humble apartment. There the two marveled that there were joys in each to unbury. We never learned her name, as the Gospel does not mention the name of the woman in the city who was a sinner, and as St. Augustine did not mention the name of the woman with whom he lived for eighteen years. And yet they all are anonymously immortalized in Scripture and verse. Years later, Thompson wrote of her these memorable lines:

Then there came past . . .
  a flower
Fallen from the budded coronal of Spring
And through the city streets blown withering.
She passed—O brave, sad, lovingest, tender thing!
And of her own scant pittance did she give,
That I might eat and live: then fled
A swift and trackless fugitive.

As later on in life he had often wondered whether or not he had thanked Lord Rothschild for the florin, so now he sought her out on the streets to renew thanks, but though in the accidents of the streets he met her, he was never destined in the same accidents to find her.

Later on, living with the Meynells with whom he spent nineteen years, he had a distant and spiritual love of Alice Meynell who was twelve years older than himself. In distant worship he wrote:

Each half-occulted star beneath that lies
And, in the contemplation of those eyes,
Passionless passion, wild tranquillities.

Thompson felt that he was never destined to love. Commenting on the marriage feast of Cana, he said that marriage proves "much wine is needed before man may go through with matrimony." All human love was to him a symbol of love Divine, for it was that which gave meaning to its seeming insanity. He had such a reverence for the love of woman that he believed a woman repels the great and pure love of man in proportion to its purity. Woman, he claims, has an instinct which man lacks—the power to analyze. Woman's love is so deep and so vast that she is reluctant to give, knowing that she could never pay it back if reciprocated. Her recoil, therefore, is an instinctive fear that she could not match the love she receives. She assumes that man's love is as great, as deep, and as sacrificial as her own, and this makes her hold back a total surrender. Of such noble woman love, he wrote:

Love that falls not when man beleaguers it;
Love that never breaches their walls corporeal.

In "The Hound of Heaven" he describes this escape of sex as follows:

I pleaded, outlaw-wise,
By many a hearted casement, curtained red,
 Trellised with intertwining charities;
(For, though I knew His love Who followèd,
 Yet was I sore adread
Lest, having Him, I must have naught beside)
But, if one little casement parted wide,
 The gust of His approach would clash it too.
 Fear wist not to evade, as Love wist to pursue.

The "hearted casement" was reminiscent of a little cottage where, when he was young, he made friends with a little girl. But as the wind closes a shutter, so the rush of the Hound of Heaven slams it shut. He could not fly as fast as the Pursuer.

Children: The Flight Into Vicarious Innocence

It is not often that frustrated man, when drugs and flesh fail, seeks escape in the love of children, but it was so in the case of Francis Thompson. In a beautiful poem to Olivia, who was one of the Meynell children, he expresses his great love of a child and the fear of the contrast between her innocence and his own spoiled life. Being with the pure made him feel both pure and wicked—pure by association, wicked by contrast:

I fear to love thee, Sweet, because
Love's the ambassador of loss;
White flake of childhood, clinging so
To my soiled raiment, thy shy snow
At tenderest touch will shrink and go.
Love me not, delightful child.
My heart, by many snares beguiled,
Has grown timorous and wild.
It would fear thee not at all,
Wert thou not so harmless-small.
Because thy arrows, not yet dire,
Are still unbarbed with destined fire,
I fear thee more than hadst thou stood
Full-panoplied in womanhood.

Then he tells the story of meeting a little child in the fields of Sussex; his heart went out to her in deepest love. As he put it in the above poem, "Love's the ambassador of loss," she would go away, not knowing that she had broken his heart.

Her beauty smoothed earth's furrowed face.
She gave me tokens three:—

A look, a word of her winsome mouth,
And a wild raspberry.

A berry red, a guileless look,
A still word,—strings of sand!
And yet they made my wild, wild heart
Fly down to her little hand.

For standing artless as the air,
And candid as the skies,
She took the berries with her hand,
And the love with her sweet eyes.

The fairest things have fleetest end,
Their scent survives their close:
But the rose's scent is bitterness
To him that loved the rose.

She looked a little wistfully,
Then went her sunshine way:—
The sea's eye had a mist on it,
And the leaves fell from the day.

She went her unremembering way,
She went and left in me
The pang of all the partings gone,
And partings yet to be.

She left me marvelling why my soul
Was sad that she was glad;
At all the sadness in the sweet,
The sweetness in the sad.

Still, still I seemed to see her, still
Look up with soft replies,
And take the berries with her hand,
And the love with her lovely eyes.

Nothing begins, and nothing ends,
That is not paid with moan;
For we are born in other's pain,
And perish in our own.

But the Hound of Heaven would not let his unhappiness find repose in innocent children; they did not belong to him; they really did not belong to anybody but Him Who became a Child.

I sought no more that after which I strayed
In face of man or maid;
But still within the little children's eyes
Seems something, something that replies,
They at least are for me, surely for me!
I turned me to them very wistfully;
But just as their young eyes grew sudden fair
With dawning answers there,
Their angel plucked them from me by the hair.

The Condition of Surrender

If a man sues a woman for love, and he is already laden down with excesses and infidelities, she will ask him to purge himself of that which will stand between the mutual commitment of love. In a lower order, too, man understands the necessity of cleanliness. The great care that used to be taken of the soul is now transferred to the body. Common drinking cups chained to a well have been done away with; there must either be fountains or individual cups, lest any physical germs should enter the body. This is right and proper, but it also testifies to the fact that the soul itself must undergo some asceticism to be worthy of the Pursuer.

Paul's first word, when the Pursuer caught up with him, was: "What shall I do?" Thompson's first word is: "Naked I wait Thy love's uplifted stroke!" He realizes that he has nothing. Samson, brought into the temple of the Philistine god Dagon, shook the pillars of the temple and killed the princes and the people therein. So Thompson, looking back upon his wasted youth, muses:

In the rash lustihead of my young powers,
  I shook the pillaring hours
And pulled my life upon me; grimed with smears,
I stand amid the dust o' the mounded years—
My mangled youth lies dead beneath the heap.

At one time the earth seemed to be wholly his own. As Shelley put it: "His playthings are those that the gods give their children. The universe is his box of toys." In a magnificent passage of mastery over the things of earth, Thompson writes: "I swung the earth a trinket at my wrist . . . the linked fantasies . . . with heavy griefs so overplussed . . ." The dark night comes when all seems lost, but actually it is only a Good Friday preparing an Easter Sunday, a purgation of the sensate and the erotic from the window of life to let the light shine through. As Thompson put it in an essay: "The gates of the beatific Love are guarded by the purgatorial Love."

Now comes that moment of dread, because purgation is necessary before one can enter into love. Calvary is frightening. As Shelley had asked: "Is there no drinking of pearls except they be dissolved in biting tears?" Thompson then uses three figures of speech to describe the haunting specter of purgation. The first figure is that of a purely imaginary flower that never fades called amaranth. It was supposed to absorb all of the moisture which surrounded it, thus causing death to every flower and herb in its environment. Milton referred to it in his *Paradise Lost*. Thompson now asks:

  Ah! is Thy love indeed
A weed, albeit an amaranthine weed,
Suffering no flowers except its own to mount?

The second figure of speech which he uses is that of charcoal, as wood must be thrown on the fire before it can become charcoal with which one can trace, sketch, and draw: "Ah! must Thou char the wood ere Thou canst limn with it?"

The third picture is one in which he pictures his heart as a broken fountain; no refreshing waters pour down on it from above, but a great tree overhanging it lets fall the drops of rain making his heart a stagnant pool:

And now my heart is as a broken fount,
Wherein tear-drippings stagnate, spilt down ever
*   From the dank thoughts that shiver*
Upon the sighful branches of my mind.

And summing up all the figures he asks, "The pulp so bitter, how shall taste the rind?" If the life of youth has been so full of sadness, what shall be old age?

Though it is not generally known, Nietzsche, in his loneliness and beyond all his denials, invoked the company of the God he had denied:

Away!
There fled he surely,
My final, only comrade,
My greatest foe,
Mine unfamiliar—
My hangman—
God! . . .
—Nay!
Come thou back!
With all thy great tortures!
To me the last of lonesome ones,
Oh, come thou back!
All my hot tears in streamlets trickle

Their course to thee!
Oh, come thou back!
Mine unfamiliar God!
My pain!
My final bliss!

Man's ideas of God are not always accurate. Therefore, the atheism of a man like Nietzsche and his consequent denial of Christianity contain a truth in so far as they reject a false idea of God. Sometimes this rejection is a necessary step toward one's return to God.

There is something hidden in man which is like the brand that was put upon Cain when he killed his brother Abel, the mark of mercy which shows that man, even when he is evil, is protected by God. St. Teresa of Avila said, "For those who offend Me are very close to Me though against their own will."

Man is like the toad, very ugly animal which has a constant drive to return to its origins. Some people have taken a horned toad fifty miles away from home and marked it in order to be sure that, if it returned, it would be the same creature. After weeks and weeks it always comes back to the rock under their house. Man is like that toad, twisted and grotesque, torn away from God but really wanting to go home. As the trees twist and turn in the forest in order to be in the sunlight, so man is constantly twisting and turning in order to recover his origin and return to his home.

Those who think that religion is an escape should try the Cross. There are various kinds of cheap mysticism, expressing themselves in drama and poetry in which the soul is in perpetual search of God. There is, however, seldom any depth to these, because they allow the heart to be complacent. Thompson takes the reverse step: It is not a soul searching for God, but, far more terrible, God searching for the soul. Very few people know what they are letting themselves in for when this happens. There can be nothing leisurely about what follows. In the cheaper mysticism of man's approach to God, everybody knows the questions, but nobody wants to know the answers.

The questions are now answered by the Hound of Heaven:

> "Strange, piteous, futile thing!
> Wherefore should any set thee love apart?
> Seeing none but I makes much of naught" (He said),
> "And human love needs human meriting:
> How hast thou merited—
> Of all man's clotted clay the dingiest clot?
> Alack, thou knowest not
> How little worthy of any love thou art!
> Whom wilt thou find to love ignoble thee,
> Save Me, save only Me?
> All which I took from thee I did but take,
> Not for thy harms,
> But just that thou might'st seek it in My arms.
> All which thy child's mistake
> Fancies as lost, I have stored for thee at home:
> Rise, clasp My hand, and come!"

Finally, come some of the most consoling words ever written to those who suffer. Inspired by the fact that there would never be a shadow if there were no Light, and hence never a sorrow were there not a Hand to wipe away the tears, the poet asks:

> Is my gloom, after all,
> Shade of His hand, outstretched caressingly?